— THIS — MIGHT GET A LITTLE HEAVY

A Memoir

RALPHIE MAY

with **NILS PARKER**

ST. MARTIN'S PRESS   ❦   NEW YORK

www.stmartins.com

The Library of Congress Cataloging-in-Publication Data is available upon request.

ISBN 978-1-250-08574-0 (hardcover)
ISBN 978-1-250-08575-7 (ebook)

Our books may be purchased in bulk for promotional, educational, or business use. Please contact your local bookseller or the Macmillan Corporate and Premium Sales Department at 1-800-221-7945, extension 5442, or by email at MacmillanSpecialMarkets@macmillan.com.

First Edition: December 2017

10 9 8 7 6 5 4 3 2 1

CONTENTS

ACKNOWLEDGMENTS

Thank you to my family most of all, for putting up with me. My babies, April and August, this book is for you. The Comedy Showcase. All the comics along the way that I've met—the friends and not so friendly. Jamie Masada, JP Williams, Comedy Central, Netflix, UTA, CAA, WME, and Levity Entertainment Group. Andrew and Brian Dorfman, and Aaron Distler—the Protector of Good and Defender Against All Evil. Jay Mohr, Jeff Ross, Doug Stanhope, and Joey Diaz. Thank you to the clubs, the theaters, and the promoters. The DJs—specifically, John Holmberg, Mike Calta, Paul Castronovo, and Mancow. Lahna Turner. Mitzi Shore and the Comedy Store. The Laugh Factory and the Improv. Bob Read and Ross Mark at *The Tonight Show* and, of course, Mr. Leno and Jimmy Kimmel. Also, thanks to Nils and Anthony Mattero for putting up with my shit, and Kevin Currie, who dove in and researched everything I've ever done or recorded to help put this book together.

PART 1
ARKANSAS:
1977–1990

1.

MY MOM KILLED
SANTA CLAUS WITH
A PAIR OF SHOES

Comedians come in all shapes and sizes. We have different backgrounds and different upbringings, but the one thing we have in common is that we are all skeptics. None of us take as gospel what we are told by teachers, parents, employers, politicians, media, anyone in a position of power. We approach all of it with a healthy dose of caution—actually, cynicism—including when it comes from the audience. Especially if the audience is shitty.

This attitude touches every part of life. *Breakfast is the most important meal of the day. Milk does a body good. Pork is the other white meat.* Every time I see a slogan like those, my first thoughts are "*Really?* Says who? How do I know? Which lobbying group paid for you to say that?" And sure enough, it's always some organization with a name like Cereal Producers of America or American Dairy Council or America's Greatest Pig Fuckers.

I'm not saying that I am Neo from *The Matrix* after that scene when Morpheus gives him the option to take the blue pill and return to his normal life or take the red pill and fall down the rabbit hole to see what the world is really like. But stand-up comedy is the only profession I can think of where *everyone* involved has chosen the red pill. You can't really even get in the game until that pill has made its way through your system and replaced your entire blood supply; because comedy, if it's any good, is about trying to see the world as it truly is. It's about spotting the bullshit and the lies, then seeing behind them at what is really there. It's about asking *Why?* And then making fun of whatever the answer is.

This isn't a natural way to live your life, with the constant need to ask why. The truth is painful. If I've learned anything in life, it's that most people will do anything to avoid pain (including causing themselves a lot more of it in the long run). I'm a fat guy with a Southern accent who grew up poor, now living in Los Angeles who grew up poor. How long do you reckon a fella like me might want to hold on to the belief that "it's what's on the inside that counts"? Avoiding the pain of those hard truths is why some comedians come to the red pill (and therefore, comedy) later than others. And once they do, they gulp it down and chase it like a drug. They don't just swallow it, they crush it up on the tray table and snort it like the plane is going down.

I don't think it's a coincidence that most of the comics we've lost to drugs and suicide over the years started in comedy in their twenties, while those of us who started in our teens or were obsessed with comedy growing up are still kicking. Those comics who got started when they were older endured more pain under delusions for longer than we did. They had bought into the system more, and it made the truth on the other side of the red pill harder to deal with. That extra experience gave them more reasons to regret their choices, while we didn't have to choose the red pill at all—it was chosen for us.

We have known our whole lives that pretty much everything we're told is total bullshit. Authority figures sounded like frauds, rules were totally pointless, and doing things because "that's the way you're supposed to" drove us crazy. We rebelled for spite and because we enjoyed seeing the look on their faces. We'd get slapped with labels like *depressive* or *antisocial* or *problem kid*. When we asked "Why?" too often, we'd be told "Because I said so" by parents and guidance counselors who were popping blue pills like blueberry Tic Tacs.

Most of us can trace our awareness of the *real* reality to some kind of traumatic event in our childhood that ripped away our innocence—that shoved the red pill right down our fucking throats.

It happened to me when I was eight years old.

The year was 1980. The world was in flux. The Iranian Revolution had gone down the year before, and a bunch of students had taken fifty-two Americans hostage. Global oil production plummeted, and gas prices more than doubled, creating an energy crisis across the country. We were boycotting the Summer Olympics in Moscow that year too because the Soviets had invaded Afghanistan like a bunch of idiots, and Ronnie Reagan was kicking Jimmy Carter's dick in the dirt up and down the campaign trail as a result.

Despite all that chaos, life in the May household hadn't changed much. We were still poor, my mom was still working two jobs, and I was still a kid with no other responsibility besides being a kid. We lived in the little town of Clarksville, Arkansas, about an hour and a half southeast of Fayetteville, where the university is located. My mom was born and raised in Clarksville. I was born in Chattanooga, Tennessee, but we moved to Clarksville when I was five years old, so really, Clarksville is my hometown too.

That summer I didn't do anything different from what I did any other summer growing up. I rode my bike around town with my friends, we made up games, we played in the woods along the banks of the Arkansas River, getting filthy, coming home when the sun went down. It was like *The Adventures of Tom Sawyer*, except with BMX bikes and nobody had any money to pay me to paint their fence. And just like good ol' Tom, most days you couldn't tell where the tan skin ended and the dirty skin began on any of us. No one cared. That's what kids were supposed to do.

Today we lube up our kids with Purell and carry them around in an invisible BabyBjörn, but back then summer was one long unsupervised playdate. Except for dinner or trips to the water park that required a car, we didn't see our parents for days at a time. They were generally useless until the week before Labor Day, when it was time to load up on school supplies and figure out how you were going to come correct in the one area more important to a child than the freedom of youth: pimp-ass new school shoes.

Every kid has to start the school year with a new pair of shoes. It's a civil right. It's a tradition. As parents, we can't ask our kids to roll into their new classroom on the first day of school wearing some busted-out sneakers from the previous year with those little thingies on the ends of the laces all cracked and frayed. We sure as shit can't ask them to wear their church shoes to make a good impression on the teachers—not unless we want their classmates to put those shoes in a trash can, with our kid still in them. They have to be on point the first day, with their shoelaces tight and white, just like their first girlfriend. (I'm kidding, they can also be Velcro.)

As a kid, this is easier said than done when you are poorer than the dirt you rolled around in all summer. First you have to be smart, because your feet are still growing. You have to get a pair that's at least a half size bigger, otherwise you'll be short-toeing it all spring. Then you need to be strategic. Your parents are obviously going to push you down-market to a nonpremium brand, but you can't let them make you go straight generic because then everyone will know you're a charity case. This limits your options and is where things get tricky. Cheaper brands try to use flashy colors and gimmicky designs to imitate the quality of the premium brands. It's easy to fall for this ploy. More than a few kids I knew came home with the neon-green plastic hightops with blinking lights in the soles. Some of them pulled it off. Others, who lacked the appropriate swagger, spent the next nine months enduring enough torment to put anyone into psychotherapy. The safest play for a poor kid in the new-shoe game is to find something understated, nondescript, and clean. Shoes that no one will notice, good or bad.

Of course, I didn't know any of this when I started third grade in the fall of 1980, but I would learn it the hard way by the time the year was over.

A week before the first day of school, my mom sent me to Mr. Brown's shoe store to get my new pair for the year. We didn't have much money, but Mr. Brown and my mom grew up together, so he let her have a credit account that she could pay off over time. As the father of two young kids, I recognize how crazy that might sound to anyone born after 1990 or so. I just don't know what the craziest part actually is: that there aren't local shoe stores anymore, that lines of store credit still existed in 1980, or that a responsible parent would send an eight-year-old out to do his own shopping. Regardless, my budget was $35.

As an eight-year-old, I had no idea what $35 meant. What kind of shoes could I get with that? How much coolness could I buy? Michael Jordan was still in high school and the Air Force 1s were still a couple years away, so Nike wasn't on my radar screen. Adidas and Puma were doing some cool stuff. Reebok too. There was always Converse. As I rode my bike downtown to Mr. Brown's, I felt like I had a lot of options. Then, as I turned across Cherry Street and pulled up in front of the store, all those options disappeared from my consciousness.

There, staring back at me from the other side of the storefront window, sat the most epic shoes my little eight-year-old eyes had ever seen: burgundy-on-burgundy, velvet-on-suede KangaROOS with two-strap Velcro and a zipper pocket on the side. Hotness, personified. I was transfixed. I dropped my bike, marched inside, pointed to the window display, and announced to the entire store, "Those! I want *those*!"

I was never a lucky kid, but this one time the spirits aligned for me. Mr. Brown not only had a pair in the back that was a half size up, but the shoes were in my price range too.

"How much money are they, Mr. Brown?"

"Don't worry, son, you have enough." My mom had called ahead to give Mr. Brown a heads-up and let him know my budgetary constraints. She wasn't worried that I would try to pull a fast one on Mr. Brown, she just didn't want me to get my hopes up, so she made sure Mr. Brown was prepared to steer me toward the more reasonable options if my eyes got bigger than my stomach. Maybe that's how the ROOS made it into the front-window display in the first place. They were a deliberate diversionary tactic to draw my attention away from the expensive shoes. I can't be sure. All I do know is that when Mr. Brown slid those shoes on my feet and I stood up in them for the first time, I felt like Fonzie pulling on his leather jacket. They were velvet-plated coolness.

The first day of school was a few days later. But it wasn't just the first day of third grade; it was also our first day at a brand-new elementary school. In God's continuing attempts to prevent Arkansas from learning how to read, the old elementary school had been blown away by a *tornado* the year before. In a completely new environment, where lunch tables and benches and spots on the playground had not already been claimed by hardened and grizzled fifth graders, the social stakes were especially high.

All those times I had peed my pants or cried like a little girl or finished last in a race could be erased. This is no small thing. This was my chance at "cool." The reputation you create for yourself in elementary school sticks with you until you get pubes in middle school. That's when you start making a name for yourself in entirely new ways; when the stuff you can't stop from coming out of your pee hole changes from yellow to white and stinky to sticky. If you're a girl, it's a little different. Your reputation starts to hinge not on what comes *out* of your pee hole, but what (or who) goes into it.

I was as aware of all these social pressures as an eight-year-old could be, and I handled it by treating my new shoes like they were made of glass until school started. I wouldn't put them on. I just stared at them and touched them like an antique book that might crumble into dust if I yanked the Velcro too hard. I visualized every detail of what the first day of school was going to look like. I was like that crippled Stark kid from *Game of Thrones* who has visions every time he touches a weirwood tree.

What actually happened was better than anything my third-grade imagination could create. Full of confidence, I walked into this new school like John Travolta carrying that can of paint in the beginning of *Saturday Night Fever.* The opening song played in my head like it was my own theme song:

> *Music loud and women warm,*
> *I've been kicked around*
> *Since I was born*

Kids from every grade level stopped and stared. Every day for a month I would go up to my friends for the high-five/low-five combo with that song playing on a loop. I would do a bunch of Electric Slide run-stops on the linoleum floor of the hallways, pointing down at my shoes as I hit the brakes and made the screeching sound effect with my mouth. Sitting in class, I'd quick-pull the zipper back and forth like a hip-hop DJ scratching a record. I'd play with the Velcro straps and lean over nonchalantly to whoever was sitting next to me: "Velcro. NASA invented it. That's space stuff, betchu didn't know nothin' 'bout that, huh?" And they'd be, like, "Whoa, oh my goodness, you're so cool, will you be my friend forever?" Everybody loved my shoes and told me all the time how awesome they were. I was boy king of third grade. Kiss the zipper, bitches!

The burgundy ROOS were my own ruby-red slippers. Dorothy clicked her heels and got to go home. I did a couple run-stops and I got to make out with third- *and* fourth-grade girls. A few zipper pulls and I even got a couple of fifth-grade girls to touch my wiener. I was a smooth operator, playing girls against each other, movin' and shakin'. These shoes were so pimp Kanga still sells the exact same shoes in kid sizes, like a Lil Baby Baller starter kit.

In the thirty-five years since I got those shoes from Mr. Brown, I have shared the stage with legends, been nominated for an Emmy, made millions of dollars, been certified four times platinum, and done three Netflix specials. And still, that first month in the burgundy ROOS was the coolest I've ever felt in my entire life. When I'm going through a rough patch or feeling down about myself, I don't think about the fame and the fortune to pick myself up, I think about the sound of Velcro straps and wicked run-stops in an elementary-school hallway.

———

Two weeks after Halloween, all those run-stops caught up with me. The foam soles began to rip away from the fabric body of the shoes. The tearing started at the toes, where the room from being a half size larger gave my feet space to jam into the seam with extra force. The separation grew along the seam, like a fault line, until I was basically wearing high-top flip-flops. It was miserable. I tried gluing them back together, but that lasted for exactly one run-stop. They blew out again like a retread tire on a tractor trailer and I nearly face-planted into a water fountain. I went from Electric Slide to Electric Slip & Fall. So glue was out.

I tried duct tape next. Duct tape is the penicillin and Ctrl+Alt+Del of redneck DIY home repair. It's not pretty, it might ultimately do more harm than good, but in the interim by golly those silver sticky strips are going to hold everything together. The duct tape lasted until morning recess my first day wearing it. Not because it wasn't holding, but because everyone started calling me Robot Feet and Franken-Fatty. It was humiliating. All my coolness evaporated just as quickly as I had earned it. I was Icarus, and I had run-stopped too close to the sun.

I was not equipped to handle such a violent fall from grace. I needed someone to blame. It couldn't be *my* fault, I was just a kid. Knowing nothing of globalization and the poor quality of sweatshop labor, I turned my attention to the shoe store. They'd taken advantage of a poor child by putting these shiny, shitty shoes right there in the window, priced to sell. What was I supposed to do, *not* buy them? Eight-year-olds don't have that kind of self-control. Hell, *eighteen-year-olds* don't have it either. It was Mr. Brown's job to steer me in the right direction. Instead, he had taken me like a grifter.

What I really wanted to do was take the shoes back to the store and tell Mr. Brown, "These here shoes are pieces of shit and I want my mama's money back and a new pair of Adidas for my trouble," then maybe take a steaming shit in the middle of his sales floor. But I couldn't do that. Southern politeness would not have allowed me to come at Mr. Brown this way. Plus, I didn't have to poop and I'd worn my ROOS into the ground. I'd abused them like a Filipino maid. Covering them in duct tape, I think, was my biggest mistake. Suede does not mix well with duct tape. It's like jerking off with honey. It works for a second, but the longer you keep it on there, the more likely that soft smooth surface ends up ripped and rough.

With less than two months gone by in what was promising to be a long school year, there was only one person I could turn to if I wanted to solve my problem: the poor-kid lottery, the fat-guy savior himself—Santa Claus.

At school, when we talked about Christmas and our wish lists for Santa, all the other kids in my class wanted the biggest, coolest, newest toys—the ones their parents repeatedly told them they couldn't afford. I didn't want any toys. I had plenty of toys. From Santa, I wanted Adidas. No more of this phony-suede, tiny-zippered, no-run-stop-supporting, weak-soled KangaROOS *bullshit*! It was time for some of that fine German engineering. I wanted a little *fahrvergnügen con mis zapatos,* if you feel me. I wasn't trying to be greedy, though. I wasn't looking for the fat man to bring me a pair of the fancy Rod Laver Adidas or any of the ones the other famous tennis players wore. I just wanted the classic white shell-top Superstars with the three black stripes on the side (the ones Run-D.M.C. would make famous a few years later).

I talked to anyone who would listen about what I wanted for Christmas, but by the time Thanksgiving rolled around, it felt like Santa Claus was the only man left on Team Ralphie. If I was going to get a second new pair of cool shoes this school year, I had to get ahold of him. I had to explain what had happened with the ROOS, I had to describe exactly what I wanted, and I had to make sure he knew I deserved them—that I was on the Nice list.

I started my campaign for the Nice list by doing something that should probably have put me on the Naughty list: I stole forty or fifty stamps from my granny's desk. I've never understood why so many old people carry so much postage around with them, like at any moment a wedding might break out and they'll need to invite everyone they know *immediately,* but I'm glad my granny was one of those people because it allowed me to send Santa a letter every other day until the week before Christmas. I sent him letters about how good I'd been. I sent him short notes with pictures of the Adidas I wanted that I'd cut out of the Sunday circular from both local papers (the *Democrat* and the *Gazette*). If the sports section had a picture of a famous athlete wearing Adidas, I'd cut that out too and draw a big circle around the shoes with an arrow pointing to them and the words *I would like these please* scribbled in crayon. Then I'd draw pictures of myself wearing the shoes, so Santa would know for certain how much the Adidas meant to me. I sent so many letters to the North Pole, the post office probably had to charter a special plane just for my shit.

My granny was a whip-smart Southern lady. She knew I'd pinched her stamps and she saw what I was up to on my letter-writing campaign, so she took this opportunity to farm me out to all her old-lady friends to do chores for them: raking leaves, hauling wood, moving boxes and furniture, winterizing porches. I was still only eight years old, but she had me working like a slave. Why she didn't have these people *fucking pay* me for doing their chores so I could buy my own shoes, I will never know. At the time, I didn't mind, and I didn't ask: I was happy to do everything

I could to work my way up to the top of Santa's Nice list. Indentured servitude was a small price to pay for new kicks.

As Christmas approached, I was both excited and nervous. I knew I'd personally done enough to earn those Adidas, but as a family we'd done fuck-all to make Santa feel welcome on the big day. We didn't have any decorations or lights up, we didn't even have our tree, and some of the kids at school said if you didn't have a tree with decorations, Santa would skip your house because he'd think you were a Jew. I asked my mama about getting a tree, but she deflected and changed the subject whenever I brought it up. Like we could afford a tree. I was also worried because we were going to have Christmas at my granny's house and I'd put our house as the return address on all my letters. How in the world was Santa going to find me if we weren't where I'd told him we would be?

When Christmas Eve finally came, I had resolved all of my fears about getting skipped by Santa except for one: we still didn't have a Christmas tree. I was not going to let Santa Claus off the hook because of some weird Jew loophole, so I went out into the woods with my Cub Scout hatchet, cut down a cedar tree, and dragged it back to the house. I was a strong chubby kid, even at eight years old, but ain't no way a third grader is dragging a *tree* a half mile back to his house without doing some damage. By the time I got home, one whole side was missing its needles and half its branches. No problem. I used some of that Cub Scout ingenuity and stuffed the AIDS-y looking Charlie Brown side of the tree into the corner against the wall. I maintain to this day that it worked out better with one whole side of the tree gone because it held up against the wall really well. Once I got it in place, I put about forty feet of popcorn garland around it, used the wide-ruled binder paper from my generic Trapper Keeper to make some badass snowflakes, made an angel out of yellow construction paper that I rolled into a cone and drew a face on, then spread out an old strand of white lights that had an ozone smell to them, which, combined with the creosote from the cedar tree, was a house fire waiting to happen. I paid that no mind. This thing only had to hold out about a day and a half before it went up in flames, and the risk was worth the reward. I was not about to lose out on my Adidas because of a code violation.

Christmas Eve night was a cold one in northwest Arkansas. The temperature dropped down into the high teens overnight, and the wind was gusting above thirty miles per hour. That's a nasty combination when your house is little more than a beat-up shotgun shack with gaps between the clapboards that let heat out and cold in. In the winter we put up plastic sheeting on the walls (like Dexter fixing to kill somebody) and that helped a little, but when it's eighteen degrees outside and the oven's not on, there's no two ways about it—you're living in an icebox. We were never cold in bed, though, because my mama had us under about thirty pounds of quilts. They were so heavy and exerted so much downward pressure that when they were tucked in, you had to pick your exact comfortable spot before the quilts came down because that's where you were going to stay the rest of the night. There was no moving once the hatch was closed. I went to sleep earlier than previous Christmas Eve nights because the local six-o'clock news was reporting that they'd just spotted Santa Claus on the radar. I wasn't about to risk his passing us by after the near miss with the tree. Cookies and milk would be out, and I would be asleep before that could happen.

Early to bed also means early to rise, especially on Christmas morning. I was the first one up at the butt crack of dawn. I pried myself out of our quilt sarcophagus and made a beeline for the living room. The job of the first person up was always to turn on the oven in the kitchen to heat the house, but I ignored that responsibility. I didn't need a gas oven to warm me through because I was fired up by the Christmas spirit. Two presents with my name on them were under the tree. One looked like some kind of lumpy sweater I'd never wear, but the other was wrapped and shaped like a shoebox. My heart lifted into my cheeks.

You know how every Christmas movie you've ever watched has that one scene where the kids wake up early and scout out the presents, waiting for Mom and Dad to get up, but then they can't wait any longer, so they go bursting into their parents' room to announce that Santa came, and everyone smiles and hugs like they're creating memories that will last a lifetime and traditions they will pass down through the generations? Yeah, well, traditions can kiss my ass, I had my own memories to make! I tore off the wrapping, ripped open the box, and nearly had a heart attack. Inside was a pair of white shell-topped sneakers with one, two, three . . . *four* black stripes? As quickly as my heart had lifted into my face, it had dropped into my stomach.

Adidas only have three stripes. Not four, *three*. What in the actual fuck was going on here? I tried to convince myself that maybe these were a new line of Adidas that only Santa had access to, but I knew right well what they were. They were Winners Choice shoes from Walmart. *Poor-kids Adidas.* If you didn't grow up broke, you probably have no idea what those are. They are sneakers designed to look exactly like Adidas, except they're made out of plastic instead of leather. And to make up for the gap in quality, they added an extra stripe. A fourth stripe. A gratuitous, utterly unnecessary stripe.

Three is a perfect number: *the rule of three, the holy trinity, three-pointers, triple plays, threesomes.* It's a magical digit.

Four sucks. There are the *Four Horsemen of the Apocalypse.* The

worst music ever invented—barbershop quartet—has four mem-
bers. To the Chinese, four is an unlucky number. And they should
know, their children made these shoes. They knew when they
were making them: any kid who has to wear these shoes to school
is royally fucked. They were right too, because let me tell you
something about these plastic pieces of shit called Winners Choice
shoes: no winner has ever chosen to buy these things.

Two months of letter writing. Two months of manual labor and
being good. That motherfucker *owed me*. And he's going to do me
like this? With some generic club-store garbage? I went from ecstasy to agony in the time it took to count the stripes on the side
of a sneaker.

I stared at the shoes for what felt like forever. I counted and re-
counted the number of stripes to make sure I wasn't mistaken. I
looked at them cross-eyed to make two of the stripes merge and
hoped that if I held my gaze long enough the stripes would literally morph into one right in front of my eyes. I picked at one of
the stripes with my chewed fingernails. Maybe it would come
clean off and I'd have passable Adidas on my hands. None of it
worked. My young mind could draw only one conclusion from all
this: Santa had fucked me. I had been doughnut-holed by Saint
Nick. I was furious. The anger that swept over me engulfed the
entire house. I picked up the shoes and threw them at the tree,
which slowly fell over on its AIDS-y side. I started hollering at
the top of my lungs, cussing a blue streak: "Fuck you, Santa, you
fat fucking asshole piece-of-shit cocksucker motherfucker! You
sure ate the cookies I put out for you, didn't you, you sonuvabitch!"
I didn't care who heard me. Santa, the neighbors, God—they
could all eat shit as far as I was concerned.

That's when I looked up to find my mom at the top of the stairs
crying.

"Ralphie, what are you doing?"

"These shoes *suck*, Mama!"

"Your dad hasn't sent any money since August, honey. And since I stopped working at Junior Food Mart after Thanksgiving, things have been really tight—"

"What the hell does Dad have to do with anything?! I'm talking about Santa. He's the one that fucked me, Mama! *He fucked me!*" It was like she wasn't even listening to what I was trying to say.

"—and after paying bills and putting gas in the car so we can go see Granny later, all I had left was thirty-four dollars. These were all we could afford." She was choking back tears.

If life were like a movie and if I had the ability to empathize with other people yet, that was the moment when I would have stopped and thought about my actions, then got up and hugged my mama and maybe gone outside and given the shoes to some homeless kid sleeping in the gutter. But life isn't a movie. Life's a bitch. So instead I said, "Yeah, well, Mama, these shoes still fucking suck. They suck a big dick. Fuck these shitty shoes."

I was so absorbed in my anger and disappointment that it didn't dawn on me for at least a minute and a half what she'd really said. When it finally clicked, I turned back and looked her square in the eyes.

"Mama, what do you mean this was all *we* could afford?"

"Santa didn't bring you those shoes, Ralphie. I did."

"Why? Why didn't Santa bring me the shoes I asked for? What the fuck happened to Santa, Mom? Is he dead? *Where is Santa?!*"

That's when she said it. Possibly the worst four words one could think to say to an innocent child that one is trying to console: "Santa Claus isn't real, sweetie."

In one moment, my mother had ground my childhood into oblivion and fractured my worldview with a hammer wrapped in a velvet Santa suit. I wanted a new pair of shoes. What I got instead was some triflin' plastic nonsense and my innocence stolen from me.

Most kids would then have started to cry and sob uncontrollably, but with all the stuff I'd already been through by eight years old, I was past that kindergarten shit. I was self-sufficient enough as an independent thinker to put two and two together and realize the broader implications of what my mama had just said. My young, inquisitive brain started firing. I was like Neo as the red pill moved through his body and the revelations came faster and faster until he reached the singularity. Dots began connecting in my head, questions began rolling off my tongue at a lightning pace— the answers coming to me even before my mother could respond.

"So what you're telling me is that everyone is a liar? You're a liar? Granny is a liar? Teachers are liars? Everybody is a liar?"

How could so many people be complicit in a massive lie to America's children?

Who was that old guy whose lap I sat on at the mall up in Fort Smith? Who the fuck was that piece of shit?! We went to Long John Silver's afterward and Mama got me extra crispies like I was big-time. Cold comfort. Were the crispies how she covered up her shame for perpetrating a heinous lie on her baby boy? I was livid. Eight years old and I was flipping out like a meth'd-up long-haul trucker.

The whole goddamn reason I went to bed at 6:45 that night was because the Channel 7 news had Santa on their radar! The fucking news was in on this too? Was Doppler radar even real? It's the news! If you can't trust the news, if the newspeople are a bunch of asshole fabricators, who can you trust? You all have been feeding me horseshit and telling me it was spaghetti, but I know horseshit when I taste it and this is some grade-A horseshit, Mama! Good goddamn, Lord Jesus!

I stopped and went quiet. The calm and complete stillness of a life-changing epiphany had just overwhelmed me. This was my Neo-in-the-empty-white-room moment. I had arrived at *the* question:

"Wait, Mama . . . is Jesus real?"

"Yes, Ralphie, of course Jesus is real."

"Really, Mama, *really*?"

"Yes, honey, Jesus is real. He sits at the hand of God."

"So you're saying there's a magical bearded fella who knows everything about us, whether we've been good or bad, he keeps score, and if we're good enough, he comes and gives us stuff—that guy is not real. But there's this *other* bearded fella who is *also* magical and knows everything about us, whether we've been good or bad, keeps score, and if we're good enough, he comes and provides for us—that guy *is* real?"

"Yes."

"I don't know if I fucking believe you, Mama. I think you're full of shit. I'm calling bullshit, Mama. You just told me you're a liar two seconds ago, how can I trust you?"

My mom was an emotional person and this really got the tears flowing. "I'm sorry, honey, maybe you should ask the preacher at church. He can tell you."

I thought about it for a second. "You mean that fucking liar who told me he hopes Santa brings me everything I asked for? That sonuvabitch?! Mama, how can I trust anything an adult tells me ever again?"

———

When school came back in session after winter break, the first thing we did in class was to share what we got for Christmas. The kids who had money got the toys their parents insisted they couldn't afford. The poor kids with no dads got empty promises, and the poor kids who had dads got homemade stuff that could probably kill them. I'm pretty sure all the poor kids in America who maimed, cut, or burned themselves when I was growing up did so with a dangerous implement their fathers made for them in the garage in lieu of getting them a bike or an Atari VCS. I didn't want to tell my classmates the truth about my Christmas presents, but I had to wear the evidence to school every day, so there was no hiding it. My feet were a walking crime scene.

I tried my best to make the Winners Choice shoes look cool. I hit the extra stripe with a layer of Wite-Out. I tried taking a seam ripper to it. Nothing could help those plastic pieces of shit, and since elementary-school kids are monstrous little pricks by nature, they spent the rest of the school year making fun of me. In the span of two months I went from being the coolest kid in third grade to being a leper.

Those were my real Christmas presents: a crappy sweater and a crisis of faith.

It took me years to get some of my faith back. I've got a little now. It's important, I think. Without faith in *something* you're just a pessimist, and no one likes to hang out with a cynic for long. Funnily enough, it was *The Matrix* that helped reel me back toward a more normal version of myself. I recognized my Winners Choice shoes and Santa's empty red suit in the red pill that Morpheus gave to Neo. I hadn't actually been stripped of faith: I'd been given the power to investigate questions whose answers I had only taken on faith up to then. I learned how to ask my own questions and come up with my own answers.

It's that combination—your own questions and your own answers—that sits at the foundation of good comedy. The combination is difficult to generate if you have not had your red-pill moment. The people who have, who can do it best, are usually the best comics. They are true skeptics, riding the red-pill wave until it crashes into a half-empty room of foreign tourists who don't get their jokes. At which point they want more than anything else to believe in Santa or Jesus again because one of them might actually be able to deliver a decent audience to their gigs one day.

2.
RUSTY WAS RETARDED GOOD

One of my first friends was a boy named Rusty Dugan, who lived down the road. We met one day when a group of kids from the neighborhood were playing in the street and Rusty came out to join us. He was wearing shorts and shoes and a T-shirt like everyone else, but he also wore a hard white plastic helmet that, today, I recognize as a mountain climber's helmet. He was the only kid with one of those. We all had parents who made us do and wear ridiculous shit, so nobody flinched when Rusty came up to introduce himself. Maybe the helmet was just his parents' unique way of humiliating him in front of his friends. Still, we had to ask:

"Why are you wearing a helmet?"

"I'm retarded."

None of us knew what that meant.

I thought, "He's retarded, I'm Methodist. Cool." I just wanted to keep playing.

We were young—we couldn't have been more than seven years old—and though we'd all heard the word *retarded* thrown around by the older kids, no one had ever bothered to define it for us. I doubt they even knew.

The Clarksville school district was no help either. Clarksville is a small town that lacked the resources for a separate special-needs class of any kind. Everyone was lumped in together—smart kids, dumb kids, kids who talked funny, kids who walked with a limp, even kids who wore helmets like Rusty. There was no obvious division between all of us that might have helped us understand what it meant to be retarded.

As we got older, our teachers told us more about Rusty's condition. If someone new came to our school, they told us to say that he was mentally handicapped. If an adult asked, we could say that he had Down's syndrome. *Down's syndrome?* None of us knew what that was. How would we? *Life Goes On* didn't premiere on ABC until we were all seniors in high school.

Rusty hated being labeled with *Down's syndrome.* He didn't enjoy being made to seem different from the rest of us. Nobody else had a "syndrome," so he didn't want one either. *Retarded* on the other hand? He was cool with that because, well, we were all retarded. I mean, *we were kids.* And kids as a group are kind of retarded. Have you ever watched a bunch of children left to their own devices? As a father of two young kids myself, I can confidently report that *retarded* is being generous. They are wild animals. At my house in Los Angeles every year, I throw a block party at the end of my street that is a combination end-of-summer celebration and joint birthday party for my kids. One year my boy August—who was right around the age Rusty and I were when we met—ran around the party in a cape like Darth Vader, whipping people in the legs as hard as he could with a long tree branch that he pretended was his light saber. Nobody paid it much mind. They didn't get mad. How could they? He was a kid. Kids are idiots. Nothing had changed about that in the thirty-five years since I'd first met Rusty. So the idea that Rusty was somehow different from any of us, that he was "special," never crossed his or our minds.

Down's syndrome brings a lot of different health problems with it, but the one that afflicted Rusty the most was anxiety. His was severe. When it was triggered, he would slam his head against things—walls, desks, car dashboards, mailboxes (hence the helmet). When he'd have an episode. it was a sad sight, but none of us pitied him. He wasn't somebody who wanted or needed to be treated with kid gloves. We took the same tests, played the same games, ate the same foods. He liked when we made fun of him for screwing up, the same way he made fun of one of us when we screwed up. When we played football after school, he would brag that he already had the proper equipment and made fun of us for being too poor to have helmets of our own. That was the kind of kid Rusty was. He was our buddy.

Middle school brought a lot of changes to our lives. We moved to a new school, puberty hit, awkward phases set in, girls became a thing. But Rusty had the most profound change of all of us. His penis grew like bamboo. I swear to God Almighty, this thing was so impressive Mark Twain could have written a short story about it. It was bigger than a baby arm by a wide margin. We had him measure it in class one time when we had a substitute teacher—it was nine and a half inches long, and thick. *Way* thick. Not paper-towel-tube thick. *Spray-paint-can thick.* Frankly, I was surprised he didn't have to tie his dick around his waist like a belt just so he could walk around without stepping on it all day. It was something to behold. Like the aurora borealis, with balls attached.

I will say I did not appreciate how much joy Rusty got from

reminding all of us that his wiener almost reached the end of the ruler. We get it, Rusty: you have the biggest wiener in Johnson County. Can't you just let us fuck up with girls on our own, on the strength of our shitty personalities, without adding our physical shortcomings to the list?

In high school, Rusty didn't need the helmet anymore. His anxiety hadn't gone away, but how he dealt with it had changed. Instead of beating his head against the wall, he was now beating his meat. Sometimes, even in class. He would punish that pecker like it had stolen something from him. And there was no stopping him. Once Rusty started beating off, once he got hold of that wiener, them cums was coming out. Sweet Jesus, did he have prodigious loads. Unfortunately, precision did not accompany his production. When he finished, the area around him looked like someone had dropped a balloon full of papier-mâché paste from the ceiling.

Eventually the school staff had to develop a system for handling these incidents. You couldn't just let him take the safety off that rocket launcher in a room full of teenagers. God forbid someone gets fragged. So whenever Rusty got agitated and the kraken came out, the teacher set off an alarm to get everybody else out of the room. I don't think they pulled the fire alarm, since that seems pretty irresponsible, but in a small town maybe they could get away with it. They just had to call the firehouse and tell the boys, "Don't you mind, it's only Rusty playing with his firehose again." Once we were all out of the room, they'd let Rusty beat off, then clean him up a little bit and put his crank back in his britches.

It wasn't a great system, but what are you going to do? Things were different thirty years ago. You work with what you're given. Thinking back, I'm impressed with the patience and care our teachers showed for Rusty. Can you imagine if an incident like that happened today? It'd end up on Snapchat and the teacher would file a workers'-comp claim with their union, like *they* were the ones who needed the most care.

As a good friend, I never made fun of Rusty for these incidents. I only did what any good friend would do. I used them to my advantage.

Late in the fall of our tenth-grade year, I woke up to one of the most beautiful Arkansas days I would ever experience. By 7:00 a.m. the sky was blue like a Sandals brochure. The sun had melted the cold snap out of the fall air. There was just enough of a breeze to remind you that winter was around the corner so you should take advantage of a day like this. It was *Ferris Bueller's Day Off* weather. The kind that made you believe in infinite possibilities and made a high school classroom the last place on earth you wanted to be.

I called my buddy Duane Parnell and made an executive decision: *We're going to Big Piney.*

Every high school has a place where kids go to cut school and get high. Ours was Big Piney—a big ol' lake off the Arkansas River about thirty minutes from Clarksville with a beach and a swimming area and a couple of secluded, poorly lit parking lots where you could bring your girl at night when she was finally ready to bang. During the summer it's a hot spot for families. Every other time, it's a great spot for ditching school and hiding from state troopers. In the middle of the week, no one would be there and we could do whatever we wanted.

I called up two of our other friends, Sean and Jason, and gave them the lowdown. They were immediately in. Sean was the best looking of all of us, so I told him to find some girls to come with us. While he did that, I scraped together whatever cash I could find, I grabbed my piece-of-shit Styrofoam cooler and took my brother's new truck to a gas station/convenience store across town with the intention of filling both those fuckers up.

I might be a big boy, but don't let anyone tell you Ralphie May can't get shit done with alacrity. By the time the bell rang for first period, we were all set. The truck had gas, the cooler had booze, and Sean had four girls who were up for anything—two of whom I thought I had a chance with if the day went according to plan.

The only thing left to figure out was how to get out of class early enough to take advantage of the beautiful day. Duane was the most concerned about that:

"Ralphie, how are we gonna get outta class?"

"Ralphie, why'd we even come to school in the first place?"

"Ralphie, what's the meaning of life?"

"Relax, I'll take care of it," I said finally as we walked from the parking lot to first period. "Just wait till English class and then play along."

English class started just after 11:00 a.m. It was the first class of the day that all four of us boys had together. Waiting until then to make our move made getting to the car and getting out of the parking lot much easier. We all got to class early (for a change), and right away the other guys started bird-doggin' me, looking for some kind of cue. Then Rusty walked in.

"Hey, Rusty, did you study?" I asked as he took his seat.

"Uh, yeah," he said, kind of confused. Rusty hated being unprepared. It made him feel like he didn't know something that everyone else knew, which made him feel like he didn't belong. And that could trigger his anxiety . . . if you did it right.

"No, Rusty, did you study for the test?"

"What test?" Now he was more confused.

"The test we're having today."

"Uhhh, I don't think we have a test today, Ralphie."

"Oh, yes, we do, Rusty. We are having a fuckin' test right now. And the teacher said that if one student fails, we all fail." To a kid who wants nothing more than to feel like everybody else, that was some cold-blooded, enhanced-interrogation-technique shit.

"Oh, no, she did not," Rusty said, panic rising in his throat.

Finally one of the Rhodes Scholars I called a coconspirator caught on and chimed in to back me up.

"Yeah, Rusty, we all fail if you fuck this up."

We'd just hit Rusty's anxiety trifecta. He was unprepared, everyone knew something that he didn't, and it was all happening *right now*.

"Oh no. Oooohhhh noo!" He repeated this like a mantra, the *no*'s getting more and more guttural, until venting his anxiety verbally wasn't enough. He started pulling at that big wiener through his pants like he was stretching taffy. We'd reached the tipping point. One more little nudge and it was all over but the jerking.

I shouted across the room, "Jason, Rusty hasn't studied for the test! Now we're all fucked."

"Oooh noo! *Ooohhh nooo!!!! Ooohhh nooo!!!!*" He started shaking and pulling at his jeans.

Time to pack up and get ready to go. This class is dismissed.

Right on cue, the bell rang and Rusty pulled out the python. He started wrestling that thing like he was Jake "the Snake" Roberts. He beat the absolute living shit out of it. That his wiener was still attached to his body after all those years was either a feat of amazing durability or a testament to God's grace, because only indestructible material or divine intervention could explain how something as delicate as a penis could endure all this stress and still maintain its structural integrity. It was a terrifying accomplishment.

No one in class was more terrified than the Baptist girls from

East Mount Zion Trinity Church. Those girls were from the north side of Clarksville, the unincorporated part right along the edge of the Ozark National Forest. If they saw an erect penis before marriage, they thought they'd turn into pillars of salt right then and there, so the second the teacher came in, saw what was happening, and pulled the alarm, they ran out of there like the Lord himself was calling them toward the Rapture. They were out the door and gone faster than the four of us, *and we were the ones with the big plans.*

Within two minutes of the alarm's sounding, we were piled into the truck with the girls, the go juice, some reefer, a tank of gas, and beautiful skies. It was one of the best Big Piney trips we took that year. And it was all thanks to Rusty and his pool noodle of a penis.

If I go to Hell when I die, it'll be because of this.

Don't feel too bad for Rusty. Not only did I get in trouble when it was found out we left school grounds after the alarm, but a few weeks later Rusty got his own revenge when he got me fired from my new job.

After digging change out of the sofa, searching all my pockets for extra dollar bills, and cuffing a ten-spot from my mama's pocketbook just to make the Big Piney trip possible, I realized I needed to get an honest-to-goodness job. Something with a salary and a schedule. Clarksville didn't have a ton of options for a poor high school kid whose main skill was being a smart-ass prankster, but this was 1987 and communism was beginning to crumble around the world, so there was hope. America was starting to feel its oats again and business owners were starting to be a little more generous with their opportunities.

Eventually I landed a cashier job at the McDonald's on Rogers

Street down by Interstate 40. Back in the day it wasn't the worst thing in the world to work at a McDonald's. It still isn't in my opinion. Nothing builds ambition like working your ass off at a shitty job. Not that it was going to be all that bad. I got to handle the money, I got first pick of all the Happy Meal toys, I got free shift meals and a sweet-ass visor, and I'd be able to hook up my friends whenever they came by. It was the best two-hour job you could get.

On my first day, Rusty was the only one who came in. Like a true friend, I got him exactly what he wanted—a Quarter Pounder with cheese and a vanilla milk shake—despite all my reservations. Whenever Rusty had a milk shake he'd lose his damn mind from the brain freeze. He'd go into this eye-blinking, foot-stomping, temple-pressing spasm that was one of the only times he actually *seemed retarded.* I'd tell him he should slow down, but he didn't quite understand the concept of brain freeze, so he'd ignore me. He thought I was trying to get him to stop because I'm fat and wanted to steal his milk shake. I tried bargaining with him, but his position was firm. Retarded people really love milk shakes, according to Rusty. There was no point.

So Rusty's order comes up, I put it on a tray and hand it to him. You can tell me what happened next was accidental. You can forensically examine the facts of the case like it's the Zapruder film and tell me he didn't plan on getting me fired, and I'll call you a damn liar, because this is what he did. Holding his tray directly in front of my register, eyeballing me like a sonuvabitch, he yells:

"Thank you so much for the free food, Ralphie May. I've never come to McDonald's and gotten the free food ever. This is the greatest McDonald's for free food of all time!"

As soon as he yelled "thank you" and "free food," my boss was on me. He was not amused that I was giving away product—not even to a retarded kid. I tried to protest. I told him I didn't remember reading in the employee handbook any explicit prohibition against hooking up your friends. I wanted to tell him that during my training shift the other employees said it was cool, as long as we took care of each other's friends too, but I figured if I did that and it didn't work, they'd blacklist me, and there was only one McDonald's in Clarksville. You *do not* want to get banned from the only golden arches in your town, believe me.

So my boss fired me. I'd lasted two hours. Two and a half if you include the time it took for him to calculate my wages and cut me a check: $6.70. I've spent more time in a single visit to McDonald's as a customer than I did as an employee.

Without missing a beat Rusty announces, "If you're gonna fire Ralphie, I'll come work for you, no problem." My boss hired him on the spot. I can even understand his rationale: Rusty might be retarded, but at least he isn't fucking stupid.

I should have seen it coming. Rusty had wanted a job so badly since we all took the Armed Services Vocational Aptitude Battery (ASVAB) test in October. I don't know how he scored, but the US military-industrial complex determined that he possessed vocational aptitude of some sort. He was so proud. I was so pissed.

"What the hell are you doing, Rusty? You just got me fucking fired!"

"It's fine, Ralphie, don't worry." He had that special retard twinkle in his eye. "I'll hook you up."

That's some brazen, Machiavellian shit right there. And the worst part, if I accused him of it, no one would ever believe me.

Despite that motherfucker getting me fired *and* taking my job, Rusty was still our friend. He went everywhere with us. We hung out like he was a normal kid because, really, he was. We'd even take him to parties with us. He was hilarious in a crowd. He had a better sense of humor than half the openers I worked with coming up in Texas a few years later.

One time we took Rusty to a house party where we heard a bunch of Coal Hill girls were going to be. All the good ass came from Coal Hill, Arkansas, back in those days. Thanks to AIDS and Nancy Reagan, with her D.A.R.E. programs and her "Just Say No" propaganda, the rest of Johnson County was a dry vagina. If girls weren't already afraid of getting pregnant, now they were afraid their pussy might fall off if they let your wiener get anywhere near it. And the ones who didn't even think that way had a bunch of stingy fuckers from the church house telling them to save their flowers for Jesus. The whole thing was a disaster.

The only people who didn't get the message were the girls from Coal Hill. Coal Hill is twenty minutes west of Clarksville and about a tenth of the size, with—at least in 1988—ten times more girls down to fuck. When you were at a party where Coal Hill girls showed up, it was like finding a bottle of whiskey in a dry county. You didn't ask questions and you didn't complain, you just tried to get a taste.

By the time we got to the party, everyone was feeling pretty good. It was the usual mix of characters at a high school party: the bros, the passed-out lightweights, the couples making out, the daredevils jumping off shit, the burners, the normal cliques of friends, the criers, and of course the crazy drunk girl.

The crazy drunk girl at this party was from Coal Hill, obviously. She was kind of cute in the way any girl in high school who seems like you might be able to bang her is cute. She was not cute enough to put up with her craziness, but her drunk screaming made her hard to ignore. All she would talk about was how much she wanted "big dick." She shouted it over and over from the top of her lungs. It was getting to be too much, and I was about to tell her what was what, when I had an idea.

"Well, don't look at me," I said, "mine is just medium. But I know the biggest dick in Johnson County."

"No, you don't!" she said excitedly, then grabbed my crotch. She thought I was being coy and talking about myself. I know what you must be thinking: "Ralphie May, are you telling me a drunk, cock-crazy Coal Hill girl misread a social situation?" I know, alert the media.

"No, I didn't mean me," I told her, "but don't you worry, just go on into the back bedroom, turn out the lights, and we'll bring in the guy with the biggest wiener you ever saw."

"You mean he's here?!!" she yelled. Nothing got by her.

"Right here at this party."

"Keep in mind," I prepped the Coal Hill girl, "he's been drinking all night and he's already a little fucked-up." I wanted to create a plausible cover story for why Rusty might look all Down's syndrome–y. "I'll tell him to go slow at first so he doesn't puncture your fallopian tubes."

"Oh my God, how big is it?!"

I held up my hands about a foot apart—basically the length of a two-pound Big Piney bass.

It's hard to distinguish between terror and excitement when you're buzzed, but I chose to believe her wide-eyed, stupefied look was born of enthusiasm because, I mean, c'mon, she's from Coal Hill.

"Go get naked and get that pussy warmed up." She was going to need all the help (and spit) she could get. She disappeared down a hallway toward the back of the house. When she was out of sight, I went into the backyard where most of the people were hanging out and grabbed Rusty.

"Hey, Rusty, there's a girl in the back who wants to fuck you." Simpler is always better.

"Oh. okay." No comprehension was in his words.

"You just gotta go in there, get your wiener hard, and put it in her. Nice and slow at first, then a little faster and a little faster. Don't shoot the cums in her, but ya know, you can put it anywhere else. Like at school. It don't matter."

Rusty said, "Okay," about twelve times, like someone repeating a filler word while his brain catches up to the concept he's trying to grasp. By the ninth "Okay" I think his brain caught up. He understood what was about to happen and was excited. We got him all pumped up. Right before he went in there, he yelled, "Go, Panthers!" He was going to do her for the team. God bless that goofy sonuvabitch.

He was in the bedroom for no more than thirty seconds before he came out with his wiener in his hand, screaming, *"There's something wrong with her. She don't got no pee-pee."* Rusty thought everybody had wieners. It had never dawned on us that Rusty had no understanding of the differences between male and female bodies. He treated everyone equally, so he thought people were equal in every way. He figured they were just like him.

"No, no, it's in there, buddy, it's just really tiny and covered up. Just have her do it. Have her put you inside of her."

I don't think he quite understood what we meant, but, boy, I tell you what, Rusty took to it like a goddamn natural. He fucked her for thirty to forty minutes straight. I mean, can you imagine? Your first piece of ass and you last for half an hour, and she's screaming in ecstasy the whole time? Rusty came out of that back bedroom a new man. I bet that girl had to sit on frozen peas for a week.

If that had happened to me, if I'd come out of the gate and

punched my v-card like a champ, I could have dropped dead right then and there, content with having lived a full life at sixteen years old.

We asked him how it went.

"Oh, she's a good girl. I like her a lot."

That was Rusty. A sweetheart of a man.

If I go to Heaven when I die, it'll be because of this.

I lost track of Rusty for a while after I moved to Houston and started doing stand-up. We reconnected a couple times over those early post–high school years when I'd come back to Arkansas for holidays or gigs, but eventually we lost touch for good. A few years later I found out from my friend, Jon Byrd, that Rusty had been diagnosed with multiple sclerosis. MS is a bitch for an otherwise healthy adult. For someone with Down's syndrome, who is already immunocompromised, it's a complete fuck job. He died not long after.

Rusty taught me more about what it means to be a good human than anybody else in my life up to the point that we parted ways. Teacher, parent, friend, mentor, you name it. None of them matched the impact Rusty had on me as a person in the world.

Thanks to Rusty, growing up, I had no idea that retarded people were that different from normal people. I learned to treat everyone the same by watching him do it.

Thanks to Rusty, I firmly believe that retarded people are the best part of our society: They don't wage war, they love everybody, and they work bad jobs and are oftentimes so happy to have them that they'll fucking steal them from you. They are model Americans. I've known this my whole life, but snobby intellectuals have tried to keep it a secret from everyone by using code words and politically correct phrases, because they don't want us to realize that they are the completely useless ones, not the retarded people. I'm pretty sure Rusty would agree.

Thanks to Rusty, I learned how simple it is to be happy if you let yourself be. You know what made Rusty happy in elementary school? His Scooby-Doo lunch box. It was one of the good metal ones with the thermos that could keep pea soup hot until four o'clock. He looked at that lunch box like he'd hit the damn kid lottery. He was genuinely happy with what he had. In high school it wasn't much different. He liked hanging out with us. That's all he needed.

Most of us will never be as happy as Rusty was while he was alive. We'll try, and we'll get close for about twenty-six seconds every year, right at the apex of a really, really, *really* good orgasm that we didn't have to beg for, but that's as close as we'll get most times. I wish we all could be more like Rusty. I try every day. It's not easy, but it's worth the effort, because Rusty was retarded good.

3.

THE LORD GIVETH AND HE TAKETH AWAY

By the time I entered high school, my granny had been diagnosed with Alzheimer's disease and begun to deteriorate rapidly enough that my mom had to quit her job to take care of her. This meant that we May kids were on our own most days. That was no problem for my brother, Winston, or my sisters. They were older and already doing their own thing. They had jobs and spending money. If they didn't show up to work, they'd get fired, and nobody else would have to know about it. For me, it was a little trickier. If I didn't get out of bed on time to make first period every morning, I'd have teachers and administrators up my ass, which meant they'd call home or come around asking after my mom. Her plate was full already, I didn't want to add more to it. So to give myself a little bit of flexibility and get around the potential inconvenience of administrative interlopers, I convinced my mom to let me get a hardship driver's license—at fourteen years old.

A hardship license is basically permission from the state to drive before the technical legal age because circumstances outside your control have left you high and dry. Depending on the state you live in, a few criteria determine your eligibility: Do you need it to get to school? Do you need it to get to work? Do you need it for a long-term health issue? Yes, yes, and, unfortunately, yes. There are usually only two stipulations: One, you have to keep a C average. Okay, fine, whatever. Two, no pleasure driving whatsoever. Well, fuck you very much, Uncle Sam.

I was psyched to be able to drive myself around. It wasn't the driving itself that was so cool. Most kids from rural areas grew up driving tractors and work trucks around their property as soon as their feet could reach the pedals. What was cool was being a freshman pulling into the school parking lot in your older brother's 1986 blue-on-blue Chevy Silverado, blaring the Eagles' *Greatest Hits* album out of the tape deck while eyeballing the sophomore girls like you were a senior, all before you were old enough to shave.

The government said I couldn't drive *for* pleasure; they didn't say I couldn't drive *with* pleasure.

In the beginning, I followed the rules. Home to school and back. That was it. Then I got a job. Home to school to work and back. For a time, the euphoria of being one of the only kids in my class who could drive on the streets was enough to sustain me. But eventually, like any kids who are given a little bit of extra freedom and responsibility before they are ready for it, I started to test the boundaries.

"Well, depending on how you look at it, Deputy, the bowling alley with the bitchin' arcade *is* between my house and my school."

Slowly but surely over my freshman year, the rules governing my underaged driving vanished like brownies at a potluck. I was third-generation Clarksville, after all. Everyone knew what was going on with Granny and my mama. They had sympathy for us when they saw me cruising around at a time and a place that was clearly not school or work related. As long as I didn't run over anybody's kid, nobody asked any questions.

When you're poor, nothing beats earning your own money to buy your first car. It's a particular achievement when the alternative—borrowing your brother's truck—becomes too difficult to coordinate and you actually *need* a car as much you *want* one. I was able to earn enough money to buy and fix up my own car by the time I got my real driver's license in February of my sophomore year, thanks to my buddy Duane Parnell's dad and a Chevy truck full of drugs.

Duane's daddy worked in the regional office of a federal drug enforcement agency. His division did all manner of raids and property seizures, so anytime we were out of school, he'd bring home cars that they'd seized and impounded on drug raids or traffic stops and pay us to clean them up real nice for auction. We'd set up a cleaning station at the end of the Parnell family driveway just in front of their garage, and Mr. Parnell would let us run the cars through our little setup. Over the summer between our freshman and sophomore years, he ran cars through like they were on a conveyor belt. I wasn't complaining—more cars equaled more money—but even then it seemed like we had a lot of business for a place as out of the way as Northwest Arkansas. Was this whole detailing gig even part of Mr. Parnell's job? Were these cars *really* going to auction? Or was he running some kind of side hustle out the back gate of the agency's impound lot? Neither of us was ever really sure.

On the one hand, Duane's older brother ran with a notorious

biker gang who I will not name since I like staying alive, and they say the apple doesn't fall far from the tree, so maybe Mr. Parnell was a fence. On the other hand, an *actual* part of Mr. Parnell's job that we knew about was to go around to all the schools in the surrounding counties and scare the hell out of kids about drugs. A man like that isn't running a chop shop out of his driveway, right? Mr. Parnell was straight. He was all-in on the antidrug thing. He had a whole presentation with a display case full of drugs and stories about all the bad things each offender had done while on the drugs. He even let you come up and get a close look at both the drugs and the mug shots of the people the troopers took the drugs from. He really wanted it to sink in. *This could be you.*

For a good number of the God-fearing Johnson County youth, Mr. Parnell's display case chastened them just the way he hoped. For some, it made no impact. For Duane and me, the display case became our personal drug cabinet. On days when we had multiple cars to wash, we'd race through the first one, then go into the garage where Mr. Parnell kept the case, grab some of the drugs (only the smokable types), then fire them up in the backseat of one of the cars at the back of the line. That way, if he came outside unexpectedly, we could quickly stuff the drugs under one of the front seats and blame the druggies whose car it was.

"Wooo-eee, Mr. Parnell, this one here's a real stinker. They must've been some serious druggers you took this from, huh? It's gonna be extrahard to get clean, I think. We should probably get paid double for this one."

"Nice try, May," he'd say, shaking his head. "Dinner's at eighteen thirty sharp, son. These best be done in time for you to wash up before."

"Yes, sir," Duane would say. Then, after Mr. Parnell went back inside, we'd use whatever we could find to replace the drugs we'd taken.

One time we replaced a chunk of hash with a piece of petrified dog poo from the neighbor's yard. This little butt nugget looked *exactly* like the Kush we'd just smoked. And it was sitting right there in front of us, like the face of Christ in a piece of toast. It was amazing. Duane stood watch while I carved off a piece of the turd with his mother's garden trowel. He picked it off the tip with a napkin from the glove box of the 1986 Ford Mustang GT we smoked its doppelgänger in, then replaced it in the display case while I made a production out of getting started with the next car.

We thought we were so slick.

A few weeks into the summer after freshman year, we discovered that Mr. Parnell's cabinet of delights wasn't our only source of good times. Early one afternoon we were going through a cherry 1972 Chevy truck, buffing out every scuff, polishing every chrome knob and handle, when Duane bumped a hidden switch and a secret compartment popped open underneath the passenger-side dash. At first I thought it was just the glove box that had accidentally fallen open, but the compartment was too big and opened too far to be a factory install. Duane reached over to close it back up, but it was too heavy to move with just a flick of his fingers like a normal glove box. I bent down to investigate. There staring back at us were ten half-pound pouches of marijuana, a small brick of cocaine, and $8,000 in cash.

I would like to say that when Duane and I set our eyes on this bounty, we were so cool that all we saw were dollar signs and images of porny debauchery. The reality is, we fucking panicked. *Somebody* wants those drugs back—could be a bad guy, could be a good guy—and somehow they're going to know that we are the people who have them. That's how the thinking goes in the mind of a teenager whose primary frame of reference for drug dealers is episodes of *Miami Vice*.

Duane ran to get his dad. I stood there frozen. When you've never seen that kind of weight before, it feels like you're staring into a crystal ball that's showing you a future of getting butt-raped in a jail cell.

I shook off the flash of paranoia just in time to stop Duane before he reached the back door.

"Duane, don't!"

"Don't what?"

"Don't tell your dad. Not yet." Duane saw the gears turning behind my eyes. He knew that look. "We should keep it, " I said as he came back over to the Chevy truck.

"We can't do that, Ralphie. Those are *drugs*."

"No, that's money. And that's just a little reefer."

"Yeah, but that's cocaine!"

"You're right. We should give him the coke."

"Thank you. Okay—"

"But we keep the rest."

I understood the pickle Duane was in as the son of a federal law enforcement employee. Yes, cocaine is worse than marijuana, so it's good that we were telling his dad about it, but keeping the weed wasn't somehow *less* illegal. Something is either legal or illegal, that's it. That's how Duane was taught.

I was not interested in that kind of black-and-white distinction—not back then. Life was shades of gray. Or in this instance, shades of green, and the only distinction I cared about was the one between "kind bud" green and "cold hard cash" green. Ours was Mexican dirt weed, which sat somewhere in the middle.

Before his dad came outside and stumbled on our mother lode,

I needed Duane to understand where I was coming from: mainly that ever since my granny got real sick and my brother started being a dick about letting me use his truck, I needed to find as many ways as possible to make money. Washing cars for Duane's dad was a good start, but it wasn't nearly enough. I needed to get a car. I needed to buy clothes and shoes for school, and school was right around the corner. I needed to pay my Boy Scouts dues for the World Scout Jamboree in Australia later in the year. And most important, we needed to party our balls off before summer ended.

"You don't really think it was a coincidence that you just happened to hit the exact right spot in that moment for the compartment to open, do you?" I pleaded. "No, sir, Duane Parnell. This is a sign. We were *meant* to find this stuff. You and me, nobody else."

As a baptized-but-lapsed Methodist I was prepared to go full Christian Revival on Duane to make him see the light. If I had to conjure the spirit of our Lord and Savior through John's earthly vessel to convince him that the secret compartment in this 1972 Chevy truck was our personal Ark of the Covenant, well then, it was time to testify. As a good Christian, a great American, and an even better friend, Duane didn't let it get that far. He was in. We split the cash, sold a bunch of the reefer, went to tons of concerts, and what we didn't spend throwing big bonfire parties in the woods with a bunch of kegs, I used to buy a 1979 burgundy-on-burgundy Oldsmobile Cutlass Supreme with notchback velour bench seats and a 5.7-liter 350 Rocket V-8 engine. A bona fide all-American fuck machine.

The fall of 1987 passed like my first month of third grade . . . *times a million*. Our football team was good, I still had a bunch of weed left over from our summertime fire sale, and best of all I had a girlfriend who I could drive around in my very own car. When you've got all 350 of the horsies in that Cutlass pulling you around sweeping country roads as smooth as a ribbon of silk, with the ass end sunk into the road and your girl's ass sunk in right next to you, you can't help but feel like the king of the world.

Riding in the Cutlass was like floating in a cocoon forged out of freedom. It provided a sense of security and comfort that had largely been missing from other areas of my life up to then. When I was behind the wheel, all felt right in the world. I drove it everywhere, every day.

One weekend early in the spring semester, just after my birthday, central Arkansas experienced an unseasonable warm spell, and a group of us decided to go camping down south at Lake Ouachita to take advantage of it. The Cutlass is good for cruising, it's good for screwing, but it ain't no good for camping. So I begged by brother, Winston, to switch cars with me. His Silverado was ideal for hauling a bunch of gear.

Friday morning I grabbed his keys and headed out. The plan was to go to school, *ditch* school, pick up supplies, then head home to get some sleep before an early drive Saturday morning to the campground. Easy-breezy.

On the way home from the store I was cruising down a country road I'd traveled a thousand times, listening to that old worn-out Eagles' *Greatest Hits* album again with my windows down and my seat belt off, and I was struck by a weird combination of excitement about my future and what I would later recognize as nostalgia (for what, I still have no idea). It felt like one of those moments in your life where everything is in sync, like you can feel yourself going with the flow, and the flow is going in the right direction.

It felt like that right up until the moment I was hit by a drunk driver.

Floating down the road on autopilot, letting "Witchy Woman" lull me into a false sense of security, a car headed in the opposite direction crossed over the lane line and hit the front driver's-side quarter panel of the Silverado at full speed. The impact pushed the truck laterally toward the shoulder of the road, then rolled it down an embankment on its longitudinal axis into a ditch between the road and a soybean field.

According to the sheriff's deputy who found me, the truck rolled between two to four times, landing on its side. It's a miracle he found me at all. You couldn't see the truck down in the ditch from the road surface until you were right on top of me, and even then you'd have to be looking because it was starting to get dark and the guy who hit me was long gone (I assume it was a guy—they never found him). Thankfully, a lady down the road heard what sounded to her like a large explosion and she called the sheriff.

When the deputy arrived on the scene, the searching beam of his flashlight shocked me back into consciousness for about ninety seconds. All I know about the accident I learned from the police reports. I remember only two things from that brief period of lucidity: the smell of gasoline and the sound of "Witchy Woman." Through the mayhem and carnage and twisted metal, the engine of the Silverado was still running, and the tape deck was still playing. I don't know if that says more about the sturdiness of Chevy trucks or the indestructibility of 1970s California country rock, but to this day if I hear "Witchy Woman" playing in a grocery store or a dentist's office, I have to leave, and it takes me a couple days to get back to normal.

I spent the next nine days in a medically induced coma with swelling on the brain from what's called a coup/contrecoup injury—basically a double concussion where your brain bounces

off both sides of your skull like a *Price Is Right* Plinko chip rat-
tling into the $0 slot.

When I finally woke up, I learned the extent of my injuries:
forty-two broken bones, sixty-four separate breaks; three broken
vertebrae, two in my neck; significant breaks in the large bones of
the arms and legs; and, worst of all, sixteen separate fractures in
my collarbone. With no air bag or seat belt, my upper chest took
the full force of the initial collision. It's been nearly thirty years
and my collarbone still isn't right.

The next forty-eight days in the hospital were an endless painful
parade of blood draws, sponge baths, sheets changes, 5:00 a.m.
doctor's rounds, X-rays, CT scans, surgeries, and visits from
friends, family, teachers, and my girlfriend. The visits petered out
after the first week—the hospital was thirty miles away and people
had to move forward with their lives—but the *physically* painful
stuff continued pretty much right up until I was discharged.

At the time of the accident, I was already a big boy. I walked
around at about 240 pounds, but I was country strong too, and in
the South, a nice fat cap on your brisket is nothing to be ashamed
of. Big boys like me—we carried our weight around with grace
and aplomb. Did you ever watch Paul Prudhomme's cooking
show? That man could slide around in a rolling chair like a prima
ballerina.

I was not so lucky. While I recuperated, I lost a fair amount
of weight, but mostly from my muscles atrophying for lack of use.
When I got out of the hospital, they confined me to a wheelchair
with braces on my legs and splints on my wrists, which just meant
more atrophy. Except now, instead of choking down a calorically
controlled regimen of lukewarm hospital food or being fed intra-
venously from what looked like a large bag of horse cum, I could
go to all my favorite places and mow down the largest, fattiest,

saltiest, greasiest plates of deliciousness imaginable. This is when the big weight gain began. Adding weight while you are losing muscle is the worst possible combination. It's like getting Eiffel Tower–ed by fatness and feebleness. You're fucked coming and going.

Then, just to add insult to injury, my girlfriend broke up with me, my mother and my aunt (her sister) got into a fight over my granny's care, and they decided to move her down to Prattville, Alabama, as some fucked-up kind of conflict resolution, and then Clarksville High School administrators tried to make me repeat my sophomore year. I'd missed so many days since the accident, they said, and since I wouldn't be getting back to regular classes until a month before school was out for the summer, it made the most sense to just stay home, recuperate fully, and run it back full speed the following September.

How thoughtful of them.

What *I* thought made the most sense was for them to fuck right off and let me finish out the year, take all the tests I missed, and let the chips fall where they may. What were they going to do? *Not* let me go to class? Bar the doors? Expel the fat kid in the wheelchair?

Good luck with that one.

There are two types of transformative experiences in life: the ones that change the way you see the world, and the ones that change the way you travel through it. My accident was the latter. Nothing would be the same for me after getting out of that goddamn wheelchair just before the end of sophomore year. Honor roll? College? Those are both great, but life is too short and fleeting to work your ass off for a piece of paper. I was fortunate to live through my accident, and I had no intention of taking my second chance for granted. If I was going to live, I was going to live *for right now*.

That is not the type of realization most people come to expect from a sixteen-year-old kid from small-town Arkansas. Yet, most sixteen-year-olds haven't been taking care of themselves for a few years already, and even fewer have survived getting T-boned at high-speed in what, at the time, felt suspiciously like a giant dose of karmic retribution for pocketing all that Chevy truck cash during the summer.

The people least prepared for my epiphany were the administrators of Clarksville High School. They had no idea I saw right through the crackerjack bullshit they called school. They didn't understand that they couldn't threaten me with grades or the fear of poor marks on my "permanent record" ruining my life. Motherfucker, I've been to the other side of *existence*, you haven't even been to the other side of the state!

I'd seen the world too. A year earlier I went to Australia with the Boy Scouts for the World Scout Jamboree. I hung out on Bondi Beach and saw topless ladies just chilling like it was nothing. I learned to flirt with Kiwi girls and play the didgeridoo. Some Maori dudes taught us how to do the haka. I didn't need a diploma for any of that shit, and I don't need your blessing to do something meaningful with my life either.

This realization was incredibly freeing to my spirit, and it couldn't have come at a better time as I tried to get back to some semblance of normalcy after the accident. The problem was, as a kid, inner freedom turns everything else into a prison because you lack the means to break out and follow your spirit. Nobody's giving you a credit card or renting you a hotel room or an apartment. You're a prisoner of the system. It only gets worse when you discover the one thing that the wardens of that prison system—principals, teachers, parents—have been trying to hide from kids for centuries: that they're all just making this shit up as they go along. They have no fucking idea what they are doing.

That's the curse of intelligence, of enlightenment, of seeing the matrix for what it really is. It strips away your delusions and ignorances. It takes away all your hiding places and forces you to confront everything—both the good and the bad.

Clarksville, Arkansas, was not prepared to have that daisy cutter of truth dropped through the roof of its self-imposed prison. Fortunately for the residents, they'd be rid of me sooner than they expected.

4.

THE LEGEND OF SWEET DICK

Sex is a lot like stand-up comedy. If you really want to do it, you can't let fear or doubt get in your way—you have to go for it. Not in the Donald Trump pussy-grabbing way, obviously, more in the putting-yourself-out-there-and-being-vulnerable way. At first you don't particularly care where you do it. If you can find some dirty hole on the wrong side of the tracks that will let you get up in there, you'll be there with bells on, because in the beginning, it's the reps—the experience—that matter most. Eventually, though, doing it for its own sake isn't enough. You want to be good at it. You want to be able to get up in all the best spots. To do that you have to develop a thing—a niche—that helps you stand out and attract a crowd. It took me several years of open mics, hosting spots, and middling at clubs all over Texas to find my footing on-stage, but I found my fuck game much earlier—on a Saturday night during my senior year, in the front seat of the Cutlass, parked behind a baseball diamond on the outskirts of town.

I was deep into my "I don't give a fuck" period when I nutted up to ask Allie out to dinner and a movie. I don't remember if that was her actual name, but Allie sounds like the name of a fun, cool, beautiful girl who is up for getting down in the front of a comfy Cutty—which she was—so we'll go with that.

Our first stop was Mazzio's Pizza for some delicious pie. Mazzio's is a chain restaurant throughout the South that has that good thick-crust pizza, which helps it hold a whole mess of meat toppings. If you don't want pizza, they also make hoagies. And if you are on a diet, they have a salad bar. For a sixteen-year-old kid with an appetite and a budget, Mazzio's was the tits.

My friend Kevin's father owned the Mazzio's in Clarksville. Besides owning a legit dinner-date triple threat, he also had the most awesome Arkansas name ever: L. Freeman Wish. Who's giving L. Freeman Wish a hard time? You hear L. Freeman Wish is on the phone, *you take that call.* Let me tell you, if you're sick of getting kicked around by fate, there are worse things you could do than make friends with people whose first names are an initial. I do believe that is one of the secrets to making an easy life for yourself. It was definitely one of the secrets to hooking up a large six-meat pie on the fly.

After Mazzio's, we drove thirty miles east to the Rickwood Theater over in Russellville. Thirty miles is a long way to go to see a movie, but back then the Rickwood was the only theater for two counties, so you did what you had to do to get your date in a dark room with no parents around. Besides, you don't follow up a majestic six-meat pie with shadow puppets on the side of a barn if you're trying to impress a gal. You procure tickets to one of Hollywood's finest new releases in THX high-fidelity cinema-quality sound.

It wasn't all bad. Sixty miles round-trip gives you a lot of time to get high and get to know each other's private parts.

In anticipation, I stuffed a sixer of Budweiser and two four-packs of Bartles & Jaymes Mountain Berry wine coolers (for the lady) into one of those shitty grocery-store Styrofoam coolers shaped like an old McDonald's, with the pagoda lid that never stayed on unless you flipped it upside down. I'd had this cooler for at least a year, so it was beaten all to hell, but it was perfect for the backseat. The angled sides and trapezoid lid pressed against the seat back, while the bottom stayed flush with the seat itself, which kept the cooler sitting upright the whole ride. I was going to get one of the new models with the red plastic handle (the ones that fell apart like a Whole Foods bag), but they moved to a square design, which would lean backward and slosh all over the seat once the ice melted. The new model was also a dollar more, and I needed that dollar for ice.

These are the things you think about when you want a date to go perfect.

I also picked up two joints from my buddy Joel Penny. Joel Penny was a Renaissance man born to the wrong era. He was whip-smart, he read books, he played the saxophone, and he had the best long hair in school. It wasn't that bleached-blond, straight-as-hay Bret Michaels eighties hair. It was more like a Glenn Frey, let's-spark-a-doobie-and-start-a-band-in-1971 type of hair. A cascade of wavy brown locks that flared at the ears and curled at the bottom and made all the girls jealous. Remember that famous Farrah Fawcett poster in the red swimsuit with the hairstyle that every woman tried to copy for like a decade? Well, they weren't

copying Farrah—that poster came out in 1976—they were copying Glenn Frey. And Joel Penny had the look down pat. He also
had a bunch of shit weed that he rolled for you into the finest
joints in all the land. Joel was a master craftsman. The joints were
as long as caterpillars and as smooth, fat, and round as silkworm
cocoons. They were a joy to smoke. Lord Jesus, they were works
of art.

With two Joel Penny joints in the ashtray—one to loosen up the
nerves on the way down to the theater, one to loosen up the mor-
als on the way back up—the table was now set for a great date. I
mean, Mazzio's Pizza for dinner, a small popcorn and a Coke at
the theater, some alcohol and some weed for the ride? Come on
now, who's better than me? I even let Allie pick the movie. Odds
were in my favor that we were going to be making out most of the
time anyway, so what did I care? We probably saw *Willow* or some
shit, I don't remember.

Sure enough, we made out the whole time: through the coming
attractions, through the dancing snacks singing, "Let's all go to
the lobby!," through the film, through the credits, all the way until
the houselights came up. It was great. The ride home was great
too. We passed the second joint back and forth. We broke into the
second four-pack of wine coolers. As we pulled into Clarksville,
things could not have been going better. This presented me with
a decision: take Allie home or take our relationship to the next
level.

"Wanna go to Cline Park?" I asked.

"Sure, yeah," she said.

Cline Park is on the northeastern edge of Clarksville, right
where the big road that winds through the Ozark National Forest
dumps down into town and ends. The park was a favorite of kids
from my high school because it's out of the way and has a good

amount of privacy thanks to a couple of baseball diamonds ringed by long, narrow parking lots, each with a single row of parking spots. There's more privacy in a single-row parking lot than a rectangular-grid-style lot because you really have to look around to see other cars in a single row, and they really have to look around to see you. In that configuration everyone is more apt to mind their own business unless they want their dates to think they're perverts. This made Cline Park the perfect spot for what would become a Ralphie May specialty—some good ol'-fashioned finger blasting.

At some point in the final decade of the twentieth century, finger blasting got a bad rap. It became the female equivalent of the hand job. Disrespected, disregarded, considered déclassé. I don't know exactly when or why this happened, but it was a sad day for America and a horrible way to end the millennium. Finger blasting, like hand jobs, is a cornerstone of sexual maturation for teenagers. It is to sexual experience what the five-minute opening gig is to stand-up comedy. For most of us, it's our first hands-on experience with the parts that make the babies. It helps us figure out where everything is, what feels good, and for how long. It's the gateway to sex. It also builds stamina that transfers directly over when sex finally happens. You think you just *inherited* the wrist and hand strength necessary for some good prolonged missionary (for guys) and doggy style (for women) fucking? Like it's a gene? Hell no. That comes from a steady regimen of hand jacking and finger blasting. It's sexual calisthenics. It's third base. And you can't play baseball without third base, now can you? That's how important finger blasting was, is, and should always be.

That doesn't mean it was easy. Those high-waisted Guess jeans from the eighties were every guy's nemesis. You popped the button at the top thinking you were home free, then these two giant bolts of stiff fabric were held together by a zipper that wasn't nearly long enough to make up for the extra distance you had to cover with your hand. They were denim chastity belts. You could be elbow deep in a girl's jeans before you hit pay dirt. It's why they called them Guess jeans. "Hey, fellas, guess where her pussy is."

Allie's jeans were no exception. I practically armbarred myself getting down her pants, navigating that wild Porky's bush, then finding my way in. Once I did, Allie was *really* into it. She was alternately squirming and convulsing and bucking. She looked like she was riding the world's slowest-moving rodeo bull. I didn't know girls could move their hips like that. I also didn't know that when their legs closed around your hand and crushed it into a million pieces, it probably meant they were having an orgasm.

Then Allie did something I'd never heard of a girl doing: she pulled down her pants so I could get a better angle. Petty, judgmental bitches might call her a slut for doing that, but I call her an angel of mercy. Ten more minutes and I would've been on the disabled list with a repetitive-stress injury. Not that it would have been such a bad thing for my reputation. Can you imagine going to school on Monday wearing an orthopedic wrist brace?

"What's wrong? Get in another car wreck?"

"Nah, got the carpal tunnel this weekend."

"How'd that happen?"

"Oh, you know, just a little too much finger blasting."

Allie and I went at it for one whole side of a mixtape. I can't explain how into it she was. I remember thinking, *Man, you're great at this! Maybe this is your thing*, your purpose. *You're the master finger blaster. That's how you're gonna get laid every weekend until you graduate. The word will spread around school, then around Clarks-*

ville, and the girls will just line up to get some before you blow this pop stand for bigger and better things.

This ridiculous train of thought was finally derailed when I had to flip the cassette and adjust myself because my boner was killing me. I'd been able to ignore the discomfort by keeping my entire focus on tenderizing that 'giner meat. Once my concentration was broken, all that extra blood my brain was using flooded down to my pecker until it felt like it might break off inside my pants if I didn't do something. So I let the python out of the terrarium and guided Allie's hand to it like I was teaching Helen Keller her first braille lesson.

It's still one of the most reckless and courageous moments of my romantic life—right up there with saying "I love you" and "I do." So many things could have gone wrong in that moment. She could have slapped me. She could have recoiled and jumped out of the car and run home to tell her daddy. She could have told everyone at school that it was small or weird or ugly. Instead, thank the Lord, Allie started tugging on it, and I instantly relaxed into the seat. My hands went to my sides, my head tilted back, I was a puddle of flesh. It felt like the only bone left in my body was the one in her hand.

Allie took this reclined pose to mean that I wanted her to give me a blow job. Now I did, no question, but I wasn't yet at the point in my crusade to give zero fucks that I had the balls to tell a girl, "Hey, why don't you suck my dick." And that's not what I was trying to indicate by leaning back into the seat. It was just a natural reaction. Being only seventeen herself, Allie hadn't learned yet that when you start jerking off a guy, it's like pulling out the king stud from a load-bearing wall: it's only a matter of time before everything around it collapses in on itself. Her response to my posture was equally naïve.

"Um, I just want you to know that I would totally suck your dick right now, but um, I just don't like the taste of dick."

Maybe *naïve* isn't the right word, because the first place my mind went was not to sympathy, but to the scoreboard. How many wieners had this girl tasted? It had to be numerous wieners for her to have such a strong opinion on their taste. She must be a cock connoisseur. My mind was spinning. I was almost offended. If this girl had already touched all this penis meat, didn't that mean I should have touched way more 'giner meat by now? Did I miss some kind of mini–sexual revolution while I was in the hospital? Maybe I was the naïve one here. It took another second to collect myself and get my wits about me.

"I've got an idea," I announced to Allie with phony authority. "Put your pants on."

I folded up my boner and drove us to the convenience store inside a Dodge's Fried Chicken shop about a quarter mile from the park. God bless the South, I tell you, because only in the Bible Belt would the good Lord Jesus make a store that could give you a three-piece dark-meat combo for $3 on one side and the Pepto-Bismol to keep it down on the other. I pulled into the first spot I saw and threw the car into park.

"I'll be right back. Want anything?"

If she did, I didn't hear it. I had a one-track mind, and the end of the line was Blow Job Town. The only stop on the way was the candy aisle. I made a beeline for it and found what I was looking for: Fun Dip.

Remember Fun Dip? Two candy Lik-A-Stix and three pouches of flavored sugar powder—cherry, lime, and grape—to dip the sticks into after you wet them in your mouth. If Fun Dip powder worked to change the flavor of the Lik-A-Stix, I reasoned, it should work to change the flavor of my wiener too. To my mind, this made perfect sense. Granted, it wasn't my mind that was doing the thinking in that moment, but the heart wants what the heart wants, dammit!

"What'd you get?" Allie asked me as I hopped back in the car.

"Do you like Fun Dip?"

"Sure."

"What's your favorite flavor?" It was the gentlemanly question to ask.

"Grape, I guess."

"Well then, grape it is."

We drove right back to Cline Park and picked up where we left off. Partly because Allie was hot, but mostly because I was a seventeen-year-old male, I was just as hard as when we left. So I undid my belt like it was the drawbridge into Blow Job Town, spit on my hand, wiped it all over, and dipped the head of my wiener into the grape Fun Dip packet. As I sat there with the Fun Dip pack in one hand and my wiener in the other, Allie gave me this confusing little look. I couldn't tell if she was put off by my presumptuousness or turned on by my ingenuity.

I got my answer when she leaned over and sucked off all the purple powder. We went dip-and-suck like that until we reached the bottom of the grape packet. When we were plum out, I tried to open another packet while she kept on sucking, because in America we finish the jobs we start! I ended up cumming in her mouth a few moments later, which she was kind of pissed about because I didn't let her know beforehand that I was close. I didn't know that's what you were supposed to do. In pornos it's always the woman who tells you you're ready. She leans back, opens her mouth, and unhinges her jaws like she's trying to catch a flying Junior Mint. Not until I was older did I learn about the head tap. And even if I knew about it, it wouldn't have mattered. I was full of Budweiser and weed. I'm lucky I knew where I was.

Allie was a trouper, bless her heart. I sparked up the last of the second Joel Penny joint, and she quickly forgave me. We drank and smoked and finger blasted some more, then I took her home.

The night was nearly perfect. The only thing I would have changed was the flavor of the Fun Dip, because grape turned my wiener into an eggplant emoji. In retrospect, my preference would have been to use lime, since cherry would have made it look like I fucked a period monster, but the last thing you want to do to a classmate who was just giving you head is leave her with a sour taste in her mouth. They say a rumor travels around the world in the time it takes the truth to put its shoes on. Imagine how fast rumors of my sour penis would have traveled in a tiny high school where everyone knew each other's business? I could kiss my newly minted finger-blasting reputation good-bye if that happened.

The next day was Sunday, the Lord's day. I went to church with my mom like usual, and afterward, while our parents had coffee and cake down in the church basement, I lied to my buddies about having sex with Allie. I also told them she blew me, and how amazing it was—which wasn't a lie—though I left out the part about the Fun Dip. That felt like maybe a little too much sin for a house of worship.

I woke up Monday morning with a spring in my step and a fire in my belly. Sure, my penis was still purple, but I had a white-hot zeal for life. Nothing was going to slow me down . . . except maybe the low-grade fever and extremely painful urination I woke up to the following morning. It turns out one night of purple penis is a neat party trick. A whole day is a cool war story. But two days? That's a medical condition.

Clearly something was seriously wrong, but I was so ignorant about sex and anatomy at that age, I had no idea what it was. I thought maybe I'd caught AIDS or come down with some exotic purple version of gangrene. The only thing I knew for certain was that my dick wasn't working right and I needed to see a doctor.

When you're still technically a minor, going to the doctor is easier said than done. No one blinks when you file for a hardship license that lets you drive unsupervised at fourteen, but an unsupervised penis evaluation at seventeen, that raises all sorts of flags. If I had no other option, I would have bitten the bullet and gone to my pediatrician, Dr. Clyde Underwood, but that would have been one of the most uncomfortable moments of my life. Dr. Underwood had known me since we moved back to Clarksville when I was three years old. He'd known my mom even longer than that. They exchanged Christmas cards. The idea of explaining to him what I had done, in an exam room covered in fire-truck wallpaper? No, sir.

Thankfully I had a car, which meant I had options. Before I left for school Tuesday morning, I called a walk-in clinic in Fort Smith and made an appointment for 4:30 p.m. That gave me enough time after school to gather together some gas money and make the sixty-mile drive west.

The doctor on call at the clinic that day was a Vietnamese man named Dr. Nguyen. There's nothing particularly noteworthy about that, except you didn't see a lot of Vietnamese people in those parts, so I had some doubts about his credentials. He could sense my skepticism too once we got into the exam room and he asked me to stick out my tongue and say "Aah."

"Don't worry, Mis-tah May, I *bác sĩ*."

What the fuck was a bocksee? He repeated himself, with emphasis, like now I was going to understand him.

"*Bác sĩ* . . . 'doctor'?"

"Uh, ok."

"He's a real doctor," the nurse who was taking my vitals finally chimed in. It sounded like a routine they had rehearsed, and it did not inspire confidence.

"What wrong wit you today, Mis-tah May?"

"Uh, Doctor, I've got something wrong with my dick."

"Ohhhhh? What wrong wit you di—?" He dropped the *ck* because I lived inside a racial stereotype. I don't know what else to tell you.

"Well, it burns pretty bad and it's hard to pee without it hurting."

"How rong rike dis?"

"It started yesterday, but it got worse today."

"You have unprotected sex?" That was a tough one. In that part of the country, sex education was still pretty primitive. I wasn't completely sure what defined *sex*, medically or otherwise.

"I guess I kind of was. . . ."

"Hmmmm." Dr. Nguyen pondered. I don't think his English was good enough to decode my totally evasive, contradictory, unhelpful answer.

"Hypothetically, what could someone catch if, to get a blow job, they dipped their wiener into a Fun Dip pouch over and over again in order to make it taste good?"

"Ahhh—"

"Grape flavor if that matters."

This was when the nurse left the room. I heard her whispering with the other nurses behind the intake desk out in the hall. Then they broke into a chorus of laughter. So much for patient privacy.

Dr. Nguyen didn't answer my question right away. He quietly made some notes on my chart; probably just a personal reminder to tell his entire family the story of the big white boy with the itchy purple penis.

"Okay, Mis-tah May, we tess foh STD." Then he ordered a scope of my urethra and left the room.

The nurse who talked all sorts of shit to her other nurse friends did the scope—a procedure she performed with a little too much glee if you ask me. With that flexible little cystoscope in her hands, *STD* should stand for "sexual torture device," because that was about as close to death as I had come since my accident.

When the test results came back, they revealed that I didn't have a sexually transmitted disease, but I did have a urinary-tract infection. Some of the Fun Dip powder had gotten into my ure-thra. Not a surprise, really. Allie and I had absorbed an entire packet between us—me up my pee hole, she down her piehole. That's sixteen grams of sugary powder, if you believe the nutritional-facts panel on the back of the Fun Dip package. Sixteen grams doesn't seem like that much when you say it out loud, but sixteen grams of cocaine (by way of comparison) is like four teaspoons worth of nose candy. You could kill a Colombian with that. And while Fun Dip powder isn't nose candy, it's not like it's made out of cotton balls and butterfly kisses either. Put that stuff under a microscope and it looks like angry daggers made out of broken glass. Imagine that up your pee hole. No amount above zero is "not that much Fun Dip" in your urethra. Dr. Nguyen prescribed me some antibiotics, sent me on my way, and a few days later it cleared right up.

That should have been the end of it. There was no reason for anyone to ask questions about my drive out to Fort Smith. No one should have been the wiser. But then I got really high at a bonfire in the woods a couple months later and told the story to all my buddies. The more they laughed, the more details I divulged. I painted such a picture for them, they should have called me Rembrandt. Instead, they decided to call me Sweet Dick. For the rest of senior year my nickname at school was Sweet Dick, or SD if a teacher was within earshot. Finger blasting stopped being my thing almost overnight. I was Sweet Dick now—*that* was my thing.

Sweet Dick didn't die when I finally left Clarksville. He came with me wherever I went well into my twenties. I was the one who brought him. You could hardly ask for a better alter ego. I used that story all through my twenties to get girls. I would have friends call me Sweet Dick in mixed company out at bars or parties, trying to get at least one of the women in the group to wonder if maybe I'd got something going on that she hadn't figured from looking at me, and that she might want to find out about. One girl in the group would always bite, her curiosity getting the better of her.

"Why do they call you Sweet Dick?"

Man, was I ready for that question. In the brief moment just after she finished talking, it felt like fishing with a pulley rig. She clamped down on the bait and the rig yanked her right out of the water. All I had to do was bring her into the boat.

"I'm glad you asked. They call me that because my dick's so sweet it'll give you cavities."

"If your drink ain't sweet enough, I can just drop my dick on in there and sweeten it up a little bit for you."

One time I said, "My dick's so sweet you won't get any S-T-Ds but it might give you di-a-be-tes."

It was so stupid, but I got a ridiculous amount of mileage out of my secret identity because the whole notion was hilarious, and I was hilarious for going all-in with it.

That, I realized, was actually my thing. It wasn't my high-fructose-corn penis. It wasn't my finger-blasting prowess. My thing was that I was funny. It always had been. Frankly, that's why Allie went out with me. That's why she gave the Fun Dip a shot. It was so ridiculously stupid as an idea that you had to see where it went, for the story. And what is comedy if not a series of stories condensed to their most potent, absurd form?

Allie could have given a fuck about Mazzio's Pizza or my 1979 Oldsmobile Cutlass Supreme. She went out with me because I was funny, and chicks love a guy who can make them laugh. If I could make her laugh enough to look past my Southern postaccident huskiness, what's to say I couldn't make whole rooms of people laugh and have them pay me for their pleasure? No matter what filthy hole they stuck me in.

5.

WHO NEEDS COLLEGE WHEN THERE'S LIFE?

When my aunt took Granny down to Prattville, my mom blossomed like a flower that had been living under the canopy of a large tree. She finally had enough sunlight to grow. A sick mother no longer overshadowed her. A recovering son at least for a few months didn't keep her rooted in place. And her other kids were old enough to do whatever the hell they wanted, so fuck them, frankly.

Near the end of my sophomore year, just as I was getting the pins and screws taken out of my arms and legs, my mom dusted off her old teacher's certificate and started applying for teaching jobs all across northwest Arkansas. That was my mama. You can't hold a good woman down. Naturally, she got the first job she was up for—a high school home-economics position in a little town just south of Fayetteville called Winslow, twenty-five miles away.

For the first time since I was five years old, I was going to be living some place other than Clarksville, Arkansas. Had my girlfriend not broken up with me, had I not gained a bunch of weight while I was in the wheelchair, and had Clarksville High not tried to butt-fuck me with their stupid rules, I might have been sad to leave. But Winslow represented the same kind of fresh start for me as it did for my mom.

Tucked into the northern edge of the Ozark National Forest, Winslow is one of those towns that you search for on Google Maps and have to zoom in on five or six times before you can see anything. Once you do, all you see is the bare bones of what it takes to be called a town in the South: post office, high school, Baptist church, Methodist church, Pentecostal church, butane depot, gun shop.

I thought I knew what it meant to live in a small town—it's not like Clarksville is Gotham—but I was unprepared for just how small the high school where my mama was going to teach and where I would finish high school was going to be. My whole grade was nine people. *Nine.* That's barely a baseball team. It's hard enough to fit in at a new school as it is, but it's even harder to fit in when your whole class can fit in your car. Even our mascot was small—the Fighting Squirrels.

Before I had to worry about fighting or fitting in with my class-mates, I had to deal with where I fit in with the school district. At least in the late 1980s, when you moved to a new county, you had to get retested on all the basic subjects so they could figure out where you placed in their system. This worried my mom a little. For most of my time in Clarksville, even before the accident, I was bad at school. I don't mean I misbehaved, I mean I just wasn't very good at it. Don't get me wrong, I loved learning. I'd get A's on most of my tests. But then every quarter I'd come home with C's on my report card because homework is a bunch of bullshit, and in normal public schools homework is at least half your grade.

This was a constant source of frustration for my mom. As a

licensed educator, she knew that my refusal to do stupid busywork would reflect poorly on her with her new colleagues in the school district. But as a teacher, she also knew that homework was, in fact, total bullshit. She *wanted* me to do my homework, but what was she going to say? She couldn't lie and pretend that it was important or real. She'd already tried that with Santa Claus, and that spiraled into a complete loss of faith in every social institution we have. If she'd tried the same thing with homework, God knows where I'd be right now.

I didn't suffer many consequences for my poor grades, ultimately. At a school that can't even afford special-ed programs for a kid like Rusty Dugan, it's not like they had programs for the gifted that poor grades would keep you out of (or cool, fun shit that good grades would get you into). Maybe there was an honor-roll pancake breakfast or something, but those activities always happened on a Saturday morning, and who the hell wants to get up early on the weekend to eat cafeteria pancakes?

My mom would never say this, but I'm sure the last thing she wanted was to come to a brand-new town to get back into the teaching game for the first time in forever, only to drag a big, fat dummy along with her. Fortunately for both of us, standardized tests like these district placement exams always came easy to me. Which is why I wasn't at all surprised when I tested out as "gifted and talented" in mathematics, science, reading, and history. What surprised me was that this designation actually got me something good besides just being the first bit of official evidence I'd ever had that I was smart.

And I have S&H Green Stamps to thank for it.

S&H Green Stamps were stamps you could collect at the supermarket or the department store as rewards for shopping there, then redeem them for *a wide array of premium housewares* from the S&H Green Stamps catalog. They were one of the first retail loyalty programs in the country—like airline miles except for stuff that breaks real easy. My mama's mama didn't raise no fool, though. Once my mama filled up one of her Quick Saver Books, she skipped past the pages in the catalog filled with flammable bedroom furnishings and children's toys covered in lead paint and went right to the page with the *Encyclopaedia Britannica.* Her babies were gonna know some shit.

For as long as I can remember, we had a patchwork collection of encyclopedia volumes in our house. Most people buy all thirty-two volumes of the *Encyclopaedia Britannica* together, as a set. I understand that. But when you're poor and you're picking up volumes on the back of your weekly grocery bill, not only do you not have that luxury, you also need to be strategic. That meant those two index volumes could fuck right off. If you don't know how to spell the thing you want to know about, you don't need an encyclopedia, you need a dictionary. From there it was all about prioritizing the letters. *A* through *D* were no-brainers, and I was a monster at those. I'd read those volumes cover to cover several times over by the time we got to Winslow. All of the *Wheel of Fortune* bonus-round letters were must-haves: *R S T L N E.* If the producers saw fit to give them to you right off the bat, you had to know there were some good nuggets in those letters. Ironically, *I* and *Q* never made the cut. Not until I was in my late twenties, stoned off my ass watching *White Men Can't Jump* for the first time, did I learn from Rosie Perez that a quince is a fruit. Going into high school, I was pretty well covered up to *N,* then there was a little gap before I found my groove again with *R, S, T,* and *W. U*ranus, *v*enereal disease, *x*enophobia, and *y*ellow fever would have to wait until I made my own money. I didn't know what a zygote was until I actually made one. My wife and I named it April.

Our encyclopedia set was a godsend. It started small when I was young and slowly grew over the years, like knowledge kudzu that I would wrap myself in every chance I had. Reading about aardvarks and the kingdom of Babylon was better than antagonizing my brother, Winston, and getting beat on, I'll tell you what. And the more I read, the more I wanted to know.

The reading and the self-education (called autodidactism—I told you, I dominated volume *A*) finally paid off the summer after my junior year in Winslow, when I was accepted into the beginning-scholars program at the University of Arkansas. If my "gifted and talented" designation by the school district was my first bit of proof that I was smart, my acceptance into the beginning-scholars program was my first bit of evidence that I was capable of a lot more than I thought.

The goal of the program was to select gifted high school kids from all over the area and give them an opportunity to take real college classes for actual college credit. We'd get to live on campus, in Hotz Hall, have legitimate Razorback student IDs, and take classes with other college students. It was the first time in my life that school didn't feel like school; it felt like *learning*. It made me want to study and do well, which I did.

The best part of the program, though, was that I made friends with some of the college kids in one of my classes. I've always been kind of an old soul, and I've always been funny. Those two qualities are a huge advantage when you're trying to get in with an older crowd, male or female. Want to fuck a cougar? Take her out to dinner and tell her you like to handwrite letters and that your favorite *Golden Girls* character is Blanche. You'll be coming before the check does.

My new friends brought me into their group by inviting me to be a part of their informal study group. We met once a week at the Shakey's along Highway 71 Business to mow down large pizzas and drain pitchers of ice-cold beer. We were all underage, but nobody gave a shit back then. This was 1989, and the federal minimum drinking age of twenty-one was still pretty new, so a lot of servers and business owners either forgot or looked the other way, especially when things got busy. Plus, AIDS was the big deal in those days, not underage drinking, so as long as we weren't gettin' all gay with each other while we knocked back a few pitchers of Budweiser, those good ol' boys could give two shits.

The impulse to get twisted with the rest of the group was strong. If this were Clarksville, I would probably have been leading the charge. But I recognized that it was a privilege to have the respect of older friends and to be in this scholars program, so I didn't want to do anything to screw that up. Instead I stuck to getting fucked-up on big red cups of soda. I thank my stars every day that I didn't drink with those guys, because if I had, there is a good chance I would have totally blown the opportunity that changed my life.

Late in the summer before my senior year, our go-to Shakey's on Highway 71 hosted a multiround open-mic competition sponsored by the local radio station KHOG for the opportunity to open for Sam Kinison on the upcoming Fayetteville stop of his college tour. When you're a young comic, opening for any headliner out on the road is a huge deal, but in 1989 there was no more popular working comic than Sam Kinison. He was a legend, a force of nature. Opening for him would be like doing five minutes on the hill above the Sea of Galilee before bringing Jesus out to deliver the Sermon on the Mount.

Here's the thing: at the time I knew almost none of that about Sam, and I had no concrete designs on pursuing stand-up as a career. So when my study group walked into Shakey's one last time before I went back to normal high school, and there were sign-ups for an open mic, all any of us saw was the $50 cash prize and complimentary food and drinks for the winner and his guests. Anyone who went to college or moved out after high school knows that free pizza and beer when you're eighteen and broke is like finding a parka in the dead of winter with a $100 bill in the pocket. It's a damn miracle. My friends immediately signed me up. Why me? I was the funny one of the group. Simple as that. What they didn't know was that this was not my first rodeo.

When I was twelve years old, I told some jokes as part of the closing-night talent show at a Methodist youth retreat in Mobile, Alabama. This was one of those sleepaway camps where parents dump their kids during the summer to teach them about the evil of all the sins their parents were about to commit with three kid-free weeks on their hands. Most campers took their counselors suggestions when it came time to choose the talent they wanted to show. They sang hymns or played instruments or did a choreographed dance routine to some shitty Christian rock song, and they all got the same amount of phony applause from the counselors whose ideas they'd borrowed. It was one of those places where the counselors were bigger dorks than the campers, because the campers were there against their will at the command of their parents, and the counselors were there by choice, because they wanted to be of service to the Lord instead of their loins. Even at twelve years old I knew if I was going to have any chance of winning this talent show or not dying of boredom before it ended, I'd have to take a different path and do the only thing I'd ever been complimented for: being funny.

Five years later, and I was in the same exact position. After three decades in comedy, so much about this evening is a blur, but I will never forget the one joke that killed. It was about how Vanna White is the dumbest person on television because she basically cohosts a game of hangman, she knows what the words are, and she *still* needs them to light up the letters for her so she knows which ones to turn. What's funniest to me about this joke today isn't that it was some kind of inspired comedic genius, it's that things have only gotten worse for Vanna. They still light up the letters for her, except now *she doesn't even need to turn the letters!* All she has to do is touch them and they appear. Dumb and lazy is no way to go through life, Vanna. But you did *Playboy* when I was fifteen, so I forgive you.

I won the first round of the open-mic competition on the back of my Vanna White joke. Ironically, the free food and $50 cash prize would be a close approximation to my daily wages for the next ten years.

Shakey's had video games in the back, so after the results were announced and the prizes were distributed, my friends and I hung around for a while talking, laughing, and blowing through my prize money on the arcade games. It was just another fun late-summer night.

As I got ready to go, I noticed a group of college girls at another table. Some of them were cute. Not just late-night Shakey's cute either. These girls were light-of-day, show-your-friends cute. And they were looking our way. Only one of them was unattractive, so of course I was her favorite. The realization that she was my only shot to score was my cue to leave.

I said good-bye to my buddies and exited out the back of the restaurant where I'd parked the gutless Cutlass. I didn't even get to the driver's-side door before she made her move.

"You were so great."

"Thanks."

"I totally laughed a lot."

I opened my door.

"Is that your car?"

If I were older and more experienced I would have known that a question that fucking stupid really meant "Is your penis ready for touching?" Instead I said, "Uh-huh."

"Can I sit in there with you?"

"Umm, sure."

Once we got in the car, it took her all of two seconds to open up my pants and start blowing me. I didn't even have a chance to turn over the engine or turn on the tape deck to distract her from the overflowing Dumpster we were parked next to. It didn't matter. She was laser focused and I wouldn't have heard the music anyway. My mind was elsewhere—on my immediate past and my long-term future.

In the previous two hours, I'd made fifty bucks, ate a bunch of free food, and now I was getting a blow job from a girl I'd never met. (A groupie, I guess you'd call her.) If I could get all that just for telling a few jokes, what was the point of going to college? Isn't that the whole reason people go to college in the first place? I thought I just stumbled onto a better way. I mean, no offense to higher education, but no one ever sucked my dick for getting straight A's or acing a test, so what good are you to me?

I realized right there onstage, after my first big laugh with the Vanna White joke, that everything in my life had felt wrong until right then. It just clicked. It was an amazing realization. For a few moments at the Shakey's Pizza on Highway 71 Business, I was a king. My path forward was set from that moment on. There was zero chance that I would ever go to college.

I continued to fly high in the two weeks between my initial victory and the finals. I'd found my calling. I'd also made a much grander realization: I didn't need to listen to anyone or anything that didn't relate directly to my future in stand-up comedy. Why would I? Out of respect? Do you think any of those people would have respected my choice to pursue comedy?

One of my first decisions, with the blessing of my mom, was to move back to Clarksville to finish out high school. Winslow was great, but with a class that small, you can't avoid scrutiny. If I was going to coast through my last year without getting kicked out for truancy, disrespect, or just plain not giving a fuck, I needed to go back to a much-bigger school, with my old group of friends, and teachers who had different (i.e., lower) expectations for me. If a high school could pass someone into college like Dexter Manley, who was functionally illiterate, so he could one day become a famous football player, surely a smart kid like me could find a way to game the system and get the fuck out of there.

Shortly after my first victory at Shakey's, I moved in with Winston in our old house in Clarksville while my mom stayed up in Fayetteville working at Winslow High. Like any red-blooded guy in his midtwenties intent on tearing the world a new asshole, Winston was in and out, gone for days at a time. And like any high school senior with basically unlimited freedom, I followed right in his footsteps. It didn't take long for the house to become equal parts ashtray, recycle bin, flophouse, and toilet. In many ways, our house perfectly reflected my attitude toward school and would be a microcosm of my living situation as a stand-up comic before really making it: me, a guy several years older who was going nowhere and living like a slob, and no one with enough interest to clean up or keep the refrigerator full.

A lot can change when you're gone for a year. It's out of sight, out of mind. So when I told my Clarksville friends what had happened over in Fayetteville and that I had the finals coming up that Friday, none of them believed me. They were like those dudes who believe the earth is flat because they can't see the roundness with their own eyes. They hadn't seen me perform, so it must not be real. I didn't care. Let those small-town, small-minded fucks doubt me. It's their loss.

When Friday came, I was a nervous wreck. After school, I went home and worked on my jokes in the mirror. I had what I thought were four or five good ones, with legitimate setups and punch lines, but I had no earthly idea if they were any good. None of my friends believed me, so I didn't get to use them as an audience. This was totally untested material. I tried not to think about it too much. To ease my nerves, I beat off like three times, then hopped in the Cutlass and drove as slowly as I could to Fayetteville without getting stopped by state troopers or being late.

When I pulled into the Shakey's parking lot, a big shiny black limo was parked out front. *Holy shit, that's* THE *limo.* Somehow in my drive over, I'd completely spaced out on how Sam Kinison and his brother Bill were going to be *in the audience* at Shakey's to help judge the contest and would then immediately take the winner *in their limo* to the show on campus only an hour later.

Thank God I'd beat off before I left, otherwise the sight of that limo might have made me nut all over my steering column. It might also have cost me the victory, because my calmness on the microphone combined with my Vanna joke as the opener helped seal the deal. I was the unanimous winner.

———

The ride over to the University Ballroom on the campus of the University of Arkansas was the first part of one of the most transformative experiences of my life. If my accident was a kind of fork in the road for aspects of my personal life, opening for Sam was a springboard for my professional life. It gave me a glimpse at what was possible.

It's hard to describe Sam Kinison to people who weren't aware of him when he was still around, because he was just too complicated of a man. But for the sake of this book, what I can say is that Sam's limousine was a perfect reflection of Sam: black on black, full disco interior, cocaine on the bar, and rock 'n' roll cranked to eleven. Which is to say, to a kid from Clarksville who'd never ridden in a limo, it didn't feel like real life. And when Sam started talking to me, it all just felt like a dream.

"Hey, kid, are you nervous?" Sam asked.

I was pretty confident I had my material down since I'd practiced in the mirror, nailed it onstage, and beaten off three times. "No, sir. I think I have my jokes pretty well memorized."

Sam smirked. "Kid, there's gonna be thirty-five hundred people there, and none of them paid to see you."

"Okay, I'm a little nervous."

Sam knew what I would learn over the next God knows how many years. Memorization is one of the least important parts of comedy. It's good to be able to do, but if you have no charisma or a bad delivery, then all you get from knowing your lines is that the audience knows clearly how much you suck. I started to get visibly nervous, swaying back and forth on the side bench and sliding down the leather every time the driver went up or down a hill. It was a strange thing for Sam to have said, considering how young and wide-eyed I was. I think he could see how he'd rattled me and felt bad for trying to punk me like that.

To make up for it, he started asking me about my routine. "So run me through your set."

Set?! I had, like, six jokes. I didn't have a set. I hemmed and hawed, hoping someone might interject or shove cocaine in front of him.

"You got a closer, at least?"

"What's a closer?"

"It's a big joke to end your set with."

In hindsight I did have a big joke to end my set on a high note, but at the time I didn't know it.

"Nope, I don't got one of those."

"Okay, here's one of my old ones you can use."

I was all ears. This was like private office hours with a professor of comedy.

"In case you get into any trouble at all, like if one of your last jokes isn't hitting, what you do is you just start screaming at the audience and cussing them out. The more you scream and cuss, the more they'll love you. Then when you're done, intro me real fast, drop the mic, and walk off. These are my fans, they'll die."

"Really?"

Sam assured me that it would work.

When we got to the venue, it was already full. It was my first time experiencing the buzz that hangs in the air when thirty-five hundred people are in a room to watch a show that's just about to start. I haven't done a lot of different types of drugs in my life—mostly just weed and alcohol and acid and ecstasy—but the addictive, intoxicating feel from that buzz is why I imagine so many guys like Sam did coke (to chase the high), then started doing heroin (to numb themselves from the crash).

When I took the stage, most of the audience was skeptical. Like any audience is with an opener they've never heard of, they were willing to put up with only so much before they turned. The question they were asking themselves wasn't "Oh, who is this fine young man? He must be great since Sam has selected him." Their question was "Who the fuck is this fucking guy, and where the fuck is Sam?"

Thankfully, my first four or five minutes of jokes clicked. I got a couple big laughs and a few decent ones. Enough to confirm that stand-up comedy really was for me, that this was what I was going to do with the rest of my life. The plan was for me to do six to seven minutes of material, then bring Sam onstage with the intro his brother gave me: "Ladies and gentleman, the greatest comedian alive today, the rock star himself, Mr. Sam Kinison!"

"That's it. No fucking ad-libbing, got me, kid?" Bill said.

"Yes, sir." Like I needed to be told twice. The last thing I wanted was to have to come up with more new shit to say. Seven minutes was already a stretch.

People talk about how hard stand-up comedy is, but I was feeling myself after my first five minutes. *Maybe I really am a natural at this,* I thought. Then the comedy gods stepped in. With ninety seconds left in my set, my mouth started moving faster than my brain, and I flipped a punch line and a setup, and the joke bombed. The next joke was effectively my closer—my big finish and dismount. Its punch line was a bigger tag onto the previous joke, which meant that its success was predicated on the success of the previous joke. You know, the one that just Nagasaki'd my set.

All these years later I don't remember the joke I flipped, but in that moment I remembered exactly what Sam had told me on the ride over. So I went with it.

"Hey, you fucking stupid, inbred, pig-fucking, dumb, illiterate pieces of shit, you couldn't get these jokes if I wrote them down in crayon and ear-fucked them into your brain for you. You hillbilly, backwoods sons of bitches. You fuck your mothers and get fucked in the ass like Ned Beatty."

It was beautiful. It was Shakespearean. It might have even been in iambic pentameter. I was screaming and carrying on like that for what must have been thirty seconds, but felt like five minutes of full catharsis.

Immediately, thirty-five hundred people started to boo in unison. Not polite Southern booing, like their expectations had been falsely set. This was like red flag at Talladega booing. These crackers were pissed. In later years, I would get the crowd riled up like this on purpose, just to see if I could win them back before my set was over. But this was literally my fourth time doing stand-up comedy. I was decimated. I got offstage as fast as I could, fighting back the tears so the spotlight didn't catch them shining in my eyes—which is like blood in the water for an audience that has decided to hate you. I didn't even introduce Sam. That was my one job, and I couldn't do it. All I wanted to do was get the fuck out of the venue and back home as soon as possible.

With no introduction, no music, no fanfare, just booing that was slowly morphing into a mob mentality and general sense of lawlessness, Sam came out. He grabbed the microphone and waited for the reaction to die down.

"*Can you believe that kid?!* Talking to you good people like that?! He will never work in comedy again! I'm gonna squash him like a bug! Oh oh *ohhh*!!!"

The biggest guy in stand-up besides Eddie Murphy was trashing me onstage.

I. Was. Crushed. My idol had just said I'd never work again. My calling had lasted two weeks. The disappointment was overwhelming. Backstage I found the house phone and called my mom collect to come pick me up before anybody saw me. I'd taken my fair share of shit over the years, but this kind of intense, focused public humiliation was too much even for me.

My mom picked up on the third ring. I couldn't get any words out. They were stuck in my throat like a dam, holding back a river of tears. Just as the dam was set to break, a hand came from over my shoulder, grabbed the telephone receiver, and hung it up. It was Sam's brother, Bill.

"Kid, don't take it so bad. Sam thought that was hilarious. He never thought you'd have the balls to do it. He and I were laughing our asses off, and trust me, we were the only ones laughing. We're proud of you."

"You're what?" All the words Bill was saying were English, but none of them made sense in the order he was speaking them.

"Hear that?" The audience was howling. "They love you now."

"They what?" I'm trying to suck up tears and snot bubbles, trying to get my shit together enough to respond in a way that didn't make me sound like a child.

"Sam wants you to come to the after-party. Stick around."

I was so confused. Did Bill and Sam think I was genuinely funny? Was Bill still just fucking with me like Sam had on the ride to the venue? Was this all some big sadistic joke to get their rocks off? Were they just inviting me to the after-party so they could keep fucking with me?

It turns out another dynamic was in play. At the time of the Arkansas gig, Sam was under tremendous pressure. His ticket-buying audience expected him to be extremely controversial at every show. But he was being protested everywhere he went by people who hated him and what they thought he stood for. Initially the hatred stayed outside in the parking lot, but in recent weeks it had made its way inside clubs and theaters. People would buy tickets just so they could jump up in protest and interrupt his show. Every gig on the tour felt like a trek through a minefield, and this stop in Arkansas would be no different. Sam knew that doing his bit about Jesus getting nailed to the cross was not going to fly here without some serious consequences.

Driving to the auditorium with this seventeen-year-old kid who had no experience and no closer, Sam sensed an opportunity. I could be a human shield. By giving me a closer that was certain to incite the wrath of all these people, I'd absorb the lion's share of their moral outrage, which would not only ease the burden on him but also reduce the likelihood that some asshole would jump up to interrupt the show.

I knew none of this until years later. At the time it just felt like they were fucking with me for the sake of fucking with me. It felt like I was being hazed. Still, I took the brothers Kinison up on their offer and went to the after-party at Sam's hotel. I'm not sure what possessed me to say yes beyond lacking the words and the will to say no, but I'm sure glad I did. A local TV weatherman was there, some radio guys from KHOG, some minor celebrities from the University of Arkansas, and a bunch of girls. So many girls. This was no place for a seventeen-year-old kid, which meant it was the coolest party I'd ever been to in my life. I still haven't been to a party that crazy in Los Angeles. I mean, rails of blow, booze everywhere, group sex all over the place. These women made Coal Hill girls look like sexless pig people.

I had no idea what to do. There's no handbook for parties like this. Basically the rules are don't do anything to make the cops come, and don't die. I stood off to the side and sipped on a beer, discreetly pouring half of it out as I talked with girls who thought I was part of the crew. After a while Sam came out of a room with two women. He walked over to a table, snorted three huge lines into one nostril, then finished half a huge line in the other nostril, before looking over at me with my little baby beer.

"Hey, kid, order some pizza."

You mean you can do cocaine and eat at the same time? According to my advanced knowledge of *Miami Vice* and *Scarface*, that was supposed to be impossible. But who was I to doubt Sam Kinison? He was a legend for a reason.

So I call up the Shakey's on Highway 71. It was the only place I knew the number to, and I ordered like ten pizzas. They laughed. We were way out of their delivery zone. When I told them who it was for, they got real serious. I'd never seen pizzas made and delivered so fast.

It was like the delivery guy drove a DeLorean back through time to get us our pizzas. When Sam finally came to the door to accept delivery, he paid the driver in cash and tipped him in three little baggies of coke. Thirty minutes later we got a phone call. It was Shakey's Pizza calling us back: "Hey, you guys need more pizza? We can be right back over there, no problem!" It turns out that you may not actually be able to eat lots of pizza when wired on cocaine (we went through maybe three of the ten pies), but you sure as shit can make a bunch of it.

It was the best pizza I never tasted.

Stand-up comedy is one of those businesses where no matter how talented you are, you will never make it as far as you could have unless you have someone in your corner championing you, opening doors you could never open yourself. In the 1980s, Johnny Carson was that guy for a lot of comics. If he gave you the okay sign or called you over to the couch, you had a TV show within a year. Club owners like Jamie Masada, Budd Friedman, and Mitzi Shore gave extra stage time to comics they thought had "it."

Sam Kinison was, in a way, my first comedy mentor. He kind of took me under his wing after my baptism by fire. He was the first guy who believed that I had actual talent. He said I was ballsy enough that I could really do something in stand-up comedy if I wanted it bad enough. But most important, he told me to get the hell out of Arkansas and go get started where he did—at the Comedy Workshop in Houston, Texas.

"They're not gonna be nice to you, kid," he warned me, "but you'll learn a hell of a lot."

PART 2

HOUSTON:
1990–1998

6.

THE SHOWCASE WAS
THE WORKSHOP

America was at the end of a golden age for stand-up comedy when I left Clarksville for good. In the 1980s and early 1990s, every big city had multiple clubs that were filled nightly. Every bar, café, and restaurant that had a couple slow days during the week—like the Shakey's on Highway 71 Business—would host an open-mic night to draw in customers and double or triple their sales. Even television was getting into the act. HBO debuted the *Comic Relief* fund-raiser in 1986. Then in 1989 they started *One Night Stand*, which aired half-hour stand-up specials. In 1991, the Comedy Central network started, and at least half the programming in the first few years was stand-up clip shows. When network executives started throwing sitcom deals at comics, that's when everything really started to heat up.

The sitcom boom started slowly at first in the 1970s, with Redd

Foxx and *Sanford and Son,* Bob Newhart and his two shows, Robin
Williams with *Mork & Mindy.* Then in the mideighties, Bill Cosby's *Cosby Show* debuted and blew the doors off everyone. Once
network executives realized you could take a stand-up comic and
translate what he or she does onstage to the sitcom format, they
started scouring the big clubs for people who they thought could
replicate the model. Roseanne Barr got her self-titled show in 1988.
Jerry Seinfeld got his in 1989. Lenny Clarke and Kevin Meaney,
both out of the Boston scene, got a crack at their own shows in
1990. Then Tim Allen got his, with *Home Improvement,* in 1991,
which was when my eighteen-year-old baby face rolled into Houston after a brief and unremarkable stint in Baltimore living with
my sister Melanie to save money after I got kicked out of high
school.

Houston is a culture shock for a kid from Clarksville. Not only
does the Houston metro area have twice the population of the entire
state of Arkansas, but the city itself is probably one of the most
diverse in America. It has large populations of Vietnamese, Indi-
ans, Puerto Ricans, Mexicans, blacks, whites, and everyone in between. You can get Tex-Mex one day, creole the next, Ethiopian
food the day after that, Salvadoran *pupusas* the day after that,
then finish the week with the best steak you've ever had. Then you
could do it all over again every week for fifty-two straight weeks
and almost never have to go to the same restaurant twice. The city
has a place for you whether you're white-collar, blue-collar, or no-
collar people. Whether you're a cowboy or a roughneck, a gang-
banger or an arts patron. Whether you listen to country music, rock
'n' roll, or rap—all of which are being made in Houston.

Basically anyone or anything that Archie Bunker ever went on a
rant about in an episode of *All in the Family* you can find in Houston. The city is so diverse it has at least a half dozen nicknames:

Space City, Bayou City, Capital of the Sun Belt, Energy Capital of the World, H-Town, Hustle Town, Syrup City.

Clarksville? We've hosted a peach festival every summer since 1938.

The landscape is no less different in Houston. I was used to seeing mountains and green forests every day, but there are no mountains in Syrup City. There are skyscrapers, everything is brown, and the air is so humid in the summer—which starts in mid-February and goes until November—that you can chew it. Houston was a strange place to live in, but it was the perfect place to move to for a young kid starting his career in stand-up comedy.

By 1991, Houston had become the biggest and arguably the most important city (along with Boston) for stand-up comedy outside of New York City and Los Angeles. Within a couple years of my arrival, two Houston-based comics—Brett Butler and Thea Vidale—would have their own shows, and one of the funniest men alive, T. Sean Shannon, would become a writer for *In Living Color*, before eventually moving on to write for *The Tonight Show* and *Saturday Night Live*. On top of it all, two of the greatest stand-up comics who have ever lived—Sam Kinison and Bill Hicks—called the Houston clubs their home.

The club at the center of the Houston comedy universe was a place on South Shepherd Drive in the Montrose section of the city, just west of downtown, called the Comedy Workshop. Opened in 1978 by some people from Minnesota, it was one of the first dedicated comedy clubs outside New York and Los Angeles. In the eighties it was home to a group of guys that called themselves the Texas Outlaw Comics. It was Sam and Bill Hicks, Carl LaBove, Ron Shock, Riley Barber, John Farnetti, and a handful of others that came in and out over the years. They were all great Texas comics.

I knew none of this at the time of my arrival. All I had to go on was that Sam had said I should go to a place called the Comedy Workshop once I got the fuck out of Arkansas. So once I got settled in with my other sister, Camelia, and her husband, who were thankfully living in Houston proper at the time, I set about finding the address for this magical place. This was no easy feat in the early 1990s. We didn't have Google or Uber. Hell, we didn't have the internet and cell phones. At least not in the form or with the ubiquity that we have them today. I couldn't just type in *Comedy Workshop* and *address* and wait for an answer to be served back to me. I had to . . . <gasp> . . . *look for it.* I tried the yellow pages (aka Paper Google) first, but I didn't know what category to search under: jokes? Stand-up comedy? Nightclubs? No matter where I looked, I couldn't find the listing. Next I tried 411 (aka Telephone Google), and again I came up empty. There was a Comedy Showcase, but no Comedy Workshop. *Man,* I thought, *this must be some supersecret special spot to not even be listed. I wonder if I'm gonna need a password to get in, or something.*

Eventually I found the address for the Comedy Workshop and gathered my nerve to finally show up at its front door and start my career in stand-up comedy. That's how I thought about it. I wasn't just "giving this a shot." This was my first day at the office. This was the first day of the rest of my life. The drive from my sister's house to the club was a brutal internal struggle. Part of me wanted to hammer the accelerator and blow all the red lights to get there as fast as I could. The other part of me wanted to make a hard U-turn at every light I hit. Either approach would have achieved the same result, ultimately, because when I pulled up to the address I'd been given, the Comedy Workshop was gone.

In its place was a goddamn dry cleaner's.

———

It turns out running a profitable comedy club is very difficult. Even under the best circumstances, even at the peak of the comedy boom, it's hard to recoup all the costs related to running a business when you're in an industry that operates primarily on the weekends and only after dark. I can't even imagine how hard it was during the 1980s and early '90s, when cocaine floated in the air like glitter at a titty bar. I had no idea what combination of factors brought the Comedy Workshop to a close (though there were plenty of rumors), and I had no interest in finding out, because I had bigger issues to deal with: my nonexistent career in stand-up comedy had ended before it had even begun. I mean, Sam cut his teeth at the Comedy Workshop. It's where Bill Hicks became Bill Hicks. This was *the* place. Obviously, it wasn't the *only* place. Houston probably had eight or nine legitimate spots for comedy at that time. I needed to figure out not *what* to do, but *where* to do it. Sam hadn't given me a Plan B. The path as my eighteen-year-old hillbilly brain understood it was to go to Houston, then to the Comedy Workshop, then to *The Tonight Show*, then get famous, then get all the 'giner meat. I'd done step one, but if I was going to become . . . whatever I was supposed to become . . . where the hell was I supposed to go now that step two was a dry cleaner's?

The answer was the Comedy Showcase, another reputable developmental club that sat, conveniently, in a strip mall three miles from my sister's house, next to a Kingboat Chinese restaurant.

I showed up on a Tuesday. The place was closed.

Did you ever have one of those periods in your life when you were younger when you figured some shit out and came to some realizations about who you are and what you wanted to be? Remember how that felt like you'd actually done some shit? Like you'd *accomplished* something? Remember how you thought that if you started checking the boxes people told you to check, everything would start opening up for you, like the levels on *Legend of Zelda*? Remember how it never worked out that way, and at the first sign of struggle you started to look around for something to blame, for an escape hatch and an excuse to quit? I was almost there. I was starting to feel like the world was conspiring against me, like maybe a fat kid from Arkansas isn't allowed to do something like this, not for real anyway.

Something told me not to quit, though. Being a broke-ass motherfucker with no meaningful skills was probably part of it, but that wasn't all of it. Something else was pushing me. Something that I would realize much later in life was called drive or passion or purpose or obsession, depending on who you talked to.

I gave it another shot the next day. This time the club was open, and I met a woman named Anne Emerson. I told her that my name was Ralphie May, that I was a stand-up comic, and that I wanted to work there. I have no idea what was going through her mind when she heard those words come out of my mouth. I was eighteen years old at the time, but with my rosy, chubby cheeks and my impish, toothy smile, I must have looked like a thirteen-year-old trying to scam my way into a place with liquor everywhere and people saying "fuck" all the time. She knew better than to turn me away out of hand, though. Great comics were coming from everywhere and nowhere back then. You couldn't risk not at least hearing a fella out. You might miss the next Sam Kinison or Eddie Murphy or Rita Rudner or Andrew Dice Clay. Anne told me to come back that night and ask for a guy named Danny Martinez.

———

Along with his wife, Blanca Gutierrez, Danny Martinez owned and operated the Comedy Showcase. They opened it together in 1983 after Danny fell in love with comedy a couple years earlier, doing open-mic nights at the Comedy Workshop, of all places. The first thing I noticed about Danny was his great radio voice (which is where he started). It had just a hint of Texan behind it that made him sound even more trustworthy than he already was. As I got to spend more time around him and got to know him a little better, I watched how he carried himself. He had this incredible gravitas and quiet confidence that you would not expect from someone who stands five feet four and a half inches tall. Back in the day that last half inch really mattered to Danny too. Don't you dare shortchange him and call him five feet four inches. *Short people are five feet four inches.*

Even as a young kid, I quickly realized that Danny Martinez is about as good as they come—truly the salt of the earth. Onstage, it was no different. I'd never seen a comic as smooth at transitioning between jokes, or as unflappable, as Danny was when working audiences. On nights when he felt like getting up and doing fifteen minutes, he'd regularly earn standing ovations from the crowd. It didn't matter what kind of show he was on, he always had something to say behind his jokes, and he never had to curse. He was like a tiny Mexican Cosby minus the raping (allegedly).

The night I met Danny, I introduced myself the same way I did to Anne:

"My name is Ralphie May, I am a stand-up comedian, and I want to work here."

"You're not a comic." He didn't say it like it was a challenge; it was just a fact. "I'm sure you're a funny kid, but it'll be a while before you're a comedian."

"How long is a little while?"

"If you really want it, you just have to respect the process." Like some little Mexican Yoda.

This was the process: Come to the Comedy Showcase every night. Hang out. Don't get any stage time. Just watch other comics who had, presumably, done what I was now supposed to do. Do this for weeks. On Mondays, go to the Laff Stop over in the River Oaks Shopping Center* for open-mic night and work on some jokes. Wait for Danny to give you a shot. You get five minutes. Don't fuck it up.

Eventually, Danny let me get up. Most good comics have a great origin story about the first time they got onstage at a real club in front of an actual audience. Usually it involves bombing like the *Enola Gay* yet feeling the addictive rush of getting their first laugh that kept them coming back. My story wasn't quite like that because I didn't even get a chance to bomb. Only eight people showed up to the Thursday-night early show that Danny put me on, so he canceled it. My first time . . . wasn't. It was like the stand-up comedy version of "just the tip." What made it worse was that Friday and Saturday are headliner nights, when the shows are stacked with seasoned pros, so I had to wait until Sunday to get my shot. Those were the longest sixty-six hours of my life. Fuck Baby Jessica and her fifty-eight hours stuck in a well. This was *real* suffering.

When I finally got up, I did okay. I didn't kill, but I didn't bomb either. In my allotted five minutes I managed to avoid flip-flopping any setups with punch lines, and I even got a few good laughs, mostly with lowest-common-denominator shit and fat

---

* This was the original Laff Stop location, only a few blocks from where the Comedy Workshop used to be. In 2006, it moved to a spot on Allen Parkway and Waugh Drive. It closed in December 2009.

jokes full of curse words. Imagine a sweeter-sounding nineteen-year-old version of me slinging fat jokes at my own expense. On a Sunday night at 8:00 p.m., of course that shit's gonna get some laughs. I knew that, even then.

But that wasn't good enough for Danny. He wasn't interested in developing comics who got mostly cheap laughs. He wanted you to get the good laughs, the *right* laughs. When I got offstage, he button-holed me and pulled me into the greenroom so he could yell at me:

"Ralphie, what the fuck are you doing out there? Quit cursing!"

Danny explained that anyone can get a laugh from a well-placed *fuck, shit, asshole,* or *cocksucker.* Anyone can write dirty. The problem is, once you've gotten used to writing dirty, it's next to impossible to learn how to write clean. And writing clean is how you find your best six minutes for *The Tonight Show* or Letterman if you get that far. Once you learn how to write clean and you can put together a solid twenty minutes, then you can think about working in some dirty shit.

The next night I went up, I cut out the curse words but continued to lean on the easy laughs from the obvious fat jokes. I was young. I had no real life experience compared to these other guys. At least it felt that way. What else could I possibly talk about?

Danny buttonholed me again.

"Listen, Ralphie, you have a choice. You can be a fat person who happens to be a comic, or you can be a comic who happens to be a fat person. Which one do you want to be?"

For a self-educated high school dropout with no father to speak of, the importance of Danny's willingness to mentor me and share his wisdom cannot be understated. He wasn't just teaching me how to be a comic—a real, good comic—he was showing me how to be a man. He was telling me, by virtue of spending his time on me, that I had value. Not many things in this world can make a man feel more vulnerable than standing alone on a stage three feet from a room full of people who are expecting you to make them laugh. The only way you can get through it and persevere toward success is to have confidence in yourself. Danny injected that into me like the cheese into a chile relleno.

Over the next eight years, I basically went to college at the Comedy Showcase. Danny Martinez was my professor. My itty-bitty Mexican Socrates. He worked on jokes with me. He told me what I was doing wrong, and most important, he taught me what it meant to be truly, authentically funny. I was not the only one he did this for. A laundry list of hilarious comedians and writers owe some amount of their success to Danny, the classroom that was the Comedy Showcase stage, and the office hours that were those straight-shooting greenroom chats.

It's funny when you think about it: I came to Houston looking to get my start as a comedian at a developmental club called the Comedy Workshop, at the urging of a short, funny man who got *his* start there and who was great at yelling. Instead I got my start at a different developmental club called the Comedy Showcase, urged along by the short, funny man who started the club and who was also good at yelling.

I know there's some serious *hakuna matata* circle-of-life karma shit in there somewhere, but all that matters to me is that Danny Martinez, who I still call my great friend, turned out to be one of the most positive forces I've ever had in my life, and his club became my new home.

7.
YES, AND . . .

Wednesday-, Thursday-, and Sunday-night shows at the Comedy Showcase were dedicated to local comedians. Brand-new people did five minutes. New people with a little experience maybe did ten minutes and hosted the shows. They were the warm-up guys, so to speak, responsible for getting the audience pumped and introducing each comic on the bill. As you got better and developed bigger bits, you got more time and better spots during those local shows. Eventually, maybe you even closed the show, doing thirty or forty minutes if you were planning on going on the road in the near future.

It was a great system, and pretty soon I started getting regular spots during the week. To get more reps, I volunteered for spots that nobody else wanted to take. In the beginning, I couldn't believe that was even possible, that open spots were even a thing. In the early nineties, there was no shortage of young comics hanging around at any of the clubs. How could there be open spots? I couldn't understand for the life of me why anyone who was trying to get good at stand-up would turn down stage time. Comedy is a muscle after all—you have to work it. If you don't, it atrophies. And the stage is your gym. In my opinion, as a young comic at eighteen, nineteen, twenty years old, there was no such thing as a bad spot.

Eventually, after talking to Danny about it, I figured out what was going on. The spots I was volunteering for were open because they were between some of the funniest fucking people anybody had ever seen in their lives: Thea Vidale, Brett Butler, T. Sean Shannon, his brother Charlie, Frank Lunney (aka Captain Rowdy), and a handful of other local legends. These comics could come in any night of the week and get standing ovations every time. Even when they were working out new material onstage, they'd kill. And when they brought twenty or thirty polished minutes, Lord Jesus, they would *destroy*. Going on between two of those people was like asking to perform in the eye of a hurricane. On either side of you is this whirlwind of energy produced by an awesome force of nature, and then there you are, standing in the middle of it, everything eerily silent, surrounded by destruction. The local comics who had been around awhile and felt the hot, stifling panic of comedic death that came from trying to follow Thea or fill time before Charlie had decided, almost as a group, that the emotional pain of a silent crowd wasn't worth the money or the experience you'd earn from enduring it.

I was still too young and too green to make that calculation. I didn't know what I didn't know. To me, every spot was a good spot, so I took every spot Danny was willing to give me and then asked for more. I was like a guest in a Greek grandmother's house: as long as you keep eating, she's gonna keep feeding you.

I took what you might call an improv approach to my career. One of the fundamental principles of improvisational comedy is this idea of "Yes, and . . ." When you're in a scene, your job is to accept the premise of what your partner is doing (say yes to it) *and* then build on it. You're a needy, codependent God? Okay, and I'm a dyslexic angel who thinks you're a dog and keeps calling you a "good boy" and trying to make you sit.

Beyond the crowd work I do now at the beginning of my sets, I have never done much in the way of actual improv. Don't get me wrong, I love watching it. It's hilarious. But I'm a joke guy, an observation guy, a story guy. I like writing bits and building an hour with jokes and stories that transition seamlessly and call back to one another. Still, this idea of "Yes, and . . ." helped me with my career choices, especially in the beginning. For nearly all of my time in Houston, I "Yes, and . . ."–ed the fuck out of every opportunity that came my way, no matter where it came from, who brought it to me, or where it sent me.

I'd been settled in the Houston scene for a while when I heard that Sam Kinison was coming to town for a run of shows at the Laff Stop, so I decided to get ahold of him through the club. When I asked the Laff Stop general manger to connect me, he looked at me sideways like *Who does this fucking kid think he is? You don't just* call *Sam Kinison. He's famous!* Why wouldn't I reach out? I legitimately knew the man. I wasn't trying to fanboy him or anything. What's the worst thing that happens—he says no? Make the fucking call.

All the GM would tell me was that Sam was scheduled to do radio the Thursday morning at the beginning of his run. That's all I needed. The GM didn't have to tell me which station, there could be only one place: Rock 101 KLOL. Home of the legendary morning drive-time *Stevens and Pruett Show*, starring the "Radio Gawds" Mark Stevens and Jim Pruett, along with my man Eddie "The Boner" Sanchez and Brian Shannon (no relation to Charlie or T. Sean). Only a show with as many FCC fines as *Stevens and Pruett* racked up could host a man like Sam Kinison in Houston first thing in the morning.

I went down to the station that Thursday at 6:00 a.m., when the show started, not knowing what to expect. Sam rolled in at seven, reeking of pussy, booze, and burnt Styrofoam—which I'm pretty sure are the three base ingredients for Drakkar Noir. The pussy smell meant he'd had a good night. The booze meant the night hadn't ended. And the burnt Styrofoam meant he'd been smoking cocaine. So clearly he was in great shape.

When he saw me, he told me to come into the studio with him and help him out on the show. I was more than happy to oblige however I could—writing him quick jokes, giving him stuff to riff off of, whatever he needed. When you're nineteen and you don't know shit, you do whatever a guy like Sam Kinison asks you to do. Of course the guys on the show had no fucking clue who this baby-faced fat kid was trailing behind Sam, so almost immediately I became the topic of conversation:

"This is the kid," Sam said. They looked at him a little confused, like they were supposed to know who "the kid" was. "Kid, what's your name again?"

"I'm Ralphie May."

"Guys, I pulled a joke on this kid up in Fayetteville a couple years ago that you wouldn't believe." Sam told them, and a million other people (more probably), the entire story of me opening for him and screaming wild curses at his loyal fans. Stevens and Pruett loved it.

"I gotta give it to him," Sam concluded, "he rolled with the punches like a pro. Kid's got a bright future. Remember that name, guys."

I was floating on a cloud.

"Hey, kid," Sam said, "what's your name again?"

They all got a big kick out of that one. So did I, because Sam had just vouched for me to the whole world, or to *my* whole world at least. I'd been in Houston less than a year, and I was already an anointed man. It was like *Donnie Brasco*—a friend of Sam's was a friend of ours. Getting spots at the other six clubs in town immediately got easier. They weren't better spots than I deserved based on my skill level, but they were spots that could have gone to other local comics with the same amount of experience. The way I looked at it was that they were extra reps working that comedy muscle.

Stevens and Pruett liked me enough to invite me back all by my lonesome a couple weeks later. They wanted me to sit in and do kind of what I did with Sam: write jokes for them, give them stuff to riff on, all sorts of other shit. This wasn't stand-up comedy exactly, but it wasn't *not* stand-up comedy either. There was a microphone and a captive audience who were listening because they loved to laugh. How could I not say, "Yes, and . . . anything else you want me to do too?"

The station couldn't afford to pay me to start, or they weren't willing to, I never found out which, but it didn't matter because I didn't care. This was high-pressure experience on a show that pulled a 29–34 share of the local market. Do you have any idea how many people that is in a city the size of Houston? It's approximately a fuckload. And all of them, by virtue of listening to a show like *Stevens and Pruett*, were comedy fans. They were my people. So I threw myself into it. Soon enough it got to be that I was a regular and I was sitting in five days a week. I worked for no money that whole first year, though that didn't mean I wasn't paid. The exposure and practice I got, the people I got to meet, those things were worth ten times what they could have paid me in American dollars.

Where I really made my mark on that show, though, was in my willingness to do all sorts of crazy stunts. Man-on-the-street stuff, on location, in the studio, out in the parking lot—you name it, I did it. I remember in 1994 hometown hero and greatest pitcher of all time, Nolan Ryan, came into the studio for an interview. He'd retired the year before, *at the age of forty-six*, after tearing a ligament in his pitching elbow during a game up in Seattle.* In the production meeting that morning, Stevens and Pruett thought it would be a great idea to deck me out in catcher's gear and get Nolan to throw me a fastball. Not only would it be cool to see if the hardest thrower in the history of baseball still had his stuff, but it would be *hilarious* to see the fat kid who never played organized baseball try to catch a missile from sixty feet six inches away.

Nolan arrived right on time dressed in a sharp suit and tie, looking as fit as a fiddle. Once he got comfortable, Stevens and Pruett ambushed him with the stunt idea. He reluctantly agreed and followed them outside to the parking lot, where he found a regulation pitcher's mound, a home plate, and me wearing a mask, two chest protectors, a very large cup, and a brand-new catcher's mitt that looked like someone had carved the vagina out of a large cow, spread it open, and lacquered it in place with some pottery glaze. This thing was stiff as a board.

Good sport that he is, Nolan threw a couple of warm-up pitches to get me ready, then climbed on top of the pitching rubber and

---

* He hadn't lost his stuff. He threw one more pitch after the injury. It clocked in at 98 mph. Sweet baby Jesus.

told me to get down in a catcher's stance. I have never been to a bullfight, but I imagine staring up at Nolan Ryan from sixty feet away must feel similar to staring into the eyes of an angry bull that has just fixed on your cape as its target. Nolan rubbed up the ball a little, waited for Boner Sanchez to get behind me with the radar gun, then went into that patented high leg-kick and unleashed the Ryan Express right down Broadway. Somehow I managed to catch it, though it's probably more accurate to say that it caught me. Boner showed everyone the radar-gun readout: 98 mph. It was insane. A forty-seven-year-old man had just walked out into a parking lot in a business suit, in the middle of the morning commute, and fired a bullet. If that pitch were a car, he'd get a ticket for reckless endangerment.

As impressive as the raw speed, was the sound of the ball, hitting the fresh leather of my mitt. It was the combination of a gunshot echo and a bullwhip cracking through plate glass. The sound was scary loud. The pain was just plain scary. It felt like I'd just tried to catch a fireball that cut a hole through my left palm. I pulled my throbbing hand from the glove, and already I could see the blood blister forming. I couldn't move my hand either. The guys insisted it was just numb, but when you've broken forty-two bones in sixty-four places, you know the difference between numb and broken. When something's numb, you can move it and you don't feel anything. When something's broken, you *can't* move it and you can feel everything. This was broken—two bones right where the base of the fingers meet the top of the hand. All part of a day's unpaid work.

That was the kind of shit I did on the regular, until one day Jim Pruett got busted flying guns down to Mexico and they needed me to fill in as a cohost for a while. I started getting honest-to-goodness fans then—and a paycheck. I was barely old enough to drink, but because I took a flier and reached out to the Laff Stop general manager, then said "Yes, and . . ." to Sam, to Stevens and Pruett, and to the Ryan Express, all the club managers and head-liners were now willing to throw prime spots my way on the best shows all over town.

Houston had seven major clubs—all with seating for more than three hundred people—as I started to make a name for myself: the Comedy Showcase, two Laff Stops, three Spellbinders, and the Hip Hop Comedy Stop. Would you like to guess which of those clubs featured the fewest pasty white-boy comics?

That's right, jack. The Hip Hop Comedy Stop was *the* black club in town. It was opened by a Houston comedian named Rush-ion McDonald at almost the exact same time in the late eighties as another black comedian in Dallas by the name of Steve Harvey opened a club there called the Steve Harvey Comedy Club. Those two would play each other's club back and forth, bringing sup-porting acts with them and creating a hell of a scene for black com-ics in East Texas. It was a rare thing to see a white guy or even a brown guy on one of the regular shows at the Hip Hop Comedy Stop. They weren't racist about it, they just didn't need our asses, so if you got to play the room, it meant they thought you were a legit comic and a good fit for their crowd.

The first night I was invited to play the Hip Hop Comedy Stop I totally bombed, which I was told afterward was pretty typical. It's hard to hit the bull's-eye of a target you've never aimed at before. The next night I switched some things up and did well, which I was told afterward was not pretty typical. White guys who bomb the first night in black rooms usually bomb for a reason—a reason the crowd is insistent on loudly vocalizing for you. Because of that, most comics will bomb the second night as well, if they even come back. I didn't kill my second night, but I connected with the audience and they liked me well enough that I got invited back to start playing the club regularly. There was no way I was the first white comic this happened to—not with the guys whose footsteps I was following in—but apparently I was one of the few guys to accept. I was definitely the only white guy to regularly play the black rooms during the time that I called Houston home. All of which helped me stand out and distinguish myself.

It's always good when a crowd likes you as much as they like your jokes, but there is no experience quite like a good black room when that happens. Anyone who has watched an episode of *Def Comedy Jam* or *Showtime at the Apollo* knows what I'm talking about. The place fucking ignites. You could power a city block with the energy created in a black room by an audience that likes the comedian. There is no better feeling—not drugs, not sex, not even the sex you don't have to pay for.

These moments have a downside unfortunately, and it's with the other comics in the room. Comics can be petty, jealous dicks. We're insecure by nature, so when somebody whose material we don't like or respect does well, our instinct isn't to figure out what he or she is doing right that we might be doing wrong, it's to lash out at the crowd, lament that the world is going to hell, and assume the comic in question is a piece-of-shit joke thief. That's not all comics, but it's definitely a lot of the working club comics whose names you'd never recognize.

I remember one show at the Hip Hop Comedy Stop specifically where I had just killed and gotten a raucous standing ovation, and the emcee came up after me to introduce the next comic and started making all of these fat jokes about me. One or two fat jokes? Whatever, that's fine, it's part of the game. But this motherfucker kept going. What he didn't realize is that no one who isn't fat has more than a couple good fat jokes. Unless you spend every second of your life fat, doing fat things, thinking fat thoughts, there's no way you can develop the kind of arsenal of fat jokes I'd written and perfected over those first couple years in Houston. The emcee's jokes got tired real quick, but he couldn't stop himself, I think, because he was jealous that the room liked me so much and he was pissed that the white guy did better than he did in a black room.

Eventually the crowd started getting restless and annoyed. Bad fat jokes are bad enough, but at a show with this much energy and this much straight fire getting spit, people only have so much patience for the emcee. They want you to do your two minutes and bring up the next comic. You're the sizzle, not the steak. This dude just wouldn't quit. Then suddenly, from a booth at the back of the room, a drunken one-eyed, four-foot black man walked down the center aisle to the front of the stage holding a nickel-plated, pearl-handled .45-caliber handgun. He raised it to just the right height so the stage lights would bounce off it in multiple directions, then pointed it directly at the emcee and yelled:

"Put the fat white boy back onstage and shut the fuck up, nigga!"

You'd think that when a charbroiled Oompa-Loompa pulls a gun in a crowded club, people would run for cover, but not this place, not this time. Instead the crowd went nuts because this was not your run-of-the-mill black midget. This was Bushwick Bill from the Geto Boys—the greatest rap group ever to come out of Houston. They were at the height of their fame and influence at the time, and Bill was sort of a cult figure after getting shot in the eye by his girlfriend during a fight a few years earlier because, drunk on Everclear and high on PCP, he threatened to throw their kid out the window.

When a dude like that tells you to put the fat white boy back onstage, you put the fat white boy back onstage. It was flattering, but I didn't have any more material. Plus I didn't want to be rude to the comic who was up next. When you're famous and headlining at Carnegie Hall, you can be like Dave Chappelle and walk into the Laugh Factory unannounced on a Thursday night and do four and half straight hours. When you're early in your stand-up career, it's important to respect your stage time. So when I got back up onstage I grabbed the mic and said:

"Thank you so much, but I don't want to be disrespectful to the next comedian. Ladies and gentleman, I wasn't planning on emceeing tonight so I don't know the next comedian, but I know you're going to love him. If he's booked here, that means he's fantastic. From Chicago, Illinois, please welcome Mr. Bernie Mac!"

I brought up Bernie Mac, can you believe that? All because Bushwick Bill had seen enough of that other triflin' motherfucker.

They say the Lord giveth and he taketh away. Well he gaveth me a few minutes of feeling like I was on the top of the world, and then, by putting Bernie Mac on the stage after me, he tooketh my hopes and dreams and squashed them into oblivion. Guys like Bernie Mac are the reason you rarely find a successful stand-up comic who is a true optimist. Right when you feel like you're making strides—getting better gigs, earning bigger and more regular laughs—you let yourself start to think that maybe your comedy fantasies could become realities, and this guy you've never heard of comes up and makes you think, *I will never in my life be even close to as funny as this guy*. Bernie was so funny, you almost couldn't put it into words. He could do that thing that Thea Vidale could do and suck all the oxygen out of the room, right along with my dreams.

I was able to mute some of the existential dread for my career and start to feel myself a little again later that night when the Geto Boys called me over to their booth in the back. They loved my shit and wanted to talk to me. Willie D and Scarface were there. So was DJ Screw, the legendary DJ who pioneered the chopped-and-screwed style that was unique to Houston at the time. As they introduced themselves—like they needed any introduction—all that was running through my head were the lyrics from "Damn It Feels Good to Be a Gangsta" and "Mind Playing Tricks on Me":

> *Or is it the one I beat for five thousand dollars*
> *Thought he had 'caine but it was Gold Medal flour*

Bushwick Bill was there too, of course, but he was so fucked-up, he probably had no idea where he was. They were all so nice to me, sitting there around the booth sipping out of Styrofoam cups, getting fucked-up on codeine syrup and Sprite (aka Purple Drank).* They asked me if I wanted some, but I was barely old enough to drink then and that stuff was way above my level, so instead we smoked a bunch of weed. Right in the club, right there at the booth. Nobody gave a shit.

Houston in the nineties, man. *Comedy* in the nineties. It was a fucked-up, crazy-cool time that, despite my being a carpetbagger from up north in the holler, molded me into a true Texas comic—thanks in no small part to my commitment to saying "Yes, and . . ." to whatever came my way.

When you say "Yes, and . . ." long enough, two things happen: you become indispensable to people who need someone reliable, and you see so much that you're never at a loss for what to do when things change or something goes wrong.

I learned that watching Danny Martinez emcee a show one

---

* DJ Screw overdosed from that shit in 2000.

night at the Laff Stop as a favor to the owner, Sandy Marcus. Danny was never one to refuse a favor or say no when someone needed help, so when Sandy came up to him later in the night with a wrinkle in the program, he was unfazed:

"Look, Danny, there's a new guy on the bill. He's a magician."

"Are you serious? A magician?"

"He's got some kind of magic competition in San Francisco coming up, and he wants to run his ten-minute set. So just do eight or ten minutes, bring up the magician, and then everything else on the bill stays the same."

No self-respecting comedian wants to share the stage with a guy in a cape and a top hat, but Danny is a professional. All right, he told Sandy, no problem. So he does his eight to ten minutes and he's wrapping up, and from behind the curtain there's this voice:

"Hey, do more time!"

He wasn't even the one who heard it. A guy in the front row of the audience heard it and yelled up, "He said to do more time!" So Danny does another five or six minutes and starts wrapping it up again, and he gets the same shit from the voice behind the curtain: do more time. Like a very demanding Oz. Danny begrudgingly does three or four more minutes, and now he's reached the limit of his capability as host. Danny had a mountain of material, but being the emcee, he hadn't set any of it up right to just run it out on command like this goddamn magician was asking him to. So he does a little bit of crowd work and finally just says fuck it and brings the guy onstage.

Don't be fooled: this was no David Copperfield, Penn and Teller magician. Oh, no, this cat looked like the kind of guy you found either in the phone book or the sex offender registry. He wore a tuxedo with tails and a top hat. He carried out a small card table and draped a black cloth over it. Then he brought out some kind of bird perch and marched it over to the edge of the stage with a magical flourish. He could not have been any cheesier if he were made out of Brie.

After the standard corny magician's introduction where they say a bunch of puns and reassure the audience that there are no wires or mirrors anywhere, he went into his act. First he did some sleight-of-hand bullshit that turned a bouquet of flowers into a dove. He let go of the bird, and it was supposed to fly a circle around the room and then land on the perch across the stage, the way it was trained. But the room was so dark and the stage lights were so bright that the contrast messed with the dove's vision or homing mechanism. On its way to the perch, the dove overshot and fucking slammed into the wall behind the stage at full speed, like a live-action Tweety Bird cartoon. It dropped like a stone and started flopping around on the stage just violently enough that the audience went speechless. Had it just plain died, the crowd might have been able to convince themselves that it was part of the act, and at the end the bird would miraculously appear on someone's plate of nachos, or something. But watching a helpless animal writhe in its death throes was too much for them. It was too much for Danny and me and two other comedians at the back of the room as well, because we broke. We were crying we were laughing so hard.

The magician knew right away that he was in trouble. He started sweating profusely. He should have wrapped that shit up, scooped up the bird with his top hat, and lived to fight another day. But he'd committed to a full run-through of his ten-minute act, so he soldiered on. As he worked his way into his next trick, I immediately understood why he was sweating: it involved another bird. Sure enough, he put his stupid hat on the table, placed a handkerchief over the top, waved his hand, and, *voilà*, produced a dove. He held that dove in his hand the same way he'd held the first, only this one he held for maybe a second longer, almost certainly asking himself whether it was a good idea to let it go. I guess his answer was *let it ride*, because he let that fucker fly. It left his hand, circled around the room, lined up its approach, and then—*smack!*—right into the wall. It fell to the stage and flopped around right next to the other dove.

Danny and I had never laughed so hard at anything in our lives. The audience was in total shock, but they heard us laughing, so a little bit of nervous laughter started coming from the seats. They must have thought, *Well, if the other comedians are laughing, then this must be okay, it must be part of the show.* They didn't realize that comedians, aside from being petty, jealous dicks at times, are also sadistic assholes when someone is dying catastrophically onstage. It's the best possible kind of performance art. It is true magic.

The magician did a couple of little card stunts and rope tricks before transitioning to his big finale: a big bunch of flowers with a cover over them. Oh, no, he couldn't . . . could he? He pulled back the cover to reveal yet another dove. Oh, yes, he could. He couldn't possibly let this one go, though, right? I mean, we all got it. We knew what was supposed to happen. He could fast-forward to the end; I think we all would have been okay with that. "The Amazing Sergeant Slaughter" wouldn't hear of it. He opened his hand and let that dove go too. It left his hand and flew around the room just like the previous two, except this bird saw the carnage of his wingmen on the stage floor below, so he booked it over to the other side of the stage and the relative safety of a lighting array that, together, probably pumped out five or six hundred degrees of concentrated heat.

When the bird touched down, it went up in flames. Apparently, birds are highly combustible. Who knew? After a couple seconds of shocked silence, a ball of feathers and flames fell down from the rigging onto the stage. It was hard to tell if it was the bird flopping around or if it was the flames causing the ball of burning flesh to roll around. Either way it was a fire hazard, so a lady in the front row threw her drink on it to douse the flames. Only the drink was straight vodka, and it sent a fireball toward the ceiling that *incinerated* the bird.

Finally the magician started freaking out, which made the club manager freak out, which forced Sandy Marcus to do something. She sent Danny back onstage to save this magician from himself and try to salvage the rest of the show. But besides giving everyone their money back, what the hell do you do in a situation like that? Offer ten-cent wings? How do you follow that?

So Danny gets up there, grabs the mic, talks the magician off the stage, looks around at the bloody avian sacrifice at his feet, and says the only word that comes to his mind: "Taadaa. . . ."

8.

THE ROAD CAN BE AN ASSHOLE

There's more to being a comedian than telling jokes. Your job does not begin and end with your ability to create setups and punch lines or develop callbacks and reversals. It's more than knowing how to tell a story or do crowd work or shut down a heckler. It's not as simple as that—as just doing all your time and making sure you don't go over. Being a comedian is about understanding how and why the world works. It's about seeing the matrix. To do that, you've got to go on the road. If getting up onstage as often as you can is how you become good at comedy, then going on the road is how you become a good comedian, because the road, when it comes right down to it, is where the world is.

Successful comedians have all done their time on the road, and the best ones do it with their eyes wide open. They learn to identify what is universal about people and what things are different. They figure out what parts of their act play well wherever they go, and what needs to get tweaked and massaged based on where they are on a given night. They learn where in the country they resonate more and where they resonate less. It's a steep learning curve early in a comedian's career, partly because you just don't know and partly because when you come to the clubs in many of these towns, you're running into audiences whose reason for being there is to watch stand-up comedy, not necessarily to watch *you*. Most times you are totally irrelevant to them beyond your role as the delivery mechanism for the comedy they've come to see, which means that you have to overcome a fairly high bar of skepticism right away. They're sitting there unfamiliar with you or your act, and they're thinking to themselves, *I paid twenty-five dollars for this ticket and twenty-five dollars for food and drinks, this fat fuck better be fucking funny.*

Huge comedians like Louis C.K. and Jerry Seinfeld, or Amy Schumer and Whitney Cummings, or Chris Rock and Dave Chappelle, don't have that problem anymore. They spent years on the road turning the raw comedic strength they developed in the gyms that were their home clubs into the kind of functional fitness necessary to do bigger and better things in their careers: hour specials, sitcoms, *Saturday Night Live,* movies, TV hosting gigs, that kind of stuff. They did the work and have nothing left to prove. Now they can play everywhere because people are buying tickets to see *them*. For a good, successful comedian, that is the brass ring, and the quest to reach it begins on the road.

My first road gig was at the Funny Bone in Baton Rouge, Louisiana, maybe two years after moving to Houston. The owner of the club called Danny Martinez looking for a last-minute opener for the shows that weekend, and my name was the first one that popped into Danny's head after the other three first ones he thought of who couldn't do it. To be fair, those other comics were better than me at the time, so I couldn't get too bent out of shape about it. I just had to say yes, and then hit the road.

For an opener, not all road gigs are created equal. Your headliner can go a long way in determining the kind of experience you're going to have and the type of crowd you're going to face. If the headliner is popular, then you can craft some of your material around the kind of audience that likes the headliner's style. If your headliner isn't particularly well-known, then how he or she meshes with the culture of the crowd is the big x-factor. Before Sam was Sam or Bill Hicks was Bill Hicks, for instance, when they went out on the road to a place like Des Moines, Iowa, or Asheville, North Carolina, with their respective brands of comedy, they could kill or be killed. They could burn the house down or they could run into an absolute buzz saw of Midwestern propriety or Southern gentility. They never knew which it was going to be from show to show, so guess how they figured it out: the opening act.

The opener is the sacrificial lamb, the official food taster for the king. If the food is good, the taster gets a warm meal. If it's poisoned, he dies. As the opener, if you find yourself with a good crowd, it reminds you why you got into comedy in the first place. If the crowd is poison, you end up fighting for your life the whole time, groping your way through all the pearl clutchers to find whatever laughs you can.

When Danny Martinez told me about the Baton Rouge gig, my first question after "How much does it pay?" was "Who is the headliner?"

Danny laughed. "It's John Fox."

John Fox was a legendary road warrior and an absolutely filthy comic from Chicago.* The only thing dirtier than John's comedy was his personal predilections. He was known as a fall-down drunk who did every drug he could get his hands on and indulged in every vice you could imagine. Sometimes he'd be so drunk onstage that people in the crowd would just stand up and walk out.

John usually wore some kind of sandy-blond mullet and a mustache, but beyond that, his physical appearance changed depending on how long he'd been on the road between stints at home—which became Los Angeles, I believe, by the time I met him. If he was fresh and rested after soaking up some of that California sun, he looked like Captain Kangaroo's younger alcoholic brother. If he'd been on the road awhile, he looked like late-model Chris Farley. When he was at the end of a run, he liked to joke onstage that he looked like Nick Nolte's mug shot. If you worked with John Fox on the back half of his club tour, you were in for a rough few days, because besides performing with him, you also stayed with him at the condo provided by the comedy club.

That is the other part of the equation that determines how well a road gig can go. Pretty much every comedy club worth its salt has a furnished two- or three-bedroom apartment where they put up the comics when they come into town. We call it the comedy condo. It sounds like a nice gesture—a cool fringe benefit of the club circuit—but really, giving young comics who are typically broke a place to stay for two or three days is what allows club owners to pay African-diamond-mine wages to openers like me. In the end, it's a win-win for everyone, so no one complains.

Depending on how old and how successful the club is, the comedy condo can be nice and quiet and have clean beds, it can feel

---

* He died of colon cancer in 2012.

like a well-worn time-share unit, or it can look like the set of a buk-kake gangbang where someone forgot the mop. No matter how the place looks, it always smells like stale cigarette smoke and moldy carpet, and the refrigerator never has more than condiments, coffee creamer, and maybe leftover takeout food from the comics who came through last.

One of the most famous rumors that swirled around the comedy world while John was on the circuit was that, no matter which city you were playing, if you were staying at the comedy condo and there was a jar of mayonnaise in the refrigerator, you should not, under any circumstances, touch, open, smell, or eat from it. Because chances are that John Fox had jerked off into it, fingered out a dollop for lube, or stuck his dick straight in and fucked it like a pocket pussy. If you liked a good old-fashioned bologna sandwich after a show or if you were one of those sick fucks who dip their french fries in mayonnaise, you best be headed to the grocery store for a fresh jar straightaway.

Baton Rouge is a dead shot east from Houston, 275 miles down Interstate 10. I got there in no time flat and stopped in at the club to pick up a key and directions to the comedy condo. It was good to get the feel of the room too since I'd never been there before. Every room is different. Any chance you have to get comfortable in new surroundings you should take, since the more comfortable you are, the better you tend to do.

"How's it looking for tonight?" I asked the manager, who'd given me the key.

"Should be good," he said, "but no nigger jokes, hear me? Baton Rouge is good people, we don't like all that nigger stuff here."

I was still too young and inexperienced to have any halfway decent race material that didn't come straight out of a *Truly Tasteless Jokes* book. Even if I had something, I wasn't about to go nuclear on race in my very first road gig. That's how you get labeled and pigeonholed.

"Okay," I said, "no problem."

I got to the condo about an hour later after getting gas and stopping at the store to pick up some groceries. I was excited, having never been to one of these places before, and a little nervous, not knowing what to expect. I was still living in a room at my sister's house; this was going to be like having my own giant apartment, like a grown-ass man. I just forgot about the roommate part.

I opened the front door to the condo, and there he was on the couch. John Fox. The legendary dirty comic from Chicago, with the mullet and the mustache, butt-fucking the maid. Cocaine residue was all over the glass coffee table in front of them. John didn't miss a beat. He motioned me right over, reached out, and shook my hand.

"Hey, I'm John Fox, the headliner!"

"I'm Ralphie May. I'm the opener."

"Nice to meet ya!"

I didn't catch the maid's name. She was too busy freaking out. I thought it was because I'd walked in on them. Then I realized John's dick was still in her butt as he turned to shake my hand. That was probably not the best feeling in the world; though I cannot attest to that on a factual basis, as I have never had a pecker parked in my poop shoot like her. John started saying some other stuff, sniffing those postnasal cocaine sniffs the whole time, but I didn't register any of it. Having heard the rumors about John Fox from other comics who'd come through Houston, all I kept picturing was this maid with a butthole full of mayonnaise—like the dip cup in the center of a veggie platter.

I thought I was going to vomit. Not from the sight, but from the smell. By then, the scene had made its way through the visual and auditory cortex of my brain and finally landed in my olfactory receptors. The smells were overwhelming: sex, poop, sweat, stale cigarette smoke, the remnants of industrial bleach from the last cleaning. They combined into this gas that you could almost see with your eyes, like mist. It was like bear Mace.

There was another smell too, faint and sporadic. But when I caught wind of it, it cut right through the fog of butt-fucking. I smelled it every time John moved. It took me a second to identify, but I finally pinned it down: it was mayonnaise. *Cheap* mayonnaise, warmed by friction.

Mayonnaise is the cockroach of condiments. Leave it undisturbed in a dark, cool place and it will live forever. Only when you fuck with it and contaminate it does it grow into a disgusting monstrosity. Well, I can't think of anything more contaminating to mayonnaise in the early 1990s than using a Cajun maid's butt-hole and John Fox's dick as a mortar and pestle.

That image put my gag reflex over the top. I didn't know what else to do, so I dropped the groceries, ran upstairs to one of the bedrooms, and hid until I heard them leave. Eventually, when it was time for me to head out to the club, I had to come back downstairs. The place was still a mess. Part of me thought, *Hole-eeee shit, the legend is true, this is totally insanely awesome!* The other part of me, the one raised by a good Christian Southern woman, looked on disapprovingly, thinking, *Well, some maid she is.*

I bumped into John years later at the Zanies in Chicago, where I was doing a run of shows. We got to chatting between shows, and I told him this story. Not only did he remember it, he remembered the maid's name too—Vera. He was laughing so hard when he found out it was me who walked in on him because for years he'd been dining out on this story with other comics, but he never knew who it was that came in.

"You made the right move going upstairs," he assured me. "Vera was a nice lady, but she had a sloppy butthole."

One of the big benefits of being a young Texas comic was that I could get 80 percent of the benefits of going on the road without even leaving the state. The place is so goddamn big (larger than the entire country of France, where mime passes as stand-up comedy), when you hit the clubs in every corner of the state, you end up doing a lot of traveling and working some pretty diverse rooms. The vibe in El Paso (750 miles west of Houston), for example, is different from the college vibe in Lubbock (523 miles northwest of Houston), which is different from the college vibe in Austin (150 miles west of Houston), which is different from the roughneck oil-rig vibe of Galveston, Corpus Christi, or McAllen (all south of Houston). Texas was its own world from a comedy perspective.

One of the main bookers for clubs around Texas at that time was an older white man named C. W. Kendall, based out of the Rio Grande Valley. C.W. wasn't a comedian or even a promoter by trade; he was a piano player who'd toured and recorded with some of the most famous acts in the history of rock 'n' roll in the 1950s and 1960s—artists like Buddy Holly and the Crickets, Bobby Darin, Ricky Nelson, Johnny Cash, Sonny James, Roy Orbison. My guess is that he retired and fell into a side career as a booker since, having toured for thirty or forty years and played nearly all fifty states and two dozen countries, he probably knew every room in the country that had a permanent stage and a microphone.

C.W. was real good about getting guys work who wanted to work. He just wasn't too good about the logistics of it all. He'd call me up and book me into a Friday spot in Nacogdoches, which is way out in East Texas, then he'd say he had another great spot in Odessa the next night if I wanted it.

"That's great, C.W. Who's working the Odessa gig?" I'd ask.

"You are" was always his answer.

First of all, Nacogdoches is this tiny little ant fart of a city that's damn near in Louisiana. The place is surrounded on every side by giant forests that feel like they'd suck the whole damn town into their root system if no one mowed their lawns for a month. The entire town could fit inside the old Houston Astrodome—*twice*. To get there, I'd have to drive 150 miles north, through the Davy Crockett National Forest. A place literally named for the king of the wild frontier! That's what I'd have to get through for this gig—a giant swath of unsettled territory.

Oh, but then I'd have to get right back in the car and drive more than *five hundred miles* west to get to Odessa in time for the start of that show Saturday night. And of course as a young comic, the money was shit. Houston to Nacogdoches to Odessa back to Houston is seventeen hours in a car, and I'd have to do all of it in three days, all for $250.

I started calling these weekends my "triple runs": I'd go out to a club, then over to another, then back to Houston. It was part of the game, so I rarely said no, but all that driving busted me on more than one occasion. At times I had to steal gas from station pumps just to make it to gigs.

If C.W. sensed that you were on the fence with the spots he was offering up, he'd sweeten the pot. He'd book you gigs Thursday through Sunday and tell you that the big money was the Sunday gig, but then when you got there on Thursday, you'd find out that, *whoopsie*, the Sunday gig had fallen through. You ended up making ten times less than what you thought you were going to make. So little in some circumstances that, had you known, you would never have taken the gig in the first place because the cost of gas and food was more than you were making. C.W. must have counted on that, of course. That's why he never just put lipstick on these pigs, he slapped a pair of fake tits on them for good measure.

To C.W.'s credit, he never lied about there being a gig to play, and he worked hard to get you booked, but it was too many weekends on the road just like these that, eventually, got me into teaching defensive-driving school at the Comedy Showcase three or four days a week and selling weed on the side. Not only did I have to pay rent and car insurance, I needed money to buy gas so I could drive to all these fucking wilderness gigs that C.W. booked for me.

In due time, I became a road warrior just like that good ol' mayo fucker, John Fox. I've done at least 250 dates per year for longer than I can remember now. The more time you spend on the road, the more times you make the full circuit of clubs around the country, not only do you become a better comedian, but you also develop a lot of good long-standing relationships with fans, with club owners and managers, with restaurateurs and radio stations. When you're in a new city every week, each in its own way has the power to make your life just that much easier if the people like you.

Several years after leaving Houston for Los Angeles, I was working the Funny Bone in South Bend, Indiana, for a set of shows. I'd played that room a number of times over the years, and the general manager of the club liked me. On this trip, he booked me into the nice hotel in town and got me bumped up to the Presidential Suite. It had three bedrooms, a sitting room, a giant flatscreen TV, a Jacuzzi you could do laps in, and a whole mess of those cushiony things to sit on that aren't quite chairs but aren't quite couches either. You know what I'm talking about? They have like one arm and no back, and they're always pressed against a desk or something. Anyway, I was living the high life in this place.

I felt like John Goodman in *King Ralph* when he finally realizes he can get whatever he wants.

The first night, I get a knock on the door and the room service people bring in this giant tray of food. The GM had ordered a spread of hors d'oeuvres for me to nosh on at my leisure. Not appetizers from the shitty late-night room-service menu, mind you, straight-up hors d'oeuvres from the restaurant downstairs. Canapés for days, jack!

The next day I got another knock on the door. I figured they were back to pick up the old tray and replace it with the lunch tray. I opened the door and it was the GM and three guys in suits. Pretty fancy for a tray pickup, if you ask me.

"Hey, guys, how are you?" I said.

"Mr. May, these are agents from the Secret Service," the GM said. "They're here to do an advance sweep."

"For what?"

"We're with the vice president's detail," one of the Secret Service agents said. "There's a chance Vice President Cheney may need to stay here tonight, so we need to get you off this floor."

I looked at the GM and the three agents and said, "Uh, no." Then I closed the door. I could hear the GM laughing through the door as one of the agents started banging on the door again. I had half a mind to bring over the empty food tray and hand it to the agent through a crack in the door, but I knew that would probably be a bridge too far, so I just opened the door instead.

"Can I help you?" I said.

"Sir, maybe you don't understand me," the agent began. "The vice president of the United States of America is going to stay here tonight. I'm going to have to ask you to vacate this suite." This dude had his serious-agent face on, for sure.

"No."

"Why?" the agent said.

"It says clearly on the door PRESIDENTIAL SUITE, not VICE-PRESIDENTIAL SUITE." Then I shut the door again, which only pissed off the agent even more. He was banging on the door even harder this time, so I opened it right away.

"Sir, are you going to tell the vice president of the United States of America that he can't sleep here?" the agent asked, totally perplexed.

"No, you are." I shut the door again.

I could hear the GM crying laughing out in the hallway. I could also hear him say something to the agents in a hushed voice, after which he knocked on the door instead of the agent.

"Ralphie, let me in real fast." I let the GM in and he said, "Okay, what's going on?"

"Man, I've got weed in here. I can't be having those motherfuckers around me, all right?"

"Okay, grab all your weed and put it in one of your bags and bring it with you. I'll have housekeeping come in to clean the place real well, then they'll bring the bomb-sniffing dogs in, and if everything is clear, you'll be back here in your room by the time you get back from the club tonight."

So I packed up all my shit, went to a movie, went to dinner, did two shows at the Funny Bone, then came back to the hotel. Doing two shows when you're the headliner takes a lot out of you, or at least it's always taken a lot out of me. When you're a big boy like me, you use up a lot of energy standing onstage, focusing your mind, reacting to the crowd around you. Plus, I go out in the lobby after every show and take pictures and sign shit. It's exhausting. These shows were no different, so when I arrived at the hotel, I had completely forgotten about the Secret Service agents I'd run afoul of earlier in the day.

Imagine my surprise when I came upon the hotel ringed with cop cars, three cars deep, all the way around. The place was on lockdown. I had to show my driver's license just to get into the building. I had to go through a metal detector to get up to my hotel room.

"What's your name?" asked a state trooper manning a clipboard with the hotel's guest list on it.

"My name's Ralphie May."

The statie's face lit up. "Oh, man, that's him!" he shouted to the other troopers in the lobby. They all rushed over.

"Hey, did you tell the vice president to fuck off?" one of them asked.

"No, but I did tell that asshole from the Secret Service to go tell him to fuck off."

All the staties cracked up. They were high-fiving each other, jumping on their radios, letting the other guys out in the ring of patrol cars know what was going on in here. I was getting so swept up in the energy of the scene that I went in for a high five myself. When I did, when I raised my hand up above my head, a fat joint that someone had given me after the last show fell out of my shirt pocket onto the ground. I thought I was toast, but the staties circled the wagon around me so no one else could see.

"Look, don't smoke it, just put it away," one of the staties said. "Those Secret Service guys are looking for any reason to bust you."

"Will do." I scooped it up, hopped on the elevator to the top floor, and went to sleep in my *presidential* suite.

When I woke up the next morning, they were all gone. There wasn't a trace of them anywhere, like it was all a dream. Which is fitting when you think about life on the road for a stand-up comedian. It's a great gig that is an essential part of the path to achieving your professional hopes and dreams. It's also an experience that could easily turn into a nightmare if you don't figure out what you're doing, if you don't know how the world works, and if you don't find your place in it. The way you do that is by answering the door every time opportunity knocks. Even if that opportunity's name is Dick. And even if that Dick has a Cheney stuck on the end of it. Or worse, a butthole filled with mayonnaise.

9.

THE CHANNELVIEW
HELL GIG

I became a headliner fairly quickly, all things considered. Doing spots all over town for a couple years, getting out on the road as soon as clubs would have me, and having a rabbi like Sam Kinison vouching for me early on gave me confidence that I could pull together a solid forty-five-minute headlining set, and it gave club owners and bookers confidence that I could topline a show that people would actually pay money to see.

Just as no two road gigs are the same for an opener, headlining gigs can be a little fraught when you first start getting them. What you have to remember is that all headlining means is that you are the main act, who comes out last, closes the show, and does the most time. What it *doesn't* mean is that all your shows are now at the biggest and best clubs in the country with the most sophisticated and appreciative audiences. Eventually it can mean that if you stick with comedy long enough, but initially your headlining gigs are a total crapshoot.

Sometimes they're just plain crap. Whether it was a half-empty lodge in the Catskills in 1956 or a corporate gig full of anxious tech nerds in San Jose in 2016, this has always been the case as long as there has been stand-up comedy. It was especially true in the nineties, however, when stand-up was at a peak and every bar, club, café, and American Legion hall wanted to have its own comedy night. These venues had interest and they usually had customers, they just didn't have any money. Or if they did, they didn't have the desire to part with enough of it to draw A-list comics like Sam or Bill or Thea. So what they did was call anyone they could—club owners, other comics, venue bookers like C.W.—and fished down the comedy food chain for a headliner until someone either old and desperate or young and hungry (like me) bit.

My buddy "Spooky" Dick Williams was one of the guys who these second- and third-tier venues would call. Dick was fucking funny, but Lord Jesus did he have a dark sense of humor. That's not why we called him Spooky, though. He got that name because he was hairy and he looked kind of like a short werewolf. Plus he had crossed eyes that sat a little too close together on his face, but not so close that they were scary. Just a little spooky. It was a very Charles Manson–y look, minus the charisma and the swastika on the forehead.

Anyway, one time Spooky Dick booked me a gig headlining at a Holiday Inn in Channelview, Texas. If you're not familiar with Channelview (and who is?), it's a rough part of the Houston metro area that is also home to a lot of oil production. It's not the kind of place that people go to see comedy. It's the kind of place you end up against your will and sometimes comedy breaks out.

Three comics were on the bill for this Channelview gig. I was the headliner, a short-haired redhead named Jody Ferdig was the feature act, and a Mexican fella named Anthony Andrews was the opener. I shit you not, that was his real name: Anthony Andrews. I hadn't seen something that brown named something so white since the last time I went to a Cracker Barrel.

The room we were playing had a bar and a dance floor with a big Lone Star flag painted in the middle of it. Tables and chairs were arranged around the room, and a couple of waitresses were busy delivering a nonstop stream of drinks to the guests. The guests broke down *Law & Order* style—into two separate yet equally important groups: Mexicans on one side and Dutchmen on the other. The Dutch guys were there on business from Shell, which is a Netherlands-based petroleum company. The Mexicans were there because this is Texas. The Mexican guys were being totally cool. The Dutch guys had been drinking heavily since 6:00 p.m. and were superloud. Nobody working there wanted to settle them down, though, because they all looked like the henchmen from *Die Hard*.

So Anthony goes up onstage to get the show started and completely eats a dick. He could not have done any worse if he had literally eaten his own penis with a knife and fork right there in front of everyone. Jody goes up next, and she doesn't eat a dick right away, but the Dutch guys heckle her so much that they ruin every one of her punch lines—for thirty-five straight minutes.

Part of becoming a good comedian is learning how to control a crowd. Shutting down a single heckler who thinks he is part of the show is one thing; and most comics with a little bit of experience can do that. Getting a whole room of drunk people to turn their attention your way and focus is something else entirely. At the time, Anthony and Jody couldn't do it.

Now it's my turn to give it a try. I go up there, take the mic off the stand, wait a couple beats for a lull in the noise, and go right in at them.

"Listen up! If all you Hans and Franz motherfuckers are gonna do is heckle all night, then you can save us all some time and just get the fuck out!"

There was a brief record-scratch moment, and then one of the waitresses rushed to the front of the stage trying to read me the riot act before she was even within earshot:

"Hey, fuck you, pal. They're way more important than you are, asshole!"

I did not take it well. First of all, if she thought any of these Euros were going to tip her for shit, she had another think coming. Second, it's not like we just popped in to the Channelview Holiday Inn on a whim and decided to do ninety minutes of topical material for shits and giggles. Someone in this godforsaken place hired us to come here and tell jokes to these ungrateful motherfuckers.

This waitress had no flex. She came right back at me, which only pissed me off further. I'm not proud of what happened next, but there may have been some derogatory utterances directed at her by me that started with a *c* and ended with a *t* and rhymed with *cunt*. I don't remember specifically, but knowing myself like I do, I probably said it one or two or three times.

All of the sudden, these Dutchmen stand up and try to drunkenly come to the waitress's defense. That's not good. Dutchmen are the tallest men in the world. They *average* six feet tall, and they're built like swimmers. I'm five feet nine inches tall, and I barely float. Anthony, bless his heart, sees what's going down and immediately yells, *"What did you say about Mexicans?!"*

Of course the Dutchmen hadn't said a thing, but Anthony was bona fide Mexican and knew this would get his people in the bar whipped up into *revolución*. Sure enough, they turn and move toward the Dutchmen almost en masse, like one of those giant rafts of fire ants that come together during a flood. Before too long both sides are yelling and cussing and throwing shit at each other. I'm trying to keep the peace from onstage by using the microphone, but all I'm doing is adding to the sound of the yelling.

Finally someone calls the police. Eight squad cars with about fifteen cops show up. They immediately shut the whole thing down and drag a bunch of us out into the parking lot in handcuffs to figure out what the fuck is going on and who is to blame. You want to talk about a fat moment: they needed three pairs of cuffs to secure my hands behind my back. The most humiliating part was how unnecessary the cuffs were. I was well over four hundred pounds by then—where the fuck was I gonna go? What were they worried about? That I might just magically Carl Lewis my ass on out of there?

So there I am, standing in the shadow of a bunch of goddamn oil refineries, locked up like some kind of circus freak, trying to explain to one of the officers that I'm a comedian and we were hired to do a show, but he doesn't want to hear it. He's telling me that they're going to pin me with inciting a riot and public distur-bance. I'm madder than a wet hen and I'm trying to reason with the man, but I every time I think I'm getting somewhere, I get distracted by this blinding bright light coming from over the of-ficer's shoulder. At first I thought it was his partner doing that dickhead cop thing where they shine their Maglite in your face to mess with your sensory perceptions. But when I moved to the side, I saw that it was a film crew, and that the guy operating the boom mic had a *COPS* Windbreaker on. Are you fucking kidding me? You're trying to jam me up on some bullshit charges *and* you want to put it on television?

I looked right into that camera and said, "Fuck you, I'm union! You gotta pay me scale or I'm not signing the release."

That about sealed it for the officer questioning me. He grabbed ahold of the cuff chains and started duckwalking me toward a squad car. Just then a Harris County sheriff arrived on the scene, saw what was happening, and came right over. Turns out, he was a big fan who had seen me a bunch of times in South Houston over the years. This wasn't even his regular patrol area, he was just filling in that night, but when he heard the words "public distur-bance" and "large group of Mexicans and whites" over the radio, he hopped in his car. Imagine that.

Let me tell you: I have been butt-fucked by Lady Luck on more than a few occasions in my life, but every once in a while she does me a solid and gives me a reach around. This was one of those times.

The sheriff tells the officer to remove my cuffs immediately and then asks me to tell him what happened. I explain everything with the utmost factual precision that wouldn't also get me or Anthony or Jody in trouble. When I'm done talking, the sheriff goes in and shuts the bar down for overserving intoxicated patrons, then pins public-drunkenness and assault charges on a couple of the flying Dutchmen who were being the biggest pricks during the show. When he came back out with those assholes in custody, I told him we also hadn't been paid for our work. He turned around, marched back into the bar, and got our money.

That night I ended up doing six minutes of actual comedy and made $300. Anthony got his $50 for opening, and Jody got her $100 as the feature act. Anthony and I didn't have any complaints, but Jody was so fucking mad. She had to go through thirty-five minutes of absolute torture to earn her money, and the two of us made out like bandits. Sure, Anthony bombed technically, but he only did five or six minutes. That wasn't near enough time for those fucking Dutch assholes to zero in their heckles. Jody made me buy her drinks at the rest of our gigs that week—and I was glad to do it. As the headliner, you have to take care of your supporting acts. Even if one of them barely got a joke out and the other nearly started a race war.

I ended up learning a lot about being a headliner from that hell gig in Channelview, but if I had one regret, it was that my *COPS* footage never made it to air. What I would give now to have tape of me getting pulled out of some shit bar in Channelview, Texas, struggling against three pairs of handcuffs while screaming into the camera.

Hell, when I think about it like that, it would have been my first dramatic TV credit. Now that's how you start a television career, jack!

10.

A BUCKET OF CRABS

By the second half of the 1990s I was firmly established in the Houston comedy scene as a serious headlining act. No more Holiday Inns for me, motherfuckers. It was DoubleTree or bust, now. I was headlining all the big rooms during the week. When huge national acts came through from Los Angeles or New York, I'd feature for them. I was even making meaningful friendships with some amazing comics like Doug Stanhope and Mitch Hedberg, who started in comedy around the same time I did. By most measures, mine was a pretty fast ascendancy, though not extraordinary by any means. It just felt that way at times because I'd come up in the third- or fourth-best city for comedy and I started (and looked) young. When you looked like I did and you found a niche in a town where people five to ten years older than you come from other parts of the country to get their start, you seem somehow exceptional to people who don't know any better. If I'd started in Denver or DC, then maybe we could talk, but I just did what every other good comedian did: I wrote jokes, I got up, I went on the road, I said "Yes, and . . . ," rinse and repeat.

I would love to say that the trajectory of my career was due entirely to my movie-star good looks and God-given talent, but that would be total horseshit. Not only would it be a lie, but it would diminish the importance of hard work and the influence of all the people who helped me along the way by giving me advice, support, and opportunities. It would also diminish the importance of all the haters who drove me to succeed just to spite them. My haters were a lot like the haters in any thriving local comedy scene in that they were old, bitter, tired assholes who made fucking with young, ambitious comics their official pastime, if not their second career. (Though you sort of need to have had a first career in order to have a second one, but I digress.) What made Houston haters unique was that, with a few notable exceptions, their ranks were comprised of the hangers-on of the Texas Outlaw Comics from the Comedy Workshop days of the 1980s. Because they were inside at the bar having one more drink, these were the assholes who missed the success train when it pulled into town to pick up Sam Kinison and Bill Hicks.

They infested the clubs like bedbugs in a flophouse: they were so small you'd never see them, but you'd get up every day and they'd still be there, irritating the shit out of you. Some nights when we were on the same bill, I wanted to shove the microphone so far down their throats that when they farted you'd hear feedback. They were the kind of people who would begrudge every laugh you got because to their minds you were taking laughter that should have gone to them—like happiness and joy are finite resources. I guess for them maybe they were, I don't know.

What was so sad about them was that they were fucking funny

yet, considering how hot the comedy scene was and how long they'd been doing it, they were shockingly unaccomplished. Instead, they polluted an entire generation of young, hardworking comics by being god-awful cunts to them. Their sole claim to fame was knowing Sam and Bill once upon a time. Their prized possessions were old stories that they dined out on for as long as I lived in Houston. Their shtick never changed. Neither did their stories. Neither did they.

From the very beginning of my time at the Comedy Showcase, while these old-timey pricks were finagling free drinks at the bar and doing blow in the bathroom every night, I was sitting with Danny Martinez until 2:00 a.m. talking about comedy, trying to learn as much about the craft from him as he was willing to teach me.

One of the things Danny taught me about was topical humor. You don't come flying out of the womb spitting Bill Hicks jokes about the human condition, and when you're young, you don't have enough life experience to have a well-rounded take on the world, so in the meantime the best way to come up with material is to look around you at what is going on and figure out some interesting way to talk about it.

Shit, I can do that, I thought. All I did when I wasn't performing was hang out at my sister's house and watch TV. That made me one of the most observant motherfuckers out there, is how I looked at it.

For the first couple years, all I did was increasingly sophisticated fat jokes and topical humor. The early nineties were great for both. I was getting bigger, and the world was getting crazier. We had the Gulf War; Rodney King and the LA Riots (which sounds like a band name when you say it like that); President Bush puked all over the prime minister of Japan; the Soviet Union fell apart;

they caught Jeffrey Dahmer up in Milwaukee eating people; the Dream Team killed everyone at the Summer Olympics in Barcelona; and my main man Bill Clinton ran for president—against two Texans no less.

Clinton's candidacy and election were a real boon for me as a comic. As a fellow Razorback and a Houston resident, I got to make all sorts of jokes about Arkansas and Texas, and I got to tell the story of how when I was a little kid, Clinton went to see my granny after he lost his reelection bid for governor. Granny was a big swingin' lady-dick in the Arkansas Democratic Party back then. Anyone thinking of running for office at the state level who wanted to win made a point of coming by Granny's place and asking for advice, even if they didn't need it. Clinton was no exception. He was the consummate retail politician. He knew what side of the biscuit got buttered. Boy, did Granny have some advice for him:

"Listen here, William. If you want to win another election ever again, you best have that wife of yours change her goldarn name to Clinton once and for all. This isn't hippie-dippie California. This is Arkansas for petesake!"

Hillary changed her name from Rodham to Clinton a year later, Bill won the gubernatorial election the year after that, and the rest is jizz-covered history. My mama told me that story after my granny passed away. Who knows if it's actually true, or if Granny was the influence that put him over the top, but it was a great bit from my life that I could use to build topical material on top of.

As I got better at identifying good topics and figuring out how to write topical jokes that fit my style, I realized that I could write fast. Something would happen on a Tuesday, I'd write a joke about it that night, and I'd be performing it on Wednesday at the Comedy Showcase. A lot of times they were good jokes too. They were rough, but the premises were strong.

Make no mistake, the haters were not trying to hear that. Their hate came early and it came often. They'd be there at the Showcase on Wednesday watching, seething, judging, hating. Then one of them would inevitably perform a version of my new joke somewhere over the weekend, and come Monday, with everyone at the Laff Stop for open-mic night, some people would be saying they wrote the joke first and I was the one who stole it.

Comics stumble into similar jokes all the time. We live in the same world, and most of us have points of view that are fairly alike. It's impossible to avoid ruminating on the same ideas and not coming to similar conclusions. If you ask people who have been accused of joke thievery, this reality is at the core of a lot of the beefs in the comedy world.

That was not at all what was going on in my case. Not only was I not the fucking thief—they were—but there were no great minds on the other side of this beef. There was also literally no time for me to have heard these new jokes before telling my version of them if they had, indeed, been told by someone else at the same time. Incidents like this happened four of five distinct times that I can recall. Just out-and-out fuckery. I remember sitting there in the club, dumbfounded, thinking to myself. *I'm not Marty McFly. This isn't* Back to the Future. *What are these assholes even talking about?*

Eventually I talked to Danny Martinez about it. Not to tattle like some prison snitch, more to understand why stuff like this happened. And more specifically, why it was happening *to me*. Danny is a wonderful human being, so he was not going to stoop to their level and sling shit, but he made me understand, by saying without actually saying it, that mediocre people often become angry failures, and when they do, they don't like being around people with hope.

My youthful dewy-eyed optimism and my enthusiasm for the

work was a threat to their worldview and to the status quo. My early success, without any help from them, God forbid, was a threat to their survival. There is a saying that success has many fathers but failure is an orphan. In stand-up comedy, success may have many fathers, but that's because your mother was a whore and you were adopted. At least that's what these shit stains will tell you when they can't contain their jealousy and paranoia. If a few more guys like me showed up, after all, who was going to need them? I sure didn't.

What really drew the stink eye my way and kept it there was my relationship with Sam. My having the audacity to reach out to Sam through the Laff Stop when he came to town after I first got to Houston was my first strike with them. They acted like I had breached some sort of etiquette, like there were rules for human contact that I needed to learn. If that's how they were with other comics, I can only imagine what they were like with women.

Wait, wait, wait. Do you mean to tell me that you met a girl, and you hit it off, and then you just . . . CALLED HER??? Like, on the phone?! Who the hell do you think you are, pal?

That Sam vouched for me on the radio and it led to a regular paid gig that got me a lot of exposure was strike two. It must have pissed them off to no end. How could some fat, young backwoods hillbilly come into their town, take their laughs, fill all their radio appearances, *and* have a working relationship with the one man who was keeping them relevant? No, sir. I don't reckon that's going to work. It didn't compute for them. Things aren't supposed to happen like that. I hadn't paid my dues. There's a process—not the process Danny told me to respect, mind you, but the process by which these bitter drunks rationalized their failures. I realize now in hindsight that *pay your dues* was just code for "give up," but back then their anger toward me stung.

Unbeknownst to me, by even knowing Sam I had painted a bull's-eye on my chest. When he came back to town a year or so after our KLOL appearance and picked me to open for him during his run of shows, that was strike three, and it just tattooed the bull's-eye on me permanently. Sam was their compadre, their peer, and he chose me over them? This fucking kid had to go. They would run me out on a rail if they had to.

Still, despite their obvious hostility, I tried to be friends to them. I couldn't help it. It's an unhealthy habit that fat kids and stand-up comics share: our insecurity combines with our black-sheep tendencies to make us want to be liked by everyone we meet.

On the weekend of my twenty-first birthday a bunch of us went to the dog track to enjoy the weather and hopefully win a little money betting on the races. We spent the whole day there getting fucked-up. Being newly legal, I bought drinks for everyone like I was a boss and even scored some weed for us. Kill 'em with kindness, right?

After the final race, we all decided to go to the Comedy Showcase to hang out. I was the last to arrive because I had some birthday stuff to attend to at home. When I got there, Danny's wife, Blanca Gutierrez, met me at the door. One of the comics from our group was in the parking lot annihilated drunk, stumbling around pissing everywhere, crassly propositioning a girl he'd basically trapped inside her car. Blanca was imploring me to go rescue him because the girl's boyfriend was a Harris County sheriff's deputy, and he was on his way down to the club with handcuffs and a large stick.

I was conflicted. This guy, who I will call the Asshole (I'll be goddamned if he ever sees his name in print on my watch), had called me a hack and a joke thief on more than one occasion—many, many times actually. I had zero incentive to help him and every incentive to grab a lawn chair and some popcorn and watch him get his dick kicked in the dirt. I couldn't do that. That's not how my mama raised me. When you see someone in distress, you help them, even if they're a god-awful cunt. It's the Golden Rule. So I went outside and the Asshole was so fucked-up, you couldn't even talk to him. I had to pick him up, sling him over my shoulder, and carry him into the club like a bag of dog food.

Mostly I did it for Blanca and Danny because they'd been so great to me for as long as they'd known me. But I also did it for the Asshole. Getting arrested sucks, especially when you're not in your right mind. There's nothing worse than waking up in a jail cell and having no idea what you did to land yourself there. What was the harm in extending a little bit of humanity to the Asshole when he was clearly in a dark place?

That was the last time the Asshole ever drank. He's been sober since that very day. As a human being I feel good about that. Who knows what would have happened if the sheriff's deputy got there before I did and put a baton across the base of the Asshole's neck? As for the Asshole himself, he still calls me a hack to this day and has never made amends to me. I guess he was busy being a miserable piece of shit the day they taught that step in the program, but there's nothing I can do about that, so I have to let it go.

Trying to be friends with everyone worked well enough with a few of the comics who hadn't become complete sociopaths yet. We weren't in the greenroom braiding each other's back hair between sets or anything, but they didn't openly hate me, so I counted it as a win.

That all stopped in 1993 when Bill Hicks came back into town for a set of shows at the Laff Stop. Bill Hicks was the Michelangelo of stand-up comedy. The way he structured a joke, the way he used imagery, his wordsmithery, his articulation, the way he leaned into the audience when he was delivering an uncomfortable truth—everything was flawless.

Bill was an artist and a truth teller. The first time I saw him perform, I almost quit comedy altogether. I knew I would never be as funny as Bernie Mac, and I made my peace with that. But with Bill, I knew I could never measure up, no matter what metric you put in front of us, except maybe a scale. That's a hard pill to swallow when you're in any creative or artistic field. Part of what keeps you going is continually getting better at whatever your art is, but a part of you eventually always wants to be the best at some small aspect of it. When that no longer seems like a possibility, like it did with Bill, it's gut-check time. Thankfully Danny Martinez (who was the best at smooth transitions) pulled me aside, bless his heart, and reminded me that nobody should compare themselves to Bill Hicks, in any way, shape, or form. Danny said there was nobody like Bill before and wouldn't be another one like him for a long time, decades probably.* That made me feel a little better, in the way that getting punched in the stomach distracts from the pain of getting kicked in the balls.

I don't remember if Bill had already been diagnosed with pancreatic cancer when he came back to Houston, but I do recall that he was absolutely on fire. The year before, his *Relentless* album came out and crushed; then his *Revelations* special that he did in London followed it. Everything he was doing, he was cooking with gas. He was as sharp as anyone had ever seen him. The only

---

* The closest I've seen since Bill Hicks passed away has been my friend Dougie Stanhope.

problem with his recent round of club dates was that his openers were constantly fucking everything up. They were doing Bill Hicks for fifteen minutes before Bill Hicks had a chance to come on-stage and do Bill Hicks. It wasn't their fault. They weren't doing it intentionally. Bill was such an amazing comedian that young comics who watched him would become overly influenced by his style. We called them Hicksians. The only reason I never became a Hicksian was because I was smart enough to know I wasn't smart enough to pull off his kind of material. I was twenty-one years old, what the hell did I know about the world?

Bill gave it a shot with whoever Sandy Marcus had booked to open for him. Like the others, this one did not pan out. The very first show, the opener was yet another young comic trying to emulate Bill, which just pissed him off, especially in the town where he got his start.

I've heard people say stuff like "You should be honored" and "Imitation is the sincerest form of flattery" when I talk about joke thievery and style biters like the Hicksians. What those people don't understand is that a guy like Bill Hicks dedicated his entire adult life and thousands of stage hours to figuring out who he was, what he felt about things, and what style felt authentic to his personality. The Bill Hicks who people saw onstage wasn't just a person, it was a masterwork, like the statue *David,* meticulously chiseled from the mind and the hands of a genius. Yet here was this group of young guys coming up who saw Bill and wanted to become that kind of masterwork themselves, but instead of putting in the hours to find their own version of it, they tried to take a shortcut and sculpt their own version *of him* with some Play-Doh and duct tape.

After the first show, Bill asked Sandy if she had anyone else who could open for him who wouldn't step on all of his punch lines before he had a chance to use them. Sandy threw out my name. This was her pitch on my behalf (if you can even call it that):

"Well, he's young and all he does is himself."

"Perfect," Bill told her, and so I opened for Bill Hicks on all of his remaining Houston shows.*

I like to think I opened for Bill more than just once because he loved me and thought I was funny, but deep down I know that if he did love me, it was because I wasn't trying to be Bill Fucking Hicks. And that was good enough for me.

It was also good enough for the remaining friendly comics in Houston to effectively turn their backs on me. I don't know what I was to them anymore, but I was definitely not a human being. As it turned out, all that animosity turned out to be just a prelude.

For a good stretch of time, I had a steady gig closing for a wonderful comedian (and an even better person) named Marty Schilling on the last weekend of every month. We played North Houston on Friday and Saturday nights, then Galveston on Sunday night. We'd stay the night in Galveston after the Sunday show, paid for by the club, and then wake up the next day on the beach. It paid $250 per show, so it was a $750 weekend for me, which I counted on to make rent each month after I moved out of my sister's place and got my own apartment.

One Thursday, right before one of my Schilling weekends, I got a call from C. W. Kendall. He wanted to know if I could do three shows down in Brownsville that weekend for $1,200. Brownsville is a port city 350 miles south of Houston right on the Mexico border. It's basically the foreskin on the mushroom tip of south Texas. It takes six hours to get there by car from Houston. It's not the

---

* Bill Hicks died less than a year later, on February 26, 1994.

longest hike C.W. has had me make for a gig, but it was up there. The $1,200 took a lot of the sting out of it. I hated to bail on Marty, but this was nearly twice what I would make doing her shows and I needed the money.

I called Marty and asked to get out of the gig. Saint that she is, she said not to worry. She had someone on standby for situations just like this, so there was no problem. She was happy for me that I was going to be making more money and assured me that I could come back and do the Friday–Sunday shows with her next month.

So I called C.W. back at the number he gave me and told him to book the gig. The next morning I hopped in my Dodge Dakota pickup and hit the road. Six flat, miserable, desolate hours later I pulled up to the address that C.W. had given me for the club, and it was closed. Not *not open*. Closed . . . like for good. I asked around and found out it had been closed down for weeks. I jumped back into the Dakota and drove to the address C.W. had given me for the hotel I was supposed to be staying in. It didn't exist. There wasn't even a building there.

Something was royally fucked here. I was panicked. By agreeing to do this Brownsville gig I had not only passed up my regular $750 with Marty, but I'd also given up an additional $300 from the defensive-driving classes that I was supposed to teach at the Showcase on Saturday morning. It was the end of the month. I had no money. This was going to pay my rent—*all my rent*. I wasn't sure what to do. There was no way I could pay for a hotel now that I was down here, that much I knew. But I wasn't sure I even had enough money for gas. I had some weed on me I could sell, and I had the pistol I carried under the seat that I could try to move if it got really bad.

I had two options: try to find a buyer for some of that weed and sleep in the cab of my truck overnight if I didn't find one; or roll the dice and drive straight back to Houston, hoping I could find a gas station where I could steal some fuel or sell the weed to a cashier. I chose the latter. I already had a spot at the Showcase on Sunday. If I could make it back on the early side, I could get some sleep and maybe grab some spots around town on Saturday to make enough to pay my rent.

I didn't get back to Houston until Saturday night. I ended up limping into a truck stop about halfway home and off-loading my pistol to a trucker for barely enough to fill my tank and pay for some Whataburger. When I got to town, I went straight to the Showcase and found Danny Martinez to tell him everything that had happened. I needed advice on what to do. I was out twelve hundred *actual dollars* and it wasn't my fault.

"There's no way C.W. would do that," Danny said. "He may reroute you to God knows where, but he's an honest man." That's what made no sense to me, because I agreed wholeheartedly with Danny. C.W. has sent me to the middle of West Texas to perform for what amounted to a bunch of dead armadillos on the side of a frontage road, but the gig was there.

Sunday I woke up madder than a hornet's nest, alternating between furious and frantic about paying my rent and my utilities and my car insurance. I called the number C.W. had given me to ask him what had happened and to give him a piece of my mind, but his phone just rang and rang and rang. I did my spot at the Showcase that night as scheduled, but instead of hanging out afterward like usual, I came straight home. I had too much anger and negative energy in my system to hang out at the club. The club was my real home, and I didn't want to contaminate that.

The next night, Monday night, was the open mic at the Laff Stop. I showed up about 9:00 p.m., later than usual for me, because I picked up a defensive-driving class at the Showcase to make back some of the money I'd lost. A bunch of comedians—including a number of the really mean ones—were sitting around a table, and they started asking me how my weekend went. I told them that it was shit and that there was no gig and that C.W. had fucked me and that they should watch out for that guy because he might fuck them too.

They let me finish my diatribe, then burst out laughing right in my face, making fun of me for being a sucker. C.W. hadn't booked me in Brownsville. C.W. hadn't called me at all. The guys at the table had gotten drunk on Thursday night and thought it would be hilarious if they called me pretending to be C.W. and sent me on a wild-goose chase. One of them had played the last Brownsville show before the place closed, so he knew it would be the perfect prank. Worst of all, the guy who impersonated C. W. Kendall called up Marty Schilling right after he spoke to me and took my North Houston/Galveston gigs. He was the guy she had on standby.

It was one of the meanest, dirtiest, most hateful things I've ever experienced. It pretty much confirmed for me that I had to get the fuck out of Texas. Besides that realization, the only other thing I am thankful for from the incident was that I sold my pistol before I got home. If I hadn't, I would have marched out of the Laff Stop that Monday night, grabbed the gun from my truck, walked back in, and killed every single one of those evil cunts. The rage inside me was so complete I don't know if I, or anyone else, would have been capable of stopping me. You can push a man only so far before his dignity requires that he respond in kind.

During the year I spent in Baltimore before coming to Houston, I did a fair bit of crabbing and got to understand crabs pretty well. How they defend themselves, how they often seem to move as one, how they turn red when you put some heat to them. They remind me a lot of the miserable local comics I had to deal with all those years in the nineties.

If you put one blue crab in a bucket, for example, it will crawl out. But if you throw two blue crabs in a bucket, neither crab will ever get out. As soon as one of them starts to make progress toward the lip of the bucket, the other one will drag it down. They will do that over and over until they exhaust themselves or someone bigger comes along and eats them for lunch.

That's exactly what Houston comedy was. As soon as anyone made a step forward, they'd get dragged down by the comedians behind them. It's hard to break that cycle. Even today Houston is rich in comedy talent. Some kids coming up should be superstars, but they might never make it if they don't figure out how to break free from the throng below them and reach for the top.

In making a name for myself in the Houston comedy scene, I stood on the shoulders of giants like Sam and Bill and Danny. In getting out, I instead stood on the shoulders of giant assholes whose bitterness, malice, and deceit propelled me west. The irony is, they thought they'd won when I finally moved to Los Angeles in 1998, but they didn't win. I had no peers when I got to Houston (I knew no one), and they made sure I didn't have any when I left or at any point in between. They did me a favor by eventually making Houston unbearable for me. Just like with forging steel—bend it, fold it, hammer the shit out of it—when they beat me up, all they did was make me stronger. It's the best thing they could ever have done to prepare me for the next phase of my life and my career in LA.

PART 3
LOS ANGELES:
1998–2010

11.
LOS TRUE ANGELES

Like every good modern story about struggle and success in Los Angeles, mine begins with a Mexican who needed a ride to work.

His name was Joey Medina, and actually he was Puerto Rican, but that's less funny, so just ignore that part. Joey is a great comic from New York City who has always done a little bit of everything: a little bit of acting, a little bit of producing, a little bit of hosting, a little bit of radio, and obviously a little bit of touring. He's a hustler, which is probably why we hit it off.

In June 1998, Joey flew into Houston from Los Angeles, where he was living, to do a week of shows in the run-up to the third annual Latino Laugh Festival in San Antonio. Showtime had turned the previous two years of the festival's stand-up program into a television series, so the gig had become a real draw. Agents and managers were coming in from LA for it; so were studio and network executives. In the first half of the decade they'd struck gold with sitcoms built around white stand-up comics, and they'd had some success with shows around black comics like Thea Vidale and Steve Harvey. I guess they figured they could do it again, this time by turning down the toaster and going a little less brown.

Joey and I got to talking about it after his last Laff Stop show. He'd just finished up a three-year stint hosting a radio show in Tucson the year before, and this sounded like a great opportunity for him to take the next big step. I was happy for him and was heartened for myself. If Joey could make it happen—if he could go big time—maybe I could too. Our paths weren't dissimilar, and here he was hopping flights, crisscrossing the country doing club and festival dates. Joey laughed. *Flights?* He wasn't flying unless he absolutely had to. Flying costs money. He was taking the bus to San Antonio.

The bus? Joey Medina was a popular comedian and a successful Puerto Rican man. The only greyhounds he should have been dealing with were the ones you race, not the ones you ride. Besides, this was central Texas in the summer. I'm pretty sure four or five hours on a bus full of poor people trudging across that stretch of land violates the Geneva Convention.

"You know what, you shouldn't be riding no bus. I'll take you," I said.

I was making good money by then, what with all the defensive-driving classes I was teaching on top of my regular spots and my now-thriving smokable-horticulture distribution company. I could take a day or two off to drive him and hang out. It's not like I wanted to hang out with any of those fucking pricks in Houston, anyway.

When we got to San Antonio, Joey introduced me around and immediately started telling everyone that I'd given him a ride all the way from Houston. They were blown away. I considered it doing a solid for another comedian and, more simply, basic Southern hospitality. But I guess from their perspective, when a good ol' boy from Arkansas gives a Hispanic fella a free ride across Texas, it's usually not out of the kindness of his heart, and the Hispanic guy is definitely not sitting in the front seat.

To show their appreciation, the organizers gave me an opening spot for one of their big showcases that night on the River Walk. This was one of the shows that all the executives and managers were coming into town for. The festival had quickly turned into an opportunity for both Joey and me. I was nowhere near prepared, but a comedian is never *not* a comedian, so of course I said yes.

I did eleven minutes . . . and crushed. It was an amazing feeling, but it couldn't hold a candle to what happened *after* the show. Executives were stuffing their cards into my hand, telling me that they'd never seen anybody like me before. Managers were buying me drinks, asking me all sorts of questions like "What the fuck are you still doing in Texas?" I met Carlos Mencia, who was a giant in the Latin comedy scene then, and he told me to go to the Comedy Store on Sunset Boulevard. I also met a fat little kid named Gabriel Iglesias, who was hilarious. Before the night was over, with that one set, I walked out of the club with management and representation and marching orders: get your affairs together and get to Los Angeles.

A week later, I was in California.

Getting my affairs in order on the Houston side of this little transition was the easy part. All my worldly possessions fit into the back of my Toyota 4Runner. All the question marks were on the LA side of the equation. I didn't know anybody. I was only vaguely familiar with the town from a few isolated trips out there over the previous few years. I had no idea how I was going to make money, and I knew I was going to need a lot more of it given how high rents were compared to Houston. I didn't have a weed connect in LA either, so I couldn't even bridge the economic or the social gap with that right away. The one thing I did have was a place to stay.

Originally, I was going to stay with Joey Medina on the floor of the apartment he shared with a Mexican comic named Alex Reymundo (Alex is an actual Mexican, not just Mexican for the sake of this story). I'd stayed with them before on one of my visits, and they were willing to let me crash with them while I figured out my next move. But when I was talking to Doug Stanhope about it, he told me to put a pin in the plan because he might know of a better place for me. His buddy Matt Becker, another good comic, had a small apartment in a building that a bunch of other comics lived in. He was leaving to work in Alaska for a while and wasn't going to need it, but was going to continue paying the rent because he needed a place to store the stuff he didn't bring with him. I could stay there if I wanted; all I had to do was make sure that the place didn't burn to the ground and that none of those dirty fucking comics stole his shit.

Deal.

The apartment was in a building at 1440 North Gardner Street, three doors south of Sunset Boulevard. It could not have been in a better location for what I was trying to do. It was three-quarters of a mile straight down Sunset from the Laugh Factory. Another three-quarters of a mile farther was the Comedy Store. The Improv was on Melrose Avenue, almost two miles away, but I could literally just roll my ass down the hill and slam into Melrose without breaking a sweat.

Doug Stanhope and I started in comedy at almost the exact same time, but Doug is a few years older than me, and by virtue of being better and crazier than me, he'd already gone fairly big-time nationally by the time I got to Los Angeles.* It put him in a position to take me under his wing a little bit during my last couple years in Houston; a position I appreciated very much. The one thing he said to me after he hooked me up with the place at 1440 North Gardner, where I ended up living for free for a year, was straightforward:

"You have to be in comedy clubs every night. When you first get to LA, you gotta go to every one of those fucking clubs every fucking night."

It was good advice, because my very first Saturday in town I met the Cuban comedy colossus Joey Diaz, who took me to the Comedy Store and introduced me to Mitzi Shore. Mitzi founded the Comedy Store in 1972 and has been the owner-operator ever since. Her roots go so deep into comedy that her name has become synonymous with stand-up comedy. She even married one of us—a stand-up named Sammy Shore, who she eventually divorced. By the time I met Mitzi, she'd been in the business for three decades. She was the be-all and end-all of stand-up comedy in Los Angeles—probably even the country. She knew what worked in her room, and if you were one of the people who worked, it meant you could work anywhere. In that sense she was the most powerful noncomedian force in stand-up comedy. Without her there'd be no Richard Pryor, no Robin Williams, no Jim Carrey, no Paul Rodriguez, no Louie Anderson. She saw their "it" before anybody else. Her direction and advice was so good that George Carlin would headline at the Comedy Store for three weeks before doing one of his specials just so he could have Mitzi help

---

* The guy won the legendary San Francisco Comedy Competition in 1995, for fuck's sake. Dane Cook finished second that year.

with jokes. In her prime, she had so much influence that if you showcased for her and she passed you or, even better, made you a paid regular, that pretty much meant you were on the fast track to *The Tonight Show*.* That's what happened to Roseanne Barr. Mitzi passed her into the Main Room and made her a paid regular. The next week she did *The Tonight Show* and had a deal with ABC to do *Roseanne* practically the next day. That's how quickly Mitzi made careers.

Joey Diaz introduced me to Mitzi on Saturday, and I told her my whole story. The next day, Sunday, I showcased for her. She passed me into the Main Room and made me a paid regular on the spot. I was the first person since Roseanne to get that from Mitzi, which is crazy to me because I've never felt like I was even close to Roseanne's level. We had a similar working-class vibe to our comedy, but that big bitch could burn the house down! I think one of the big reasons Mitzi passed me the way she did was because Andrew Dice Clay and Eddie Griffin were in the back laughing their asses off during my set. People talk a lot of shit about both of those guys now, but I'd never met them before, and they both stuck their necks out and vouched for me to Mitzi. Eddie, who went onstage right after me on that Sunday show, was the most vocal:

"That white boy from Houston is a bad motherfucker, y'all! Remember his name! Hey, Jeff [the piano player], what was that kid's name?"

What is it with these comics and remembering names? It's not like my name is Carlos Alazraqui or some crazy nonsense.

"Ralphie May?" Jeff said.

---

* Being "passed" is basically comedy-speak for being hired or approved to perform at a particular club.

"Remember the name Ralphie May!" Eddie repeated. Then he went on to destroy for the next thirty-five minutes.

Two days later, on Tuesday, I showcased at the Laugh Factory and the Improv. Jamie Masada, the owner of the Laugh Factory, passed me and gave me eight spots per week. The Improv passed me too. Within a week of getting to town I was officially plugged into the LA comedy-club circuit. I'd done, like, seventeen spots at the Comedy Store alone, I had another two dozen spots lined up at the other clubs, and thanks to guys like Joey Diaz, Joey Medina, Alex Reymundo, Jeff Garcia, and Rudy Moreno, I'd been introduced to all the good Latino rooms as well.

Sam Kinison was my first comedy mentor. Danny Martinez was like my comedy Aristotle, and the father I never had. Dougie Stanhope was my comedy brother from another mother. But these Latino guys were like my guardian angels when I got to LA. *Los true angeles de Los Angeles.* I've felt a special kinship with the Latin comics ever since. Their hospitality reminded me a lot of the Southern hospitality I grew up on. They would share opportunities with me. They would have me over to their *abuelita*'s house for tamales. Later they would have me on their TV shows. I also think we shared a similar uphill climb on the comedy terrain. As a fat guy, it always felt like I wasn't going to get my crack until the Hollywood system worked its way through all the "normal"-size guys. There was a glimmer of hope when CBS gave Louie Anderson his own show in 1996, but it got canceled after six shows, and that was that. Latino comics went through a similar situation in Hollywood in relation to opportunities for black comics. *Showtime at the Apollo* started in 1987, *Def Comedy Jam* in 1992. Thea Vidale, Steve Harvey, D. L. Hughley, Jamie Foxx, Sinbad, Martin Lawrence, and the Wayans brothers all got shows in the nineties before a guy like George Lopez even sniffed a series in 2002. I mean, Lord Jesus, the Latino comedian community had to start their own festival of laughs just to remind Hollywood that they were some funny motherfuckers who'd been there the whole time.

The extra spots I got in the Latino rooms in LA thanks to Joey and Rudy and those guys were a lifesaver for a long time. I wasn't getting rich off them by any means, but they helped with rent and kept me out of the poorhouse, which is half the battle when you come to Los Angeles to "make it"—whatever that means.

12.

HOUSTON, WE'RE GONNA HAVE A BIG FUCKING PROBLEM

One of the benefits of not having to pay rent for a while was that the money I saved allowed me to fly back to Houston fairly regularly to pick up some good-paying gigs. I know that sounds counterintuitive. Hollywood is where you're supposed to go to get rich and famous—emphasis on rich. How is it, then, that you make less money in Hollywood doing the exact same thing you were doing in Houston? The complicated explanation involves the economics of the market for comedy in each city. The simple explanation is that club owners are motherfuckers who are under less pressure to pay you what you're worth than you put on yourself to perform as often as you can in order to get the big break that brought you to LA in the first place. When other comics want it so bad that they'll work for free or even *pay you* to get up on your stage, frankly what incentive do you have to pay anyone?

My first time back to Houston after moving was late in the

summer of 1998 to headline some shows at the Laff Stop. That Monday, by force of habit as much as anything else, I did a set at the open-mic night too. The guy who followed me did an awful, unfunny, off-key parody of "Blue Moon," then dropped his pants at the end and had his ass painted blue. It was total garbage and painful to watch. I remember thinking, *Did I really come back here for this?*

Then I saw this pretty, dark-haired girl with big blue eyes come in and sign up to go on. In Houston, only a few female comics ever came out to the open mics—Caroline Picard, Shayla Rivera, Valerie Thompson, Jody Ferdig—so this girl's female energy was welcome. What was not so welcome was the big-ass guitar she hauled in with her spindly Kermit the Frog arms, so I walked up to her.

"Hi, I'm Ralphie."

"Lahna."

"Can you play that fucking thing?" I nodded to her guitar.

"Yes."

"Can you sing?"

"Yes."

"Are you at least fucking funny?"

"Yes."

Take notes, fellas. Charm school is in session. In my defense, I was unreasonably mad for having just wasted several minutes of my life watching that terrible musical open-mic-er hot carl my eardrums. And I already hated musical comedy to begin with. I've seen only a few guitar acts that I liked: Steve Caliph, JR Brow out of Austin, and Rodney Carrington. The rest thought they were so innovative, but they were just prop comics, leaning on their guitar as a crutch, as a cheat for being funny. I could tell from my questions and her tone that Lahna was a little scared.

"Is this your first time?" I asked.

"Yes."

"You're not doing fucking parody songs like that last asshole, are you?"

"No," Lahna said, almost offended, the first spark coming out of those blue eyes. I was relieved too, because being a guitar act without relying on parody songs meant she was legitimately creative. She might not be *amazing*, but she wasn't a hack. That's all you can ask for at an open mic.

I left her alone after that to get ready, but just before she took the stage, another comic saw her and announced, "This is going to suck!"—loud enough for everyone in the place to hear. Real funny, asshole. Already too few women were doing comedy; now you want to chase one of them off? Why? Because she might be funnier than you? News flash: she is. She hadn't even gone onstage yet and I knew that. This fucking guy would bomb so often and so completely, he would have been better off in the CIA drone program. Eventually he read the writing on the wall, and the silence in every room, and quit stand-up. Then had the unmitigated gall to go work at Comedy Central, which should tell you everything you need to know about stand-up comedy's relationship to television.

So many things about Lahna were exceptionally hilarious that night at the Laff Stop. I'd never seen a woman go onstage with a guitar in one of these clubs, so I thought it was funny just how out of place she was. She had balls too. She only had time for two songs, but she went up with both barrels cocked and murdered. Her first song was about her and a female friend carrying on a pseudoles-bian relationship that revolved around food. Her second song was a little ditty about incest called "Daddy's Hands." I mean, holy shit. It was fucking hilarious, and just so incongruous, to see this petite thing singing about incest.

Later, I approached her in the greenroom as she was putting her guitar away.

"That was really funny," I said.

"Thanks."

"And I don't joke about funny."

She was pretty dismissive, partially because I'd been a dick to her earlier, but mostly because she thought I was just being nice, like all stupid men are around a pretty girl.

"I don't just hand out compliments about comedy. I mean what I say." I couldn't have been more insecure if I was Hillary Clinton's personal email server. "You're really fucking funny. If you have any questions about comedy or if there's anything else I can help you with, just give me a call."

Easier said than done. While I was in Houston, I was staying at a place we called the Comedy Frat House behind Star Pizza off Shepherd Drive by the freeway, and I couldn't remember the phone number there. I couldn't give her my phone number in LA either, because I didn't have one yet. I was still getting settled. So I gave her the next best thing: my 1-800 pager number that I got from JJ, the King of Beepers.* Twentieth-century baller, baby!

She called me the next day. I didn't call her back. The day after, she got the phone number of the Frat House from someone at the Laff Stop and left a message:

"I don't know why you're doing this. You told me to call. I have legitimate questions I want to ask you. Don't give out your fucking number if you have no intention of talking to the person."

She had a point. I called her back immediately.

"Why didn't you call me back the first time?"

---

* J&J Beepers ran legendarily corny radio ads for years in Los Angeles. "JJ" turned out to be a guy named Jacob "Cookie" Orgad, who was an Israeli organized-crime figure with ties to Heidi Fleiss and the ecstasy trade. So basically, he was totally awesome.

"I had to make sure."

"Make sure? Of what?"

Basically, I was testing her. I wanted to make sure that if I spent time teaching her about comedy, my time wouldn't be wasted. I wanted to know that she was willing to go after it, to chase her dream, because that's what this business is all about. The test to see if she'd call back was a snapshot of the entire business she was trying to get into, and a measure of whether she had it in her to persist and persevere.

That's what I told myself after the fact. In reality, I was probably nervous or high, or nervous and high.

I went back to LA shortly after that, and we kept talking. We'd talk on the phone almost every night. Over the next year or so, I was back and forth between Los Angeles and Houston a lot, partly to work and partly to see Lahna. Even when I was in town, though, it was difficult to see each other in person. I worked normal comic's hours, and she worked crazy hours at Channel 13 News. Her shift started at 3:30 a.m., which was pretty much when I would be getting home, and she'd get off at about 11 a.m., which was right about when I'd wake up. We were on almost exactly opposite schedules. We could make it work when I was in Houston, but when I was back in Los Angeles, we had to develop a system. Every day I'd call Lahna around noon, right before she would take a nap, then at night she'd call me before I left to do spots at the clubs. We'd talk for hours when we could, cracking up laughing the whole time. That was our routine.

Never in a million years did I think I would date Lahna Turner. She was from a rich Jewish family in Memorial—a fancy Houston suburb—and I was a dirty-white-trash Methodist from Arkansas. I was fat, she was fit. I sold weed on the side, she was a good girl. She wasn't some dizzy broad either. She had a good head on her shoulders. She didn't drink, she didn't do drugs, she just wanted to do comedy. She obviously noticed how mismatched we were (it was hard not to), but we could both tell that this was more than just a friendship developing, that something special was here, because this was back in the day before cell phones and anytime rollover minutes. These were long-distance phone conversations we were having, and that shit was expensive.

I was back in Houston for the holidays later that year when Lahna invited me to dinner to meet her parents. It was at some fancy French restaurant way out in Memorial the weekend after Thanksgiving, so her sister and brother-in-law would be there too. We weren't even officially dating, so my plan was to be casual and polite and talk about Lahna from the perspective of a fellow comedian.

"Mr. and Mrs. Turner," I said as we all sat down to dinner, "it's a pleasure to make your acquaintance. Y'all should be so proud of your daughter. She is so funny and she has so much talent."

"Who are you to tell me about my daughter?" Lahna's mother shot back.

So it was going to be one of those nights, huh?

My apparently presumptuous comment had broken the seal, and Mrs. Turner just started laying into me. Dinner turned into a two-hour volley of accusations, explanations, rebuttals, and judgments. I felt like a hostile witness in a special episode of *Law & Order*. She grilled me on who I was, where I came from, how much money I had in the bank, what I was doing with my life.

"You mean you didn't go to *college*?" she spit at me like venom.

"No, ma'am, there isn't any college for what I love to do."

Lahna's sister and brother-in-law didn't say a word. Periodically I would try to catch their eyes, but they were heads down in their meals. This place must make some great fucking bisque, I thought, because these people were silent the entire dinner, even as Lahna's mother got more and more out of line. I couldn't believe Lahna's father didn't intervene to tell his wife to knock it off. Not out of any sense of decorum, Lord knows, but from a strategic perspective.

Assuming Lahna's father felt the same way as her mother, what could they possibly expect to gain by attacking my life choices when those were exactly the choices their daughter was trying to make? I stood up for myself at every turn, which meant I was standing up for Lahna by extension. Obviously they didn't like the idea of their beautiful daughter seeing some fat goyish dude, but still the whole thing was absolutely crazy to me, because we weren't even officially dating yet, and all they were doing was pushing Lahna closer to comedy and deeper into my arms.

In the aftermath of our disastrous family-dinner date, I invited Lahna out to LA to spend some time with me and then accompany me to the Palm Springs Film Festival, where a film I had a small part in, called *On the Turning Away*, was entered into competition. Mama Turner did not like this one bit. She liked it even less when Lahna said yes.

We spent three or four days in LA together before the film festival. We went all over together. We went to the beach, we went to Beverly Hills, I took her to the Comedy Store and the Laugh Factory—it was so great.

The day before we left for the film festival, we went for a walk down the Walk of Fame on Hollywood Boulevard and ran into a woman I'd dated briefly the spring before. But this wasn't just any woman. This was Tara Weissmuller, the granddaughter of the guy who played the original Tarzan, Johnny Weissmuller. She was doing a charcoal etching of her grandfather's star on the Walk of Fame when we bumped into her. Tara was a striking figure who had worked as a model. I think she even landed a *Vogue* cover. I introduced Lahna to Tara as my friend from Houston, and we all had a good laugh when Tara pointed out how interesting it was that *the* Lana Turner's star on the Walk of Fame was close by. Like any exchange with two women you have had, or want to have, sex with, it got uncomfortable quick. I told Tara we had to get moving, and she responded by giving me her new phone number and telling me to call her . . . right in front of Lahna. No chill on that one, I tell you.

I felt like I knew Lahna well by that point, so I wasn't too worried about what her response to that exchange was going to be once we got back to my place. And even if I was, I had bigger problems to deal with at the moment—I had to piss badly. We'd been walking forever, and all the Diet Coke I'd been drinking had filled my bladder to capacity like the ballast tank of a crab boat. My car was parked up by the start of the Walk of Fame on La Brea, but I wasn't going to make it. I gave Lahna the keys and told her to go on ahead, I'd catch up.

Hollywood Boulevard is both the worst and the best place to have to take a leak. The street is infested with homeless people, so shopkeepers don't let anyone off the street use their restrooms. But since the street is infested with homeless people, it's already a urinal. The only place in the immediate vicinity that felt safe to let it rip was next to an empty building with one of those street-level window wells that had wrought-iron fencing around it so people couldn't fall in. I was basically pissing into a window, which meant I would fit right in on Hollywood. I hadn't been going for more than ten or fifteen seconds when I saw a black-and-white Caprice come rolling around the corner in my peripheral vision.

Shit, LAPD. Lahna's mom already hated me. Imagine if she had to fly her daughter home because she'd emptied her checking account to bail her not-quite-boyfriend out of jail for public urination. I quickly stuffed the yogurt hose back into my pants, with the spigot still open, and whipped around to see if I had to make a run—or more likely a vigorous walk—for it.

On the list of Worst Types of People on Earth, my top three are child molesters, rapists, and terrorists. But number four, and they don't lag far behind, are assholes who buy cop cars at auction and don't repaint them. Do you have any idea how many accidents those motherfuckers have caused? And I mean real accidents, not the kind I just had in my pants.

When the adrenaline dump finally subsided, a wave of relief overtook me, but it couldn't change the damage that had been done. I'd peed my pants. What can you do in that situation? I got back to the car, climbed into the driver's seat, turned to Lahna, and blurted it out: *"I just pissed my pants!"*

When I told her what had happened, we laughed about it all the way back to my place, which, mercifully, was only eight blocks away. Pissing yourself is hilarious right up until the water part of the urine evaporates from the fabric and all you're left with is piss crystals. The last thing you want is to be stuck on the 101 in bumper-to-bumper traffic when that happens.

Once we made it back to my apartment, I started a load of laundry, took a shower, and we just hung out, talking. Lahna tried to be casual about it, but eventually she had to ask, "So, um, who was that girl?" She didn't ask in an angry, accusatory way; more like a "Wait, do I have competition here?" way. Having this gorgeous woman essentially pursue me in front of her sort of threw Lahna, I think. Then, combined with how I stood up for her to her mother barely a month earlier, it started to click for Lahna that maybe I was somebody she could date seriously. She has never admitted it, but I'm convinced that our little run-in on the street with Tarzan's grandbaby went a long way to getting us together.

The next morning I got up early to drop a deuce, burn some incense, and brush my teeth. I wanted to present myself in the most positive light instead of running the risk of coming off like a living, breathing, shitting stink machine. When I finished, I hopped back in bed and Lahna got up. She brushed her teeth, hopped back into bed with me, and we just started making out. It was amazing to have a beautiful young girl in my bed to make out with. But it was so fucking frustrating to have a beautiful young girl in my bed who *only wanted to make out*. My balls ached so bad, it felt like someone squeezing a beefsteak tomato right up to the point that it exploded in their hand. And not in the good way. When Lahna finally went to the bathroom to take a shower I furiously beat off twice—once for each ball—just to relieve the pain. Caged monkeys haven't cum that fast.

We drove out to Palm Springs for the film festival later that day. In keeping with the spirit of the low-budget indie film I was there to support, the producers put us up at a Super 8 Motel out in Indio, not even in Palm Springs proper. I wouldn't call it a shithole per se, since the desert out there is so dry that when you shit, it just turns to dust and disappears with the wind, but I wouldn't call it the Four Seasons either. Regardless, it was good enough for us to pick up right where we left off with the make-out session in LA and maybe take it to the next level. Foolishly, I thought that with our being at a fancy film festival, as an invited guest of actual Hollywood producers, this would be the night that she gave up that monkey, but she was resolute. All we did was make out . . . for her entire visit. At the time I was in equal parts agony and ecstasy, but now I kind of believe that if she had given it up on that trip, we would never have gotten together for real.

After the film festival we were both headed back to Texas by way of Lafayette, Louisiana, for a gig. Getting ready to leave, Lahna stopped in the doorway of my apartment at 1440 North Gardner. She was wearing overalls, and her long brown hair, wet from the shower, was soaking the overalls straps.

I'll never forget the look on her face. "What's going to happen when we get back to Houston?"

"Well, we can just pretend like none of this ever happened." I knew a bunch of assholes were waiting for us back there, who knew she was out here with me. I wanted to protect her, so I gave her that out.

"I don't want that." She thought it might even be that I was ashamed of her.

"Lahna, that could not be further from the truth, sweetheart."

"Okay." She sounded relieved.

We agreed to keep on seeing each other and kissed right there in the doorway, sealing the deal. We were officially dating. January 9, 1999.

The gig in Lafayette was a two-nighter—Friday and Saturday. I was headlining, my buddy John Westling was the feature, and Lahna was doing a guest set, which effectively made her the opener. It was the first time we worked together as a couple, which could have gone any number of ways. It could have been weird, it could have been a disaster, it could have been torture. It ended up going fine. The only part that was torture was that Lahna and I shared a room and again all we did was make out. I knew she wanted to take things slow, and I respected that, but even a sloth would have been, like, "Lord Jesus, won't you people just get to fuckin' already?!"

We came back to Houston from Lafayette on Sunday morning, and I drove Lahna to her parents' house, where she was living. I knew they were out of town that weekend, so a little part of me thought that this could be the day if I played my cards right.

I knew Lahna wanted to be sure, and she needed to feel totally safe and comfortable before we had sex for the first time, so I devised a plan to expedite that if she invited me in . . . which she did.

Lahna had a pet cat named Whiskers, who was important to her. She talked to me about the cat frequently. Once she even mentioned that the cat didn't like her last boyfriend and how that was a signal that maybe he wasn't "the one." I was going to make goddamn sure that Whiskers loved me like I was made out of catnip and toilet water. So at breakfast before we left Lafayette, I saved some of my bacon and put it in a little baggie that I stashed in my pocket. This being a Jewish household, I knew this fucking cat had never tasted anything resembling the magical deliciousness of bacon. My hope was that after his first bite, he wouldn't stop following me around and he'd jump on my lap and nuzzle me, showing Lahna unequivocally that I could be trusted.

It worked on both counts.

When Whiskers took down that piece of bacon, he looked at me like one of those deaf babies right after the doctors turn on their new cochlear implants for the first time: *What is this magical world am I just now discovering for the first time?!*

Lahna looked at Whiskers looking at me, then looked at me like Whiskers looked at bacon, and upstairs we went. We ended up making love for the first time that day, right there in her parents' house, which made it kind of weird, but also just so, so karmically sweet with her mother.

You mean you didn't go to college? No, ma'am, but I did just go to town.

The next day, Monday, Lahna and I planned to meet up at the Laff Stop for open-mic night. She was going to get there early to sign up, but I was going to be a little on the late side since I was scheduled to teach defensive driving at the Comedy Showcase from 6:00 to 9:00 p.m.

I pulled into the Laff Stop parking lot around 9:30 p.m., walkin' on sunshine, and there was Lahna outside, waiting for me.

"Ralphie, everybody is talking about how you and I are having sex. Why are you telling everyone that we were hooking up when we weren't?"

What the fuck? Lahna is a composed person, but she was visibly upset, which made me upset. I knew something like this might happen with these fucking assholes, but what I didn't understand was how they found out. It hadn't been twenty-four hours since we had sex for the first time—*I barely believed it still.*

"They're saying all sorts of awful things too, telling me you're a liar and a hack and a joke thief, and that I shouldn't be with you. How do they even know we're together, Ralphie?!"

I hadn't told anybody that we were having sex, or dating for that matter. Don't get me wrong, I wanted to tell the world from the minute we kissed in the doorway of 1440 North Gardner, but I had kept everything to myself.

I went completely insane with anger. I grabbed the bat from under the front seat of my 4Runner, went inside, and told ever mother-fucker in there that if they didn't shut their goddamn mouths, we were going to have a big fucking problem. And if you had a problem with me, come on and meet me outside. I was ready to literally kill anybody who crossed me or wanted to get smart with me that night. Nine people had to hold me back from going after every single guy in there who I knew had tried to fuck me or prank me or talk shit about me or run me out of comedy. I wanted Lahna to tell me which one of these malicious assholes was saying the things she told me out in the parking lot, but she wouldn't do it because she could see the murderous rampage that was about to snap off up in that bitch.

What was most frustrating of all about that night was that it didn't need to go down like that. A large chunk of what they were speculating about with Lahna and me was actually true, but their intent was to divide and cause harm. To her immense credit, later on Lahna calmly explained to people at the Laff Stop that we actually *had* slept together and we *were* dating, but that they all needed to stay out of our relationship and mind their own fucking business, because next time she wasn't going to stop me from using that aluminum bat upside their worthless skulls.*

Our relationship remained long-distance for nearly two more years. We saw each other maybe once every two weeks—either I'd come to Houston or she'd come to LA, or we'd work together on the road somewhere—but it was never for long stretches. You have to remember, Lahna was still just a young comic in Houston trying to make headway and make a name for herself, just like I did when I first arrived in Houston a decade earlier.

She was doing it too. Unfortunately, she had to do it against a headwind of hot air being blown by all those cancerous asshole comics who were constantly trying to get in her head and under my skin. They were intent on undermining our relationship, and they nearly succeeded. After the incident at the open-mic night, Lahna was more guarded and wary of me than she ever was before. For years, she never completely trusted me because she had no way to know for sure that I didn't tell anyone. The drama and jealousy of the local club comics—most of whom are now out of

---

* Okay, she didn't actually say that last part, but God bless America I wish she had, because it would have felt *so* good.

the game or right where I left them when I left Houston—nearly cost me a marriage and two beautiful children.

Eventually it got to the point where we either had to move in together or stop seeing each other. I just couldn't keep doing the long-distance thing like it was. It was distracting from both of our careers, and it was turning me into a bitter, angry person. Despite its being the nexus of all my misery, I even offered to move back to Houston because I didn't want to lose her. She said no way, that if I moved back, she'd leave me. She reminded me that my career was taking off in LA and that I couldn't give that up. She said that she would move out to LA instead.

What an amazing woman. I was in love. So was she. Her parents, not so much. Her dad would barely talk to me. When he did, we disagreed on everything. Her mom didn't bother to use words around me; she just let her visceral hatred do her talking.

Lahna arrived with all her stuff in January 2001. One of my first memories of us together in that shitty little apartment on North Gardner was watching George W. Bush being sworn into office as the forty-third president of the United States.

"My dad likes him," Lahna said as we cuddled on the bed watching the inaugural ceremonies.

"That guy stinks," I said partly out of reflex, but mostly from a place of complete justification. "How in the world could we elect a man who traded Sammy Sosa?"

13.
1440 NORTH GARDNER

One of the first things I learned after moving to Los Angeles is that there isn't one Los Angeles, there are seven or eight. Cities like New York and San Francisco and even Houston have distinct neighborhoods with their own vibes, but the cities are still self-contained and you can wrap your head around them. Los Angeles is so spread out and its boundaries bleed so confusingly into surrounding areas that you never know where LA starts or ends. Because of that, all these different areas in the LA basin have grown up to become their own places, sometimes literally becoming their own cities, such as Santa Monica or Culver City or Beverly Hills.

What that means, once you move here and try to get acclimated, is that you can't paint the whole place with a broad brush. You have to feel your way through things. That's hard to explain to out of towners, especially about Hollywood, where my apartment was on North Gardner Street. While most people know that

Hollywood Boulevard is a filthy bum toilet littered with tourists and crazies and fat guys peeing on buildings, they also think that since you work in Hollywood, and Hollywood is glamorous, you must actually *live* in the glamorous part of Hollywood too. They think you live inside the *Hotel California* album cover.

In reality, Hollywood lost its glamour a long time ago. The western section I lived in those first years was a roughly coffin-shaped area bounded by Fairfax Avenue on the west, Hollywood Boulevard on the north, Highland Avenue on the east, and Santa Monica Boulevard on the south. When you walked through the area at any time of the day, it felt you like you were in the middle of a cemetery for broken dreams. Run-down apartment buildings, dilapidated Craftsman homes surrounded by chain-link fences, and Spanish-style duplexes with iron bars on the windows dominated. People meandered in and out of them who looked like they'd come to LA in the sixties and seventies to make it, failed, never left, and this is where the city shoved them in tighter and tighter concentration, like the western half of Hollywood was the giant trash compactor on the Death Star in the first *Star Wars* (the *real* one).

Smack in the middle of the trash compactor is 1440 North Gardner. The entire block, on both sides of the street, is still shit-box apartment buildings with the exception of the fire station directly across the street. With the prostitutes and the crackhead trannies starting their nightly runs only a few blocks down on Sunset, and the homeless constantly passing out at bus stops and getting hit by cars barreling down La Brea during the day, Fire Station #41 was busy at all hours.

It was an interesting place to be in those years. It was always just a little different from any other place my comedian friends lived. Stuff happened there that didn't happen anywhere else. Like the time I got a knock on my door at four o'clock in the afternoon in the middle of the week. I figured it was one of my comedian neighbors coming over to buy or smoke some weed. Four p.m. was about when most of them got up, and the building was access controlled, so if it were a delivery guy or a solicitor, they would have had to be buzzed in from outside.

I opened the door, and standing in front of me was a nice-looking black dude and a pretty white chick in some clothes that didn't seem like they fit too well. The brother introduced himself as Alvin.

"Hey, big man, you want to party?" Alvin said.

"Huh?" I was so confused.

"Do you want to *party*?"

Somehow I was even more lost hearing the question a second time.

Alvin shook his head, looked up and down the hall both ways, and leaned in. "Aight, man, you want some pussy?"

I had two immediate thoughts: (1) I could not believe this was happening to a comedian of all people. A pimp and his hooker were cold-calling an entire apartment complex, going door-to-door selling pussy, and of all the gin joints in all the world, they stumbled into mine? The comedy gods were smiling on me. (2) These people were criminals. Her job was to trap your dick with her mouth or her pussy, like a Chinese finger cuff, until you paid. His job was to hold money, slap bitches, and cut people for nonpayment. Danger, Will Robinson! Danger! Danger!

It took me a couple beats to process what was happening. I'd taken a couple healthy bong rips of some bona fide indica a little earlier, so my brain was still floating a little bit. Alvin thought I was trying to stall him to drive a bargain, so he upped his salesman game.

"Aight, playa, normally a half-and-half is a hundred dollars, but

I see you being hesitant 'cause you don't want to spend all that. Aight, just for you, this week only, we runnin' a special—seventy dollars for a half-and-half. What do you say? Come on, half-and-half! Seventy dollas! *Got damn!*"

You wonder why black guys make such good preachers? Forty-five seconds with Alvin and I was ready to testify! Then I realized, wait, this has now become door-to-door *discount* pussy, like he was trying to off-load a bag of day-old bagels and maybe make a couple dollars in the bargain.

What Alvin couldn't see was Lahna sitting ten feet away behind the open door. Now, Lahna was a cool chick—we'd been successfully working through some of our lingering trust issues, and she'd brushed off the Tara Weissmuller run-in like a champ—but she wasn't *that* cool. Lahna's from the nice part of Houston, not the dirty part of *Penthouse Letters*. She was not so kosher with her man getting offered marked-down pussy at the front door. How many women would be, when you think about it?

So now I had danger all around me: a pimp in front of me and a girlfriend on my rear flank. One of them was almost certainly armed, and if I said the wrong thing and gave her enough time to go into the bedroom, the other would be armed too. Armies lose wars stuck in my position. I had to think quickly. I resorted to the one technique that had served me well my entire adult life: be stupid.

"Just a sec," I said to Alvin, turning to Lahna, who he still could not see. "Um, honey, do we need some pussy? It's on sale!"

Alvin got the picture. Lahna was finally as confused as I was when I first opened the door. And our boxer, Pimp, was pushing against my leg being superaggressive toward our guest, Alvin, the *actual* pimp. Lahna tried to get him under control while I talked to Alvin.

"Goddamnit, Pimp, get in here!" she shouted.

Alvin cocked his head and peered around the doorway, looking at Lahna with crazy eyes, like, *Who is this white woman telling me what to do?*

"Pimp, sit!" Lahna commanded.

Both pimps obeyed. The dog came to heel and Alvin stepped inside while his bottom bitch stood out in the hallway. I told Alvin I wasn't interested, obviously, but I offered to sell him some weed for cheap, hoping to smooth his exit. He was interested, but he was low on cash (hence the door-to-door routine), so he tried to barter. Lahna put the kibosh on that one, and Alvin left without incident to try his hustle on all my neighbors.

By the time Lahna moved into 1440 with me at the beginning of 2001, I was slinging a ton of weed to pay the rent and make ends meet. The Comedy Store and the Laugh Factory spots were great, but they weren't cutting it. The Latino rooms and the black rooms I was playing kept my head above water, but that was about it, and you can't *live* in LA treading water like that for too long. Plus it's not fun.

Selling weed solved that dilemma for me. Besides being tax-free, it had the added benefit of bringing a social scene with it. Nearly every comic I knew dabbled in the cannabical arts. Over time, my spot became the place to come and smoke, party, and flop for a couple weeks if you'd been evicted or you were coming in from out of town for pilot season.* Comics were coming in and out of 1440 all the time.

---

* Traditionally, pilot season is the first three or four months of the year, when networks start taking pitches for new shows and pilot episodes start getting cast. Most comics, no matter where they're from, eventually come out to LA for at least one pilot season.

Then September rolled around. I had just done a weekend of huge shows in Phoenix that paid me $3,000, which was the most anyone had paid me since I did a pilot earlier that summer for USA Network called *Black Sheep*. In this reality show two comedians live with a family and try to torture them like only comedians can, but if the family can endure it while abiding by a particular set of rules, they get their mortgage paid for a year. It was a fun concept. The network was offering $12,000 per episode with a six-episode commitment, but Jamie Masada, who was my manager at the time, was holding out for more money. I was so mad—that was more money than I'd ever seen as a working comedian. I desperately wanted to take it. Jamie was right, though. The show never went anywhere. I don't even think they filmed more than the test pilot. That's why Jamie is Jamie, I guess. He knew what he was doing.

I got back from Phoenix on Monday. The next morning I got woken up by the phone ringing. I looked at the alarm clock, it wasn't even six fifteen in the morning. It was my mom.

"They're attacking us!" she screamed.

"Mom, what are you talking about?"

"They're attacking us! Aren't you watching?!?"

I'd *gone to bed* after 6:15 a.m. more times than I can count since the last time *I got up* that early. I turned on the TV and flipped to CNN and just watched as they replayed over and over and over the footage of two planes crashing into the World Trade Center towers.

"Holy fuck!"

"They're attacking us, Ralphie! They're attacking us!"

"Let me call you back, Mom."

I hung up and tried to collect my thoughts. Lahna was temping as an executive assistant at Sabon—a huge Israeli bath-and-body-products company—in a skyscraper over in West Los Angeles. There was no fucking way she was going to work that day. We didn't know what was happening or how many more attacks there were going to be that day. We just sat there watching as the sun rose and more people on the West Coast started waking up.

When the banks opened, I went and cashed my $3,000 check from the Phoenix gigs. I bought groceries, filled up my gas tank plus two gas cans, got some shells for my shotgun at a sporting-goods store. I stocked up the car with water and canned food. Then, because I just didn't know what else to do and because I'm Southern, I came home and started cooking. All these comedians started showing up. Thirty comics must have gathered at my tiny apartment over that day. I cooked all day, and Lahna fed everyone. It was the only thing that kept me from panicking and going crazy—not wanting to fuck up the food.

I don't know why, maybe because our building was so close to an essential service like the fire station, but our landline phone never cut out or overloaded. We could call people all day; we even got through to New York City on a few occasions. My first call was to Jeff Ross, aka the Roastmaster General. Back then he was just hilarious Jeffrey Ross from New Jersey to me, a frizzy-haired comedian I'd met a few times when he came through the Houston clubs and who I'd been reintroduced to more formally in LA by my buddy, and fellow New Jerseyan, Jay Mohr. Jeffrey and I were fast friends, and he was always good to me. When I hit rough stretches and needed some extra money, he'd pay me $80 per week to clean his apartment in LA. He was kind of a mess and he needed it clean for chicks, so it was more than worth it to him. I would do it all—wash and fold the laundry, change the sheets. I was like Alice from *The Brady Bunch*, except with bigger titties.

I knew Jeffrey was staying at his place in New York City that week, and having stayed there a couple times when I was working, I knew how close it was to the Towers. I called his house phone to see if he was there. Thankfully I got through.

"Man, get the fuck out of New York immediately." I didn't even say hello.

From the way he answered the phone I knew I'd woken him up, which meant he hadn't turned on the TV yet and had no idea what was going on. When he did, his reaction was a lot like mine. We hung up right away so he could make some calls to people he knew who were in New York. Jeffrey was a native, so he knew a lot of people.

I called him back a half hour later, and comics who couldn't get out had started gathering at his place. Being a good Jewish boy from New Jersey, I'm sure he did for them what I was trying to do for the people at my place. Before we hung up again, Jeffrey asked me to get ahold of the people at the Brea Improv down in Orange County. He was scheduled to do a run of shows that weekend, and he wanted to let them know he wasn't going to make it. Then he asked me to cover the gigs for him. Of course, anything I could do.

His first Brea show was Thursday, September 13. Probably one hundred people were in the audience. I have not experienced a weirder sensation in my career than going up on that stage for the first time after 9/11 and looking out at all those people. Did they already have tickets before the Towers came down and were just going about their lives? Did they buy tickets that day? Was there anyone there on a first date? Did any of that matter? It became clear pretty quickly that everybody was just stunned and numb and looking for laughter anywhere they could find it. That was a tall order, and it made me start asking questions of myself. How was I going to be able to pull off this show? How was I going to be able to keep it together? What was I going to say? I knew one thing for sure: no airplane jokes. I remember telling them the story of Alvin the Door-to-Door Pussy Salesman. I wanted to talk about what was going to happen now and how I was worried because the guy who traded Sammy Sosa was the guy with his finger on the button, but even I knew this wasn't much of a baseball audience.

After the show a woman came up to me crying and explained that her brother worked on the eighty-fourth floor of one of the Towers and she hadn't been able to reach him for two days. She still didn't know if he was alive, but she wanted to let me know that I was able to make her laugh and forget all that, even if only for a few minutes, and that she was thankful.

That's what comedy is about, I realized. Not all that other petty drama and egotistical bullshit, but people coming together to share a moment, to share laughter, to escape real-life bullshit. As a stand-up comedian, you are the one who gets to deliver it.

After a couple months, things returned to normal around 1440 North Gardner. The hookers got back to hooking, the comedians got back to doing spots and smoking all my weed, and the streets around the apartment building—of which I had a bird's-eye view from my windows—got back to looking more and more like the contents of the Death Star trash compactor.

One afternoon I got a call from my neighbor down the hall telling me to look out my bedroom window, which overlooked the parking lot for a famous Mexican restaurant on Sunset Boulevard called El Compadre.* To look at El Compadre from the front, you wouldn't know it to be particularly good or noteworthy. It doesn't have any windows, it seems more like a seedy dive bar at first

---

* LA has three El Compadres now, but until 2004 the one on Sunset Boulevard was the only one.

than a restaurant, and it's painted this mustardy-yellow color like a washing machine from 1975 that has been left out in the sun to fade for the last twenty-five years. Still, because of its parking lot hidden from the street and its discreet back entrance, a lot of celebrities will stop in to eat there.

This afternoon the acclaimed movie star and fellow Texan Matthew McConaughey was getting something out of his Porsche. I'd met him years before in Austin when he was a total unknown filming *Dazed and Confused,* but now, in the parking lot behind El Compadre, he was a huge movie star who had a couple years earlier been arrested for getting high and playing bongo drums naked and had now just begun a string of starring roles in romantic comedies to rehabilitate his reputation. I didn't know that at the time, and I bet he didn't either, but I figured it was probably a safe bet that he still liked to party. I thought to myself, *You have weed. Matt likes weed. You have Cheerios. Fuck it, I bet Matt likes Cheerios. Maybe he'll want to party with you.*

I started screaming his name: "Matt! *Maatttt! Matthew!*"

"What?!" he screamed back, looking up toward the 1440 building.

"All right, all right, all right!" I shouted, which pissed him off I think. He'd finally gotten fed up enough from my shouting to acknowledge me, and this is what he gets in return? In my defense, he said "What?" in a really dickish way. I was going to invite him in for weed and Cheerios, the real Cheerios too, not the off-brand Costco kind. The least he could have done was be appreciative.

"Hey, I just saw your movie *The Wedding Planner*!" I yelled, trying to reel him back in.

He kind of perked up at the mention of his movie, which had come out right around the time Lahna moved to LA in January. He gave me the head tilt and the little wave, like he was assuming I was complimenting him.

"It's the 9/11 of romantic comedies!"

I hadn't realized that all of these other comedians who were living in the building were silently watching out their windows, but I figured it out when, in unison, the entire side of the apartment building that faced the parking lot burst into peals of laughter.

"Fuck you!" he shouted. "How many movies have *you* made?"

"I made a porno with your mama!"

The apartment building exploded with laughter, forcing McConaughey to get in his Porsche and drive away.

I almost felt bad for McConaughey. He went with the "I know you are but what am I?" of heckling responses, and I came over the top on him with such a cheap, easy joke that, when it gets the laugh, is impossible to come back from. That's what so great about comedy: for as much time as comedians spend crafting jokes and perfecting our timing and word choice, sometimes a well-placed "your mama" joke can tear the house down.

As the sense of post-9/11 togetherness began to wear off in early 2002, so too did the camaraderie of the comedians at 1440 North Gardner. As nasty partisan divisions that had first boiled up in the wake of the 2000 presidential election returned to politics, so too did bullshit comedian drama. It was nothing near the scope of what Lahna and I faced back in Houston, but it was enough to give us that final push we needed to get out of our tiny shoebox of an apartment and find a bigger place together, somewhere not inside the trash compactor of Hollywood.

We found a great place for $1,200 per month in a fourplex on Fifth Avenue just east of Crenshaw Boulevard in a neighborhood called Park Mesa Heights, which sounds way better than "da hood" when you're telling your parents about it. We ended up staying there only for a year. I loved the people in the neighborhood, which was superdiverse, but our days there were numbered when, on our

very first night sleeping in the apartment, Lahna and I were woken up by gunshots. *A lot of gunshots.* Like thirty. It was definitely
scary, but I took some solace in that, unlike in other places, if I
was gonna get shot, it probably wasn't going to be in the back, and
it definitely wasn't going to be on purpose.

14.
BOB SUGAR CHANGED MY LIFE

A lot of your success in a new city, whether it's personal, professional, social, or economic, depends on who you fall in with during those early days. If you don't find someone or some group, the biggest city can become the loneliest place.

In Houston, I had my sister and her husband as a natural support system, I had the confidence of guys like Stevens and Pruett, and I had the guidance of my mentor Danny Martinez.

In Los Angeles, Dougie Stanhope set me up and the Latin guys had my back, but it wasn't until I met Jay Mohr in the summer of 1999 that things clicked for me. Jay wasn't a comedic idol of mine, like Sam. And he wasn't a mentor, like Danny. He was different from that. He was more than that, actually. He was a savior, a *fucking saint.*

Jay and I met after a Friday show at the Laugh Factory, where we were both performing. Jay was a longtime regular, and I had picked up a spot as still a relatively new guy. Jay was up after me, and I was following this talented young guy Dane Cook, who had crushed it on *Premium Blend* the year before.* It was almost exactly a week after John F. Kennedy Jr. crashed his plane off the coast of Martha's Vineyard, killing himself, his wife, and her sister, and they'd just discovered the fuselage on the ocean floor with all three of them still strapped in the day before. I watched every second of the search on TV riveted, because this was the same way my uncle Tommy died—being a fucking dumb-ass with a plane. It doesn't take a brain surgeon to realize that overconfidence behind the stick of an airplane gets you and other people killed; my uncle and John John were not-living proof. So I wrote a whole bit about it and performed it that night.

The entire premise of the bit was that Kennedy DNA was weak and produced the dumbest people in the history of America. I went through each and every famous Kennedy:

JFK: "Fuck a hardtop, let's take the convertible. It's a sunny day!" *Boom!* Back and to the left.

Robert Kennedy: "Come on, guys, I know a shortcut through the kitchen." *Pow pow pow!*

Teddy Kennedy: "It's okay, baby, I'm a phenomenal drunk driver!" *Blub, blub, blub, blub.*

Michael Kennedy: "It's called ski football! No, it's totally safe, throw me the ball!" *Boom!* Then I smacked my head with the microphone like I was skiing into a tree like a fucking idiot.

JFK Jr.: "Eh, fuck the second day of flight school. I'm a Kennedy!" Then I'd making a whistling sound like an incoming missile that ended with a giant splash.

The rant caught a lot of people in the crowd by surprise, but the

---

* Young guy? Dane and I are almost the exact same age. He's a month younger than me.

whole show that night was seriously fucking hot, so it managed to land. By the time the show finished, all three of us on the bill had pulled standing ovations.

Afterward we were hanging out upstairs, and Jay pulled me aside to tell me how impressed he was that I was able to turn him on the Kennedy bit. Turn him? I knew Jay as Bob Sugar from *Jerry Maguire*, but I didn't know him personally yet, so I had no idea that he was a pro-Kennedy guy, or that he even cared about the Kennedys. He said he hated all that instant Kennedy-bashing and admitted that he hated me too at first, but I carried on with the bit for a good ten to twelve minutes, and by minute eight I had him laughing a little. I think what turned him was when I said that for a country full of fat people, I couldn't understand why we didn't have a holiday for JFK's assassination. If there's one way a fat man wants to honor a fallen president, it's by grilling some baby back ribs on his day off.

The next afternoon, I saw Jay again. I was walking up Sunset Boulevard from my place to the Laugh Factory, looking to pick up a couple spots that night and maybe sell a little weed to make ends meet. I know what you're thinking: *Walking in Los Angeles? In the middle of summer? Who hurt you?* Believe me, normally I'd drive to the club and take my chances parking in the lot behind the building, where we weren't supposed to park because it's for customers of Greenblatt's, the Jewish deli next door, but I'd gotten a bunch of tickets there that I had to pay off, and its being a few days from the end of the month with rent due, things were tight. I couldn't afford to put gas in the car, and I definitely couldn't afford the $20 for valet and tip I'd need if I wanted to drive my car and not get it towed.

Technically, the walk from 1440 North Gardner to the Laugh Factory on Sunset and Laurel is a cinch. It's a left turn onto Sunset and a straight shot west for just under three-quarters of a mile. What they don't tell you when you move into the middle of the Death Star trash compactor is that this stretch of Sunset Boulevard, from about La Brea to the gateway of West Hollywood at Fairfax, has a noticeable uphill grade and is completely exposed to the sun at all times. No tall buildings cast a shadow, and the palm trees don't do shit for shade. That means in the middle of the summer, in the middle of the afternoon, right where I was on Sunset, the temperature regularly fluctuates somewhere between hot as balls and hot as fuck.

I made it to Coach & Horses, three blocks from my place, before I was sweating like a big dog.* I was waiting for the light to change when an SUV pulled up to the curb next to me and the window rolled down. It was Jay Mohr.

"Hey, Ralphie, right? What are you doing walking?" Jay did the whole New Jersey "get in the fucking car" gesture.

I climbed in, sweet merciful Jesus, where the air-conditioning was cranked. "I can't afford gas right now. I'm kind of broke."

"Why can't you afford it? You're hilarious! How are you broke? You spending all your money on food?!"

"No, I don't hardly have anything in my refrigerator. Bills are coming up and I have about nineteen dollars to play with for the next three days. I can't afford it because I can't get any work in this fucking town except for spots at the clubs, and you know how little they pay."†

"Why aren't you working any of the other rooms that pay more?"

"They tell me that none of the headliners want to work with me

---

* Coach & Horses was a popular bar that stand-ups used to go to after gigs. It's now called the Pikey.
† Spots at the clubs were only $15 or $20 apiece back then. They're not much better today.

because I get too many standing ovations, like the one last night. You saw it. So I can't open or feature for anyone, but I also can't headline myself because I don't have the TV credits. These celebrity comics are all pussies, no offense."

"Fuck that. I'm not a pussy. You won't blow me off the stage. I'm going to solve this problem right now." Jay pulled out his cell phone and dialed his manager, Matt Frost. Jay had one of those little rectangular Nokia jobs that dominated the market when cell phones first became popular. It put my J&J beeper to shame. "Hey, Frosty, the opener that I'm going to take with me on the road is a kid named Ralphie May. Ralphie, how do you spell your last name? *M-A-Y?* . . . Frosty, *M-A-Y.* We're getting his airfare, put him in my hotel, let's make sure we take care of him [click]. All right, Ralphie, now you have work. If I ever see you walking on Sunset again, it better be because you're drunk or you're doing cardio or you're turning tricks."

From the time Jay picked me up in his SUV in front of Coach & Horses to the time we got to the Laugh Factory—maybe twelve blocks—Jay had gotten me sixteen weeks of work at $1,000 per week plus travel expenses. He did it right there on the spot. It changed my fucking life.

That night before our sets at the Laugh Factory, he started needling me about material. He'd gone out on a limb for me on a whim, and I think he was a little worried that I might not be able to deliver.

"So, can you do anything besides shit all over American royalty? You got any other material?"

That was a fastball right down the middle. Fuck yes! All I got is jokes. I did a completely different twenty minutes from the night before with equal success. After our sets we were talking in the lobby of the Laugh Factory about Scrabble.

"You play?" he asked, all cocky.

"Hell yes, I play Scrabble, Jay Mohr, I'll whip your ass."

"What's your average?"

"'Bout 330."

"Fuck you, that's bullshit." Jay's high score was only like 280. What he didn't know about me yet was that I still had three-quarters of the *Encyclopaedia Britannica* shoved in my brain from childhood.

"Come by anytime you want if you ever want to play on my *dee-luxe* board and have your ass handed to you, jack."

Jay showed up the next day at my place with a bag full of CDs from Tower Records. At least eighty different albums were in that big yellow bag. That was like $1,000 worth of music back then. I didn't have a thousand dollars' worth of *anything*. We started listening to these CDs full of great hip-hop and smoking my weed, talking about jokes and playing Scrabble. It was maybe the most fun nonsexual time I had in that apartment in all the years I lived there.

Jay quickly became a great friend, but he was also my benefactor. Not so much financially, but more with respect to relationships, experience, and opportunities. He'd take me around, show me things, and introduce me to people. One time he brought Kevin Spacey to the Laugh Factory, and we were all just sitting around, hanging out, while Kevin and Jay went back and forth doing impressions. They are, to this day, two of the best impressionists I've ever seen. I mean, Jay's Christopher Walken impression is so good that most people who try to do Walken just end up doing their impression of Jay's impression. Both Jay and Kevin are true geniuses. I was just happy to be there and amazed to be around that much talent.

Another time, Jay and Jeffrey Ross took me to meet Buddy

Hackett at his house in Beverly Hills. Buddy Hackett? Are you serious right now? I don't know what it is about these Jersey comics—Jay, Jeffrey, Joey Diaz, Jim Norton, Artie Lange—but they have the weirdest, most amazing relationships of anyone in entertainment. Every time you turned around and bumped into one of them, they were doing something that felt like it was out of a Scorsese film. Maybe that's why I have gravitated to so many of them over the years: Who wouldn't want to be around that kind of energy?

When we got to Buddy's house, he answered the door wearing a Father Time nightgown-robe thing, and instead of carrying a candle to light his way, he carried a pistol in case he needed to light you up. Next thing I knew we were all drinking straight tequila, and Buddy was telling stories about *The Tonight Show* and Johnny Carson and the Rat Pack. It was the most surreal shit I'd ever been a part of. I mean, Buddy was my granny's age. *They were peers.* He was in *The Music Man* with Robert Preston! As a boy, I remember loving him in *The Love Bug* and *It's a Mad Mad Mad Mad World* and, when Granny would allow it, on Johnny Carson. Now I was standing in his house drinking tequila with him, and he's holding a pistol and not wearing any underwear!

At one point he actually talked directly to me: "You got a girl-friend?"

"Yep, her name's Lahna Turner."

"Ain't that something. I knew the real Lana Turner. Yeah, it was so crazy because you'd look up under her dress and her pussy would take a bow! She was a showwoman."

Buddy passed away a couple years later. I still have a couple ties that he gave me. I have one specifically he told me to wear when I did TV because he had worn it on *The Tonight Show* and killed with it, so it was good luck. If I ever have to do stand-up wearing a tie, which I haven't to this point, I am going to wear Buddy Hackett's green paisley tie.

Jay Mohr went from benefactor to partner in crime, or maybe a better phrase is *protector of the realm*. One night we were sitting at the tiny table in the lobby of the Laugh Factory with his beautiful rottweiler, Shirley, who was sitting on the floor under the table. Jay took that dog everywhere, and she was such a good girl that he never leashed her. I don't think he owned a leash. People were starting to file in for the show as we were sitting there, and this big Mexican guy passed the table and kicked Shirley right in the face.

The Laugh Factory is an oddly shaped place. As a customer, when you come in, you pass the doorman, who checks your ticket, and you enter this small, narrow lobby that probably fits fifteen people at one time and barely has room for the table Jay and I were sitting at. The space is about twenty feet long and twelve feet across with a ticket booth in the corner. At the other end of it you're greeted by a hostess, who takes you through the doors into the room and seats you by party at a table. Effectively the lobby isn't a gathering place; it's a narrow choke point between the street and the main room that restricts and funnels access to the club off the street. If the doorman blocked the exit and the hostesses closed off the entrance, you could easily get fucked-up far disproportionate to your size and numerical advantage.

It was basically the gates of Thermopylae, and Jay was about to go full Sparta on this Mexican dude and his friends. Jay was probably 175 pounds soaking wet back then, and this Mexican fella was yolked, but size doesn't matter when someone kicks your dog in the face. Jay went crazy. He got right up in the guy's face. It could have gotten bad right there, but the guy's friends got in between and profusely apologized, trying to defuse the situation and get their whole group to leave.

They're nearly all the way onto the sidewalk right out on Sunset when Jay sees a gang tattoo on the neck of one of the guys and goes in on him.

"Fuck you, and *fuck your set*!"

They did not like that one bit. You do not talk about a man's set like that. These dudes spun on their heels and bowed up. It was the Harbor Heights Mexican Mafia (as we found out later) versus Jay, me, and poor little Jamie Masada. Now we're fully out on the street, and the bangers are talking all sorts of threatening shit while at the same time still trying to apologize for their *vato loco*, but then he just starts straight swinging. So we start swinging. Even Jamie was throwing bombs, until he connected with his wrist bent and broke it. The Harbor Heights guys finally restrain their friend and push him back to the front door of Greenblatt's Deli fifty feet away.

I don't know what set him off exactly, but Lee, the Laugh Factory doorman, had finally seen enough. Lee is a mountainous black man. He looks like Michael Clarke Duncan's stand-in from *The Green Mile,* except he dresses like a black dandy on his way to church. His suits were razor sharp. He steps out into the middle of the sidewalk and says, "Let that motherfucker go."

And they do. He comes at Lee in a dead sprint, screaming, *"You fucking nigger!,"* over and over, and, as Jay likes to say when he tells this story, Lee hit him cartoonishly hard; so hard that the Mexican should have broken into a million pieces. Instead, it was like the scene in the hallway behind the arcade in *Terminator 2* when the original Terminator first clips the liquid Terminator with a twelve-gauge shotgun blast and he barely flinches as the hole in his chest quickly reforms. The Mexican guy took the hit, dropped down to one knee, got back up, and said, "You fucking nigger!," almost like he didn't even feel it.

That's when we realized that he was on PCP, and our little scuffle turned from "Hey, It's Like I'm Sixteen and Tough Again!" to "Holy Shit, I'm Gonna Be Six Feet Under Unless We Kill This Guy!" His buddies had enough at that point and bolted. They were, like, *Hey, it's been a good run*. That should have been our sign that this wasn't going to be simple, but Jay and I chose to ignore that and start beating the shit out of this guy. Whenever he hit the deck, I kicked him in the head so hard that my foot hurt for days afterward. It was like kicking a soccer ball filled with cement. Jay and Lee especially hit this asshole in the face for what was likely a minute but felt like thirty and didn't miss. Our hands and feet were all covered in his face blood, and still he kept coming.

We started to wonder where the hell the cops were at this point, but when we finally looked up and scanned the area, we realized that Sunset had turned into a parking lot. The Laugh Factory is right at the start of the stretch of Sunset Boulevard that most people think of when they think of Hollywood—the Chateau Marmont, Carney's hot dogs, the House of Blues, the Standard hotel, Sunset Tower, the Comedy Store, then Sunset Plaza and all the music clubs—so at night, the street is typically jammed with cars. Now on top of it, they had an awesome fight to watch. People were rolling down their windows and egging it on. When the Mexican guy heard something come from the street, he'd walk over and punch in their back window with his bare fists before turning back on us.

Lee finally got a lick in that put the banger flat on his ass, and

Lee wanted to end it for good. Lee did not suffer triflin' mother-fuckers, plus he was on the clock. He had a job to get back to. So he went over to the valet stand, grabbed one of the stanchions, and raised it up over his head like he was going to bash the guy's head in.

Jay ran over and got in between Lee and the banger: "No, no, no! Lee, no! That's five years, man, that's five years!" Jay wishes. If Lee had put the corner of that stanchion through this dude's eye socket and brained him, we'd be putting a 1 or a 2 in front of that 5. Fortunately, Lee is a reasonable man who can quickly gather his composure. So he set the stanchion back down in its place at the valet stand and kicked the banger in the face again instead.

That's when Mitch Mullany pulled up in his '62 Chevy Impala and saw what was going on. Mitch was a good comic. Mitch was also very white. On the *Wayans Bros.* show on the WB network, he played a character named White Mike, for fuck's sake. What we didn't know about very white Mitch was that he was raised in very black Oakland. You don't get out of there in one piece with-out learning how to handle yourself. He jumped out of that car, rolling up his sleeves with a look of pure joy plastered across his face. See, Mitch was a legitimate actor by then. He'd done the *Wayans Bros.* thing and he'd even had his own show on the WB for a couple of seasons called *Nick Freno: Licensed Teacher.* He was a grown-up, a professional; it had been a long time since he'd got-ten to whip somebody's ass.

When he squared up on the bloody tweaking banger, Jay and I were like Iceman and Slider at the end of *Top Gun* when Maverick reengages with the Russian MiG they couldn't shake. We could not fuck this guy up no matter what we did, and now we were exhausted. (I was winded the *next day*.) Mitch hit this guy with combos like he was Roy Jones Jr. He'd go to the body, then feint, and come over with a cross right on the button that sent spit and blood flying from the guy's mouth. It was like ballet. If I wasn't so tired, I would have been aroused.*

Finally the cops showed up and took over attempting to "subdue" the "perpetrator," except they got to use fun toys like a Taser and a couple of those telescoping batons. They beat the fuck out of him. With all the paperwork those cops were going to have to do, I would have beat his ass too even if he'd done nothing to me. Meanwhile, Shirley, the true victim of this altercation, was back inside the club, no worse for wear, getting pampered by the waitresses and watching the show.

Eventually the cops got the guy under control and took him around the corner on Laurel Avenue so they could get his statement away from us and get him treated by the EMTs, who had just arrived.

After a few minutes the arresting officer came back around the corner onto Sunset and approached us. "We need you to come identify the guy who attacked you." He motioned for us to follow him up the street. We looked at him like he was crazy. "For our report, we just need you to say 'That's him' basically."

"Yeah, is he a bloody Mexican? That's him," I said. What the officer didn't realize was that the adrenaline from the fight had almost completely worn off, and what was left in its place was sheer terror. We were so afraid of the guy now that we didn't want to go near him, even though he was handcuffed in the back of a police cruiser. With what we had seen, he could come flying through the windshield at us for more.

"Take our word for it," Jay said, "that's him."

---

* Mitch died from a stroke in 2008.

The greatest thing that Jay Mohr ever did for me was something I didn't want to do: audition for the first season of *Last Comic Standing* on NBC in 2003. Jay had been working on this show idea for at least a couple years. Originally it was called *Comic House* and Doug Stanhope was going to do it, then it became something else, then NBC got involved because CBS and Fox were eating its lunch with competition shows like *Survivor, The Amazing Race, Big Brother,* and *American Idol.* Jay worked with them to refine the idea and it became *Last Comic Standing.*

It was February of 2003 and I was doing a week of shows at the Laugh Factory in Hawaii when I got a call from Jay. It was Thursday morning.

"Remember that pilot I told you about? It's now called *Last Comic Standing* and you have to audition for it on Saturday."

"Jesus, Jay, that's not exactly down the road, bro. Can you just put me on it?" I figured since Jay created it and was going to be the executive producer, he could give me a first-round bye, so to speak.

"Technically it's a game show now, so there are rules."

"Fuck, who would I be auditioning for?"

"Bob and Ross from *The Tonight Show.*"

Now I was pissed. Bob Read and Ross Mark were the talent coordinators for *The Tonight Show.* From about 2001 until Jay Leno left in 2014, if you were a young or unknown stand-up comedian who wanted to get on *The Tonight Show,* you inevitably had to get through them first. I'd already showcased for Bob and Ross and they loved me. They knew I was funny.

"You're not auditioning for that show, you're auditioning for this show," Jay said, just like a fucking producer. There was no way around it: if I wanted to be on this show, I had to audition and it had to be that Saturday.

Lahna was in Hawaii with me as my opener. We were making it a minivacation. When I got off the phone with Jay, we looked up the airfare for a Friday red-eye to LA and a Saturday-afternoon return to Honolulu so I wouldn't have to miss any shows. First we had to see if one of those tickets even existed (which it did), then we had to find out how much it cost: $850. I was only making $1,200 for the week. This was going to be a huge bite out of my ass for what amounted to a gamble.

I wasn't sure what to do, but Lahna said not to worry. She told me she believed in me and put the ticket on her credit card. Having parents who hate you was a big downside to dating a rich suburban Jewish girl, but there *was* an upside: good credit. And thank Yahweh for that!

I landed on Saturday morning, went from the airport to my apartment to shower off the smell of poi and chocolate-covered macadamia nuts from the Honolulu airport gift shop, then went straight over the hill to NBC in Studio City. The auditions were being held on Johnny Carson's old stage, which is this gargantuan room, basically like an old hangar, where they'd set up a temporary stage. The Johnny Carson aspect of the audition was cool. What was not cool was the goddamn Walk of Methuselah you had to make from the parking lot to get there. I was already pissed off and irritable from the flight and the walk, and the twelve stairs I had to climb at the end to get in the building just put me over the top.

Still, I choked down my Southern-fried fury, summoned up some positive energy, and started in on my three minutes. It felt pretty good, but ninety seconds in, they stopped me.

I was so fucking mad. "Do you have any fucking idea what I had to do to get here today? On a Saturday! I might miss my spots because of this, Jamie's gonna have my ass, I might not be able to pay my rent!" I was just unleashing.

Bob and Ross tried to slow me down, they tried to interject, but I was inconsolable.

"Ralphie!" one of them shouted finally. "Chill out, you're in."

"Just like that?"

"Uh-huh."

Sometimes I should think before I start biting people's heads off. I was still annoyed. I had to fly all the way across the Pacific Ocean on my girlfriend's dime to spend ninety seconds confirming what I'd already told Jay. Then I had to get right back on a plane and fly all the way back.

I couldn't complain. Not because I should have been grateful that I passed the audition (which I was). I *literally* couldn't complain. Jay wasn't even there. He'd slept in.

15.
SECOND-TO-LAST COMIC STANDING

The performance part of auditioning for Last Comic Standing was fairly straightforward. You did three minutes in the first round on the Johnny Carson stage. If you made it through, the second round was at the Laugh Factory the following Tuesday. If you made it through that, they flew you to Las Vegas the next day and put you up at the Paris Hotel, where you'd audition a third and final time for a chance to get into the house.

After passing the first round, I did my shows back in Honolulu, flew back to LA on Monday, and gave myself a good twenty-four hours to prepare for my Laugh Factory spot Tuesday night, which meant sleeping. The judges for this phase of the auditions were Jay, Buddy Hackett, and Joe Rogan. It was a Ralphie-friendly crowd, on my home turf, which was comforting, but by no means a guarantee. From how they judged the comics who went before me, Jay, Buddy and Joe were clearly using the audience response as a gauge for their scores, which was fair. Fortunately, I got through that round and the next one in Vegas, which set us up for a couple days of shooting in Vegas leading up to the selection for getting into the house.

Reality shows can fuck with you. I had performed the best and most consistently across the three phases of the audition, yet I was the last of the ten people selected for the house. As the house filled up and the available spots dwindled, I was so nervous. How the fuck could I not end up in that house? I thought maybe they were doing it this way for dramatic effect, like by selecting me last they'd shake my confidence a little and give the guys they selected first a bit of an ego boost. I was incorrect on both counts.

Later that night Jay pulled me aside to explain. "Man, you have no idea how fucking hard it was to get you into this house." I didn't know what he meant. "NBC does not want you on this show. They've never had anyone as big as you on prime-time television. They think people will make a laughingstock out of them."

This was not the first time I'd felt explicit antifat prejudice in show business (the implicit kind is everywhere). I once showcased at the Laugh Factory along with twenty other comedians to go on *Late Night with Conan O'Brien*. I followed Dane Cook, which seemed to happen a lot in those early days, and was the only comic who got a standing ovation. After the show, Dane and Mitch Mullany went up to the booker to find out how everything was going to shake out.

"So when can the rest of us go on the show?" Dane said.

"Ralphie did the best, so he'll obviously go first," Mitch added, "but what about after that?"

"Actually," the booker said, "we can't have Ralphie on," and told me right to my face I was too fucking fat.*

Now it was happening again.

"You have to keep doing what you've been doing," Jay told me. "You have to get a standing ovation every time you perform. Every. Fucking. Time. Otherwise if you leave it up to them, they will kick you off this TV show the second there's an opportunity."

There is a moment when a man gets kicked in the nuts when there is no pain, just shock. The moment is just long enough for the brain to register that you've been kicked in the nuts, at which point the shock dissipates and the pain explodes. It's like a massive earthquake that sends shock waves of agony through your body. When the shock waves reach your head, creating stars and double vision and virtual blindness, they rebound back toward the epicenter like a tsunami. That's when the nausea kicks in and doubles you over, eventually bringing you to a knee and maybe even to the ground, in the fetal position.

That's what my conversation with Jay felt like. And it was only Thursday, exactly a week from when he first called me in Hawaii about coming on the show.

The final cast was me, Rich Vos, Sean Kent, Cory Kahaney, Geoff Brown, Dave Mordal, Tere Joyce, Rob Cantrell, Tess Drake, and Dat Phan. I didn't know about the others, but I was a wreck. In two days I'd gone from being nervous about getting into the house to stressed about getting kicked out of it. Worse, I didn't have any money. I knew we were going to get paid for the show, but I didn't have time to wait for their check to cycle through

---

* Because of that incident at the Laugh Factory, I think Dane even refused to do Conan's show for a while. People can say what they want about Dane and his style of comedy, but he will always be right with me. He's a stand-up human being.

payroll. I'm sure they were just trying to mindfuck us and cause drama, but I'd had enough.

"Why haven't we been paid? Why haven't any of us seen our per diem?" I was shouting this at anyone who would listen. "You're trying to purposely cause drama, and it's bullshit. Fuck this, I'm done. I'm out!"

I stormed out of NBC onto the street and called Lahna to come pick me up. For the second time in little more than a week, she was my voice of reason. She said I needed to stick with the show and that she'd take care of the rent in the meantime with a cash advance on her credit card. My Southern male ego didn't like that one bit. Paying my way once? That's a gift. Twice? Now that's charity. Lahna blew off that braggadocio right fast and said I could pay it back later when I'd won the show. Fucking women and their reverse-psychology mind tricks.

Hearing that, I calmed down enough that when the producer came outside to wrangle me back into the NBC studio, I could be reasoned with. I was still yelling, though, because I knew I had them by the balls. I'd shot at the Laugh Factory and in Las Vegas for the show, and there was no way to edit me out. I told them they needed to start treating everybody like talent. This wasn't the news, this was a TV show. They were freaking out because they knew I had the upper hand. Within ten minutes of my coming back inside, we were all being taken care of, and not long after that we were all in a limousine on the way to the house.

Our first night in the house, Cory Kahaney made dinner for everyone. She had worked as a chef in her other life, so she rummaged through the understocked, unfamiliar kitchen and busted her ass to put together a great meal. It was nothing fancy—just a good, hearty simple pasta meal—but none of us had eaten hardly anything that day, so it tasted amazing.

Sean Kent, who decided to fill the "asshole" role in this house, I guess, started shitting all over the meal. This didn't sit well with me, especially from him. He'd already gotten my hackles up with his big fucking cowboy hat and his whole Austin, Texas, shtick. I knew every comic worth a damn in the state of Texas, and I'd never once heard of this fucking guy. Even if I had, if he was cut from the same cloth as most of the other Texas comics I came up with, well, then he could go fuck himself as far as I was concerned. Thus, his shit-bagging Cory's meal wasn't his first strike, it was the last straw. I calmly got up, walked over to where he was sitting, put his fork down on his plate, picked up the plate, and threw it out the sliding glass door.

"Now you don't get any, asshole. Get the fuck outta here."

The next day was the first day we had to challenge one another. I said, "I don't know if this guy is a punk-ass bitch or a bitch-ass punk. I just know I'm funnier than Sean Kent." When that played in front of him, he completely cracked. He was twitching he was so angry. It was fantastic. Naturally, he was the first one bounced off the show.

All comedians do during the day is watch TV, so all of us knew that we had to constantly be doing crazy shit to entertain the home viewers or else NBC could cancel the show and we wouldn't get paid. The way comedians normally do that is by relentlessly trying to bust on each other. Jay, who hosted the first season of the show in addition to creating and producing it, egged us on. The easiest target was Dat Phan, because he was relatively new to comedy, he was naïve, he was kind of annoying, and, as we found out later into the show, he was also a total degenerate.

One night a few of us were sitting around talking about what we all wanted to do after the show ended. I said that I just wanted to go out and perform and headline my own shows. Rich Vos and Dave Mordal were thinking about going out on the road and performing together. Dat had different plans. He decided that after the show ended, he, and I am quoting here, wanted "to get a hot blond, fuck her from behind, and then have her piss on me."

Ooooooo-kay . . . time to go to bed.

I'd seen and heard some incredible, degenerate things in my first fourteen years in comedy, but this was right up there as one of the creepiest things I'd ever heard come out of a comedian's mouth that he intended for others to hear. And I'd worked with John Fox! All I could think about after hearing that was *We could've had Ken Jeong, by golly, what a shame.*

It was true too. Ken had been passed through the first phase of auditions on the Johnny Carson stage, but when he saw the god-awful mountain of paperwork he would have to fill out just to move forward—background checks, releases, insurance waivers, tax forms, and on and on—he bailed. He'd been doing comedy for several years by then, but he was still a real doctor at the time, and this kind of bullshit paperwork was half of his job already. Why would he ever want to bring that part of his work home with him on the weekend?

I was bummed when Ken told me he wasn't continuing on, because not only was he hilarious, but we'd become friends over the last few years through Jay and through the Laugh Factory. We'd hung out quite a bit. In 2002, for instance, he and Jay and I went to the Super Bowl together down in New Orleans. Ken did his residency down there, so he knew the town pretty well. He and I shared a hotel room, because fuck Jay Mohr and his *Jerry Maguire* money! I didn't have a goddamn dime to my name at the time, so Ken paid for me nearly everywhere we went on Bourbon Street that weekend. To show my appreciation I dragged him into what may have been his very last strip club thanks to some "dancer" who unsolicitedly showed him her 'giner meat and sent him reeling: *"I think she's got HPV on her butthole!"*

He shouted it at us over the music, right past her head. We were dying, figuratively speaking, at least. Unlike the neighborhood girl at my new place in Park Mesa Heights, aka Da Hood, who Ken saved from choking to death on a piece of meat at one of my weekly barbecues. He gave her the Heimlich maneuver right there in the yard.

We could have had that guy in the house. Instead, we got a Vietnamese kid still wet behind the ears who claimed to want nothing more after his first, formative TV experience than to have a white girl pee on him.

Welcome to Hollywood.

When the show got down to five people (me, Dat, Rich, Cory, and Tess), the producers kicked us all out of the house. The last two shows would be in front of a live theater audience, and TV viewers would be the ones voting. So from February until May, when the show began airing, we were all in limbo. I don't do limbo well, either physically or metaphorically. I called Jay to see what was going on.

"Look, I can't really talk about it, but you're going to love the results," he said. "It's going to make your career."

That was the best news I'd heard all year. On top of it, all the money that I'd earned for doing the show started coming in as well. I celebrated by treating myself to something I'd heard a lot of adults raving about over the years but that I had never gotten a chance to try: health insurance. Besides the bus I bought for touring about ten years later, it would become the best investment I ever made.

The halo of buzz from being on the show wore off after a couple of weeks, and I went back to doing what I always did: performing a bunch of shows and smoking a lot of weed. The show had completely left my head when it first started to air, in part because the show was on Tuesday night and I was working gigs on Tuesday nights. I probably wouldn't have watched it even if I could have, because I was nervous about the final shows. Besides, this was network television, there was no telling if anyone was going to watch this thing.

Two weeks later I was at a Shell station filling up my 4Runner when a guy stopped in traffic and started shouting superaggressively, "Ralphie! Ralphie May!" He left his car parked *in the street* and started my way. I had no idea who this guy was or if he was trying to carjack me. All I could think was *Please, Lord Jesus, don't let it be a crazy Mexican with a neck tattoo.* I grabbed the gas pump with one hand and cupped my lighter in my pants pocket with the other. *I hope he likes fried chicken, because he's about to be extra crispy.*

"Man, I love you on *Last Comic.* You're so damn funny! Can I take a picture with you?"

That was the first time I realized something was happening with *Last Comic Standing.* Not much later, the Improv called and asked me if I wanted to go down and work Irvine as a headliner for a *Last Comic Standing* show they were doing. I was feeling myself by then so I tried to big-time them and ask for some superhigh fee.

"Sure, I can do it for three thousand dollars," I said, convinced they'd work me down and we'd settle somewhere around $1,800.

"Done," said the voice on the other end of the line. "No problem. See you Wednesday."

We did nine sold-out shows. Afterward Robert Hartmann, the

owner of the Improv, came up to me and said they wanted to work me all around the country. "Seventy-five hundred a week. Is that okay?"

"Sure," I said. That was more money than I'd ever made in one week; the most since the weekend in Phoenix before 9/11.

My dream was finally coming true—I was making it big.

The final episodes were set for the end of the summer. A drawing was held to determine the order of appearance for our live sets.

But before that went down, Jay pulled me aside again. "Look, buddy, the way they've edited this show so far, it's pretty clear they want Dat to win." This made sense for NBC for a ton of reasons, but that didn't mean I had to like any of them. "If you want any hope of winning this thing, you have to absolutely crush your set."

Basically I had to blow the place up so completely that my victory had to be undeniable in the audience's eyes. The way to assure that was to get the third spot in the drawing. Everyone wanted the third spot. It's the traditional prime, headlining spot after the audience has been warmed up by the sacrificial lambs who had to go first and second. Nobody ever wants those spots if they have a choice. When you're first, you face a cold and uncertain audience. When you're second, if the opener somehow crushed or alternatively completely shit the bed, you've got an uphill battle to bring them to your side. In the third spot, you have a chance to read the audience mood and hit 'em with your best stuff.

I drew the first spot. How's that for luck? I couldn't get a kick in a stampede. In the past I might have let this little turn get me down, like the world was against me. This time I used it as motivation. *Fuck them, I can do this thing.*

Everyone got four minutes and forty-five seconds. By the second minute, my jokes were hitting so hard that the audience stood up and gave me a standing ovation. That may seem great, but it fucked with my head: How am I supposed to follow myself now? Maybe I just fucked my whole show up! I calmed myself down, then the audience, and brought home my set with two more huge laughs. I finished right on time, with another standing ovation and three thousand people in the Paris showroom chanting my name: *"Ral-phie! Ral-phie! Ral-phie!"* It was ridiculous, like out of a movie. This went on for seven minutes. Jay had to go onstage to try to quiet down the audience. It didn't work. Eventually he had to come backstage and get me.

"Hey, Ralphie, can you go back out there and shut these people up so we can finish filming this fucking TV show, please?"

"Hold on, guys"—I looked at all the other comedians sitting around—"I'll be right back." I felt like such a big shot. Dat Phan had drawn the second spot, and sheer terror was in his eyes. I went out and thanked the audience again and encouraged them to give as much love as they could to the next comics coming up. When the taping was over, Jay said it would have been hilarious to throw all the other comics under the bus, kind of like Sam Kinison did to me back in Fayetteville almost fifteen years earlier. I kind of agreed with Jay, but I was still a Southern boy at heart, and I knew it wouldn't have been a nice move.

The next week we were back in Vegas to do the reveal show, where we all did stand-up again. I was the only one of us who did a whole new five minutes of material. And I got another standing ovation.

After we finished our sets, we were all just sitting around talking, and Jay, in his capacity as host of the show, said, "Ralphie, do you think you've won?"

"Yes, actually I do."

"Why do you think that?"

"Well, I was the only one who got standing ovations every time I performed, and I was the only one who did different material every time I performed. Based on that alone, I think I was the obvious winner."

Jay the Host was setting me up for Jay the Producer, all for the sake of the show. And I bit, like a cocky bastard.

The final vote came down to Dat and me . . . and Dat won.

For the next I don't even know how many months, everyone and their mother and their bluetick coonhound told me I was robbed. When Jeffrey Ross called me after the finale taping to see how I did, he couldn't believe I came in second. When I went on Jimmy Kimmel's show the night the finale aired (man, did that piss off NBC, holy moly!), he flat out said I was robbed. Bob and Ross called the same day from the *Tonight Show* offices and said they wanted me on that night. They were scheduled to have Dat on, but they knew having me on instead made for better TV since everyone knew "I was the real winner."

It was all a huge ego stroke, and I started to believe what all these people were saying. I started to get high on my own supply, which made me bitter for a while.

Living through the 1980s and being a fan of pop culture, the greatest injustice I'd seen in the entertainment world was when Metallica got beaten out by Jethro Tull for the first heavy-metal Grammy in 1989. Metallica could have gotten bitter and resentful and taken their guitars and gone home. Instead, they went into the studio and created *Metallica* (aka *The Black Album*), which went on to be certified *sixteen times platinum*.

I realized that's a little bit what happened to me—the first part, I mean. People weren't used to seeing someone like me on a new type of show like this, so they went with something safer. The outcome made zero sense to anyone who understood how the business was changing, but those weren't the people casting votes. I had a choice to make: Do I take my microphone and go home, or do I put the past behind me and go make my own *Black Album*?

The choice was obvious. Right away I got a five-month contract to play Vegas with money that went through the fucking roof compared to what I'd been making just a few months earlier. I had deals coming at me from all directions, for all sorts of things. It was clear to me, to Lahna, and to my reps, that people wanted me on TV.

It was incredibly exciting. I just had something else to do first. I had to do something about my weight. Once the show was over, the implications of the stuff Jay was telling me behind the scenes started to land. My weight was making my career harder. The thing is, and I know this will sound crazy, it wasn't making my *life* that much harder. Not yet, anyway.

I knew I was big—I'm not blind, I own mirrors—but I didn't spend much time during the week thinking about my weight. I'd lived with it every day of my adult life and for most of my childhood. It felt sort of self-evident by then. I mean, you don't *forget* that you're fat, especially once it becomes one of the defining characteristics of your career as an entertainer—both good and bad. The main reason I didn't think about it, though, was because, unlike those guys you see on TLC with giant scrotums, dressed in muumuus made out of bedsheets, I was still active and out in the world. No one needed to cut away the side of my bedroom wall to remove me with a forklift. I was still going places and hanging out with friends. I was doing what I loved, performing every night for packed audiences full of people just like me. I never felt the urge to sit around and cry big gravy tears about it.

Still, with the money I'd earned from *Last Comic Standing* and all the headlining gigs that had lined up behind it, I decided it was time to give gastric bypass a shot. When you want gastric bypass, they don't just lift up a roll, cut a little hole in your belly, and wrap a scrunchie around your stomach. You have to put in some actual work, which is probably why most people my size don't do it. Part of that work is losing a chunk of weight prior to the procedure to prove you're committed. I scheduled the bypass for November to give myself some time.

The first step included figuring out how much I weighed. Easier said than done when most standard scales just kind of say "Fuck it" after 350 pounds. I ended up going to the post office just below Sunset in the seediest part of Hollywood, only a few blocks from where Lahna and I took our walk on her first visit to LA with me back in '98. I slid tentatively onto the freight scale like a container of bulk mail with, God's honest truth, no earthly idea what number it would display.

I was nearly seven hundred pounds.

If you have a hard time conceptualizing how much seven hundred pounds is, then clearly you haven't spent much time in Houston, but let me make it easier for you: it's roughly the size of a vending machine full of snacks. It's twice the size of a giant panda. I weighed twice as much as something with the word *giant* right in the name.

Talk about a wake-up call. In the space of a few months, I had the biggest moment of my career threatened by my weight, and as a reward for surviving it, I got to suffer the deeply scary humiliation of going to the fucking post office to weigh myself.

By the time I made my debut on *The Tonight Show* in March of 2004 (with Snoop Dogg as the main guest, *what-what!*), I'd slimmed down to just over four hundred pounds. I had pretty much lost an entire other fat person. I was proud of that, and I felt better than I had in a long, long time. It's weird how that works with chronic pain. When you live with it long enough, it becomes your new normal and you forget what it's like to feel good, like *objectively* good. It was an amazing feeling that led to the happiest, most productive seven-year period of my life.

Later that year, Lahna and I bought a house together at the end of a cul-de-sac in the Hollywood Hills. On July 3, 2005, we got married. I figured what better way to ring in America's independence than by locking up my dick for the rest of its life!

In 2007, my baby girl April was born. Three months later, realizing there was no way in hell we could babyproof our house for that adorable little monster, we renovated it and bought a nice suburban home in Nashville. I thought, hell, I was born in Chattanooga, and I've always had an affinity for Tennessee, why not? It didn't hurt that Nashville was more or less equidistant to 90 percent of the venues I played as a national headlining act. Federal Express is headquartered in Memphis for the same reason: they're within a four-hour flight of pretty much everywhere in the continental United States. If it works for them, it can work for me.

In 2009, April's brother, August, came along. Somewhere in this period, Lahna's parents also stopped hating my fucking guts. They agreed to accept me, as the father of their grandchildren, with only mild displeasure, like mealy okra in the gumbo of their family.

Professionally, things exploded. Between 2004 and 2010, I released a comedy album and two Comedy Central specials. I appeared on a bunch of other people's shit, and I toured virtually nonstop, raking in that paper to make sure my babies were taken care of. If there was a club with three hundred seats, a stage, and a microphone, I found it and did a week of shows there. Sometimes I did it twice in one year. In certain cities I was filling theaters. I cannot tell you the immense feeling of pride I got the first time I headlined a venue that required a bona fide sound check and did not pay part of my fee with my pick from the bar menu. The only problem with this approach to my career was that in worrying entirely about taking care of my family, I forgot to take of myself.

PART 4

BACK DOWN TO EARTH:
2010–2017

16.
SIT, DOGGY, SIT, GOOD DOGG

In 2010 at the end of September, I did a string of nine shows all around the marijuana-growing regions of Northern California. Fall is harvest season in California, so at the meet and greets I do after every show, I was getting some heavy handshakes from a lot of my fans. It wasn't out of the ordinary for me to leave a show with a half pound of weed and at least four ounces of keef* or wax or some kind of concentrate. I see other comics take pictures with fans who buy them shots or bring them cookies and make them T-shirts with their best punch lines airbrushed on. Not me. After nine shows, my fans gave me enough pot to hotbox a community college.

My last show was in Stockton, a city in Northern California that *COPS* and *Sons of Anarchy* put on the map for its gang violence

* Keef is the concentrated THC crystals from the pollen of male marijuana plants.

and meth addicts. *My people.* I was playing the two-thousand-seat Bob Hope Theatre, which is the second-biggest venue in town behind the Stockton Arena, where Snoop Dogg and Ice Cube were playing that night. Because we had the same promoter, Live Nation, we ended up booked into rooms on the same floor of the same hotel. Actually, it wasn't *all* of us. Cube took a plane back to LA after the show, but Snoop Dizzle—he parties, jack!

I don't know if Snoop heard I was in the building, or if he just smelled me there, but I wasn't in my room thirty minutes before his huge bodyguard knocked on my door and invited me down to Snoop's room. We'd met briefly backstage at *The Tonight Show* several years earlier, so I knew Snoop well enough to say hello, but it wasn't Jay Leno's giant chin that would eventually bond us, it would be Snoop's giant bag of reefer that we smoked the shit out of that night with Uncle Junebug—God rest his soul—and my opener, Billy Wayne Davis.

Conservatively, we smoked more than two ounces between all of us. Billy Wayne tapped out first, but I wasn't far behind him, because I had to get up in a couple hours to drive back down to LA and catch a flight to Guam, where I was doing a week of shows. As a parting gift, Snoop put a half ounce of his killer weed in a smellproof bag and signed it:

To: My nigga Ralphie
Love: Uncle Snoop

Stockton is a five-hour drive to Los Angeles straight down the I-5. It's mostly two lanes all the way down, with tractor trailers regularly doing 85 mph in the right lane, so if you have any sense in your head at all, you do that drive dead sober. I ended up getting a bit of a late start thanks to Snoop's hotboxing my brain, so I drove straight to LAX and had Lahna and the kids meet me there, since we were making a family vacation out of it.

This was both a smart and a stupid decision. It was smart because if I missed my flight coming to pick up everyone at our house—which was an hour's worth of LA city driving away from the airport—it wasn't like we could hop the next hourly shuttle flight to Guam. You have to fly through Honolulu, with only three or four flights a day from there to Guam. If you miss your flight, you're losing a day at least. By driving directly to the airport, I told myself, I was *smartly* playing it safe.

Stupidly, though, I was driving with two backpacks in the backseat that had a West Hollywood dispensary's worth of marijuana inside them. Fortunately, I'd installed a bulletproof safe in my car (you sell enough weed in the city of Los Angeles and you learn a few things), so before getting out of the car in the airport parking lot, I took about $6,000 worth of products out of my bags and locked them in the safe: three and a half ounces of weed, an ounce of keef, and twenty grams of hash. All good shit.

With a week of big shows coming up, and two little ones to spend time with in between, on the heels of an exhausting stretch of California shows, I knew I needed to get as much sleep as I could during the twenty hours of travel ahead of me. I don't like synthetic stuff like Ambien, so I grabbed a little packet of THC strips from the stash in the safe. These strips were great for the road. They looked exactly like Listerine breath strips, except whereas Listerine strips keep your breath smelling minty fresh, THC strips get the average person fucked-up for eighteen hours. As a 420-pound man with a high tolerance, I would get superstoned for a good twelve hours.

Ideally, this being a major international airport with significant drug traffic going through it every year, I would have taken a strip right there in the parking lot and left the rest in the safe, but these strips had an accurate forty-five minute fuse on them, and we wouldn't be even close to getting on the plane by the time the THC in the strip detonated and put me on my ass. I had no choice but to bring them with me. I stuck them in my wallet, put my wallet it my back pocket like I normally do, and headed into the terminal.

I met Lahna and the babies on the concourse, and we all went through security together, no sweat. I kept an eye on the departure time displayed on the screen at our gate, and when we got safely inside the forty-five-minute window, I pulled out my wallet and did the math: twenty hours of travel divided by twelve-hour THC effectiveness equaled approximately one and a half THC strips. I peeled off a strip, then tore another one in half, and French-kissed those skunky bitches like we were at a seventh-grade dance.

With two babies, Lahna and I preboarded. Because of my size and because I was the headliner, goddamnit, I was sitting in first class. Because she is a saint, Lahna was sitting with April and August a little farther back in Economy Plus. By the time we all got situated, the forty-five-minute fuse was burning close to zero.

When the flight attendant handed me the first-class meal menu, I just handed it back to her. "Look, I do not need anything from you on this flight. I've had plenty of water and I'm about to fall asleep and really don't want to be woken up. Send my food and ice cream sundae to my babies in the back."

This was my last clear memory.

I woke up to the sound of the landing gear screeching down on the tarmac in Honolulu. I started slowly getting it together, rubbing my eyes, asking people where we were—you know. the usual stuff. The flight attendants came through the first-class cabin returning coats to passengers. and one of them stopped at my row.

"You were so funny!" she said.

"Like . . . on TV?"

"No, on the flight!"

"Oh my God, what did I do?" Tightness filled my chest and panic rose in my voice. I was never much of a drinker, but I knew enough alcoholic comedians in my day to know the sound of a man who had no recollection of falling asleep and no clue that anything could have happened in the interim.

"All right, you just did this one thing. . . ."

Dammit, woman, I'm not a copilot, quit cockteasing me and spit it out! "What was it?"

"Well, the pilot came over the PA system and announced we'd reached our cruising altitude at thirty-eight thousand feet, and you yelled, 'Some of us are a little higher, nigger!'" Like every well-trained professional white woman I've met, she swallowed that last part and dropped the —*er,* but it did nothing to reduce the shock, because I knew how I said the N-word in my act and it was *loud.*

"*Oh my God.* Do I need to apologize to some people?"

A nice black couple were sitting across the aisle from me on their honeymoon. I thought for sure I'd committed a hate crime or something, but I guess the couple were dying laughing, and the man was taking pictures of me while I was passed out, so no apology was necessary.

You know how on some flights the flight attendants come through the aisles with mints right after you land? On this flight, after they returned coats, the cabin crew handed out pineapple samples. That's when I knew I had gotten *retarded* high because, holy shit, there is nothing better than pineapple when you're stoned, and I could have overdosed on pleasure when the first bite of pineapple hit my lips.

I zombie-walked off the plane and nearly forgot to wait for Lahna and the kids. I still didn't know where I was. I was just following people. I couldn't even read the sign for Guam correctly on the connections board because my eyes were tearing up I was so high. The same exact thing happened on the next flight. I drank some water, took a piss, gave the flight attendant the same speech about not being disturbed, passed out, and woke up on the tarmac in Guam.

When we landed, I had Lahna and the kids go ahead while I went to the lavatory to straighten myself up a bit, wash my face, freshen up with a baby wipe, your basic whore's bath. I felt as fresh and delightful as could be, which gave me enough mental clarity to realize I needed to flush the last of my THC strips before getting off the plane. I pulled out my wallet from my pants pocket and fished out the packet of strips. Holding them in my hand, I saw immediately how I got so fucked-up. Because I generate so much heat and pressure with my size, the THC strips had begun to meld to one another. No single strips were left in the pack anymore; they were all doubles and triples. So when I did the math at the gate in Los Angeles and took one and a half strips to last me the entirety of the trip, I had really taken anywhere from three to four strips. That would get a blue whale high.

Even though Guam is a US territory, everybody who passes through there has to clear customs, including American citizens. Lahna was waiting for me at the bottom of the escalator that fed into the customs arrival area.

"Do you have anything?" she said.

"Uh, my backpack."

"No. Drugs," she whispered.

Drugs were the furthest thing from my mind in that moment.

I'd just passed an amnesty box, two bathrooms, and multiple trash cans on the way down from the gate, and I was feeling all proud because I'd remembered to ditch the THC strips in the plane toilet. I assured her that, no, I'd left everything I had in my car in Los Angeles.

"Are you sure? Because there are drug-sniffing dogs *everywhere*."

"Aww, where are the doggies?" I didn't even engage with the drug talk from Lahna, that's how sure I was. Plus I hadn't seen our bulldog, Hoochie Mama, in weeks, so I was happy to see some cute dogs.

Lahna was sufficiently convinced, and we made our way through passport control into baggage claim. Right away I saw this beautiful shepherd mix, a little girl, and I whistled to call her over: "Come here, baby."

She was smelling a pile of luggage, doing her job like a good little girl, so I went eighty feet out of my way to go over and pet her. When she saw me, she sat right down.

"What a sweet little pup. You need some love, don't you? I bet nobody pets you or hugs you, do they?" She was so cute, I was sure all she wanted was a little ear rub. "You're a good doggy, yes, you are, you're a pretty girl."

Forty feet away I saw another dog and motioned for it to come over too. "Come on over here and get you some of this love!" This one, a boy, came right over and sat down, just like his sister. Obviously they weren't siblings, they were entirely different breeds, but in my mind because they were so good, they had to be related. I'm thinking, *These dogs really get it, I'm a dog lover. They know I love them. THEY GET IT!*

To the uninitiated, like me, the assumption is that a drug dog will go nuts if it picks up a scent. It'll start barking and scratching at a suitcase, or something like that. But that's not how it goes at all. When they get a positive scent for drugs, they immediately sit.

A few seconds later, the dogs' handlers come over. Both pups are seated, and I'm petting them in between explaining my unique connection to the animals. "See, fellas, you just gotta know dogs. I'm a dog person and these dogs get that."

Meanwhile the handlers—otherwise known as US Customs and Border Protection officers—stood there stone silent, just letting me talk. They must have felt like they were in the twilight zone, or like someone was trying to punk them. In retrospect, I could only imagine the conversation the two of them were having just with their eyes:

Agent 1: "Can you believe this guy?"
Agent 2: "Nobody is this fucking stupid."
Agent 1: "How much weight do you think he has on him?"
Agent 2: "I don't know, but he probably smoked half of it already."

Finally the agents interrupted my snugglefest.

"Sir, are you in possession of any illegal drugs or narcotics?" the girl-dog handler asked.

"No."

"Are you sure you don't have anything?"

"No, absolutely not."

"Sir, is this your bag?" the other handler asked, motioning to my backpack.

"Uh-huh."

"Sir, could you please pick up your bag and bring it with you over to this separate lane for us?"

Still, I wasn't thinking anything of it. I looked over and saw Lahna with an expression on her face that sat somewhere between "What's going on, Ralphie?" and "You have to be fucking kidding me, Ralphie." The handlers handed me off to another agent for screening.

"Before I open this, do you have anything in here that I should know about?" the agent asked.

"No. It's great to be here in Guam."

"You don't have anything in here at all?"

"No, I don't."

"You're sure you don't need to go to the bathroom before you come through here?"

"Nope. I went to the bathroom on the plane. Feeling fresh!" I was starting to get confused. Was this one of those Asian local-custom things, where they just keep politely insisting until you agree to whatever they're asking?

"So when I open this bag, I'm not going to find anything in here, am I?" the agent asked more directly.

"Oh, no. I had some weed in there, but I took it all out before the flight."

"Do I have your permission to open this bag?"

"Of course you do."

The agent opened my backpack and started his search. He took out some papers, then my headphones, then a book, then a sealed "smellproof" bag containing approximately one-half ounce of marijuana.* Well, shit. I thought for sure I had cleared everything out of that backpack, but I guess I didn't get it all.

---

* Pro tip: smellproof bags are not smellproof to drug dogs.

The agent held up the bag like he was lifting a bass out of a lake. Then he angled it toward the light so he could read the writing scribbled on the outside of the bag:

"'To: My nigga Ralphie. Love: *Uncle Snoop*'? What's this?" the agent said, knowing full well what *this* was. Snoop's weed must have found its way down to the very bottom of my bag on the drive from Stockton. I was caught dead to rights, so I decided to have a little fun with it while I sweated out my asshole from the humidity.

"Just eyeballing it, Officer, that looks like about fourteen grams of killer weed to me, but honestly, if I was going to sell it to you, I'd tell you it was eighteen or nineteen grams because that's how I roll."

"This looks like very high quality marijuana."

"Yeah, it's really good shit. I wouldn't open it if I were you. It's the stinkiest weed I've ever smelled." I was just trying to be helpful. Did he listen? Of course not.

Within minutes the entire customs area smelled like someone had replaced all the water in the sprinkler system with the contents of an angry skunk's anal scent gland . . . then started a fire. They had to switch on the negative airflow after that—the thing they use to clear hazardous chemical fumes so people don't die.

Another agent arrived shortly thereafter to assist, and that's when they started tearing everything apart. From their conversation it was clear they were looking for seeds, which I guess is what they screen for most often down there to prevent growers coming in. (Oh, Guam, you're so cute. No grower you'll ever need to be worried about is importing seeds.) I tried explaining to them that they wouldn't find any seeds in my possession, and if they did, it would be a miracle, because I don't smoke anything with seeds.

They weren't interested in my explanation. By the end of it, this was the most offensive part of the whole encounter. Take me to jail, do whatever you have to do, fellas, but let me keep my dignity at least.

Once they cleared all the pockets and removed the big stuff that they could see, they started shaking out the bag onto the table. A bunch of shake came out, plus some little tiny nugs of bubble hash. The THC value of really good weed is around 24 percent, but in that hash it was probably closer to 85–90 percent. If the weed was a 9mm bullet, the hash was double-aught buckshot. The agents were literally holding my bag upside down while weed kept continuously falling out. I probably had enough in there to get twenty-five people high as shit, and I didn't even know I had it. It was all just in the bottom of the bag.

The agents had a hard time believing I didn't know any of that stuff was in the bag. I understood where they were coming from. When you're a poor stoner you're acutely aware of your weed stash and its whereabouts. No nug, no bud, no bit of keef, goes unaccounted for. But I wasn't a poor stoner anymore. I was a *rich* stoner, and when you are a rich stoner every day is like Easter—you find random weed Easter eggs *everywhere*. If you're really unorganized, you can lose more weed in a day than you used to smoke in a week when you were poor. Those are some uptown weed problems, let me tell you.

The lieutenant in charge came over to the table just as the other agents finished shaking out my backpack and the marijuana shower stopped. He had the first agent hold the bag up, then took out a little club from his utility belt and gave the bag one last hard smack. A whole bunch more weed that had been lodged in the seams and crevices of the backpack fell out, along with a torn foil packet and what looked, at least to the agents based on their reactions, like large chunks and crumbs of hash. But the lieutenant and I knew better, and we both started laughing.

Lord Jesus, this is such a fat-guy move: the torn foil packet was not some ingenious drug-storage method that contained the large crumbs of a brick of smuggled hash. It was the broken Mylar wrapper of a commercial-grade, American-manufactured toaster pastry. It was fucking Pop-Tarts. Fat-guy stoner that I was, I had grabbed it from the hotel's complimentary breakfast buffet in Stockton the morning before and stuffed it into my backpack on my way out the door, thinking that it was a viable breakfast option for the road. In all the traveling over the previous twenty-four hours, the Pop-Tarts had gotten crushed at the bottom of the bag and the Mylar wrapper had torn open.

The two agents began scrambling through what was now a sugary jigsaw puzzle, trying to distinguish between weed remnants and pastry crumbles. They actually thought I put weed in the Pop-Tarts.

"Officers, why would I put marijuana in a Pop-Tart? In America people don't eat those to get high, they eat them because they *are* high." Besides, I'd heard that everyone in Guam smoked weed and it would be supereasy to score. Why would I bother packing any?

The next thing I heard was "Mr. May, please come with us."

A third agent, a big Samoan-looking dude, led me into an eight-by-eight-foot room off to the side of the customs area. It was all white, almost antiseptic. I had a bad feeling about this room. It felt like the kind of place where rights get violated. I walked through the door and was met by the handler of the shepherd mix who started this mess. He was putting on a latex glove.

Oh, fuck, a strip search.

In the moment, my primary concern wasn't for me. When you're a fat guy, there are no such thing as flattering, loose-fitting clothes. When you get dressed and walk outside, everyone knows exactly what shape you are. You don't need to be a mentalist to envision the folds and the rolls.

My concern was for the agent tasked with conducting the search. I had been sitting on planes for sixteen hours, breathing in that stale recycled air. I was in a car with leather seats for five hours before that. During the initial search of my bag, I'd been sweating like a nun in a cucumber farm. I tried to freshen up a little when I landed, but there was no getting around that I still stank. My titties smelled like vinegar. I had a nut sticking to a thigh, and I was in dire need of some powder. It was brutal.

They made me strip everything off: shirt, pants, belt, shoes, all the way down to my underwear. Wisely, the agent started with my head and worked his way down. You do not want to start the night in Funkytown; you want to end it there and get out before the lights turn on.

We started in total silence. When he got to feeling up my titties, he finally spoke. "Do not make any sudden movements." He lifted my arms. Sudden movements? I haven't made a sudden fucking movement since 1987, unless you count that time in '96 when I tripped on the ice in Toronto at the comedy festival. What the fuck are you talking about "sudden movements"? Like I'm a ninja, like I'm going to pull a sword out from under my titty meat? Stop.

When they didn't find the katana scabbard I was using as an underwire full of drugs, I thought for sure we were done. Wrong. The underwear had to go. That poor man who had to search my underwear. I caught him out of the corner of my eye examining the waistband. It seemed like my underwear went on forever.

"Sorry, man, ain't nothin' brief about them things."

Apparently genital inspection is a different job in whatever union these agents were a part of, because the first agent stepped aside and the big Samoan motherfucker took over.

"Turn and face the wall and place your palms against the wall."

Oh, God, this was about to go from strip search to chocolate-star search.

"Listen, Officer, if we're gonna go more than one knuckle deep here, can we at least get a little grease on that finger or something?"

The first agent cracked, which I felt was a good sign, but the Samoan dude didn't flinch. That got me good and scared. It was a small request, a courtesy more than anything else, since Samoans are not known for their thin, dainty features. He ran his finger along the entire length of the crack of my ass. Right at the butt-hole, he gave a little push, like he was pressing an elevator button, just to remind me I was alive, you know?

Again, I assumed we were done. I mean, where else could drugs be hiding? Again, I was wrong. Fucking Magellan over here took his fingers straight down the Cape of Good Hope headed for my little horn of Africa, stopping just long enough to check my taint. There was nothing there—nothing anyone would want to smoke or sniff anyway.

Then he grabbed my balls. Well, *grabbed* is too strong of a word. He took them gently into his hand like little baby bird eggs. If you were going to check out some dude's balls for drugs or paraphernalia, how long do you think that would take? Three seconds? Not according to the Customs and Border Protection inspector's manual, apparently. This guy needed much, much longer. He had my balls in his hand for a good twenty-five to thirty seconds. He gave them a nice slow roll, like they were Baoding balls that he was trying to make sing. I've picked ripe peaches that I've handled less softly than this Samoan handled my balls. It was actually quite professional. I think he could tell his extended inspection was getting a little uncomfortable for everyone in the room.

"Hey, man," he said, "I really love you on Comedy Central."

What the fuck? What do you say to that? To a large government official with your balls in his hand, no less.

"I bet you never thought you'd be holding my balls, did you?" That's about all you can say.

He finally cracked, which made me and the initial agent crack, and for the first time since walking into the room, I wasn't worried about going to fucking prison for the rest of my life. Turns out I had much worse things to worry about.

"Okay, you can turn around," the Samoan agent said.

I turned around expecting the other agent to hand me my clothes so I could get dressed. Instead, the Samoan agent quickly double-checked his partner's work and went through my hair, my ears, and my face. *With the same gloved hands he'd just run through my butt.* Those gloves were full of musty twenty-four-hour travel ass and ball juice! He finished by checking my mouth with his pinkie. I was horrified. I had literally just teabagged myself and eaten my own ass. Is this how they greet everyone in Guam?!

They didn't end up finding anything, like I told them they wouldn't, and both agents pronounced me clean, which I certainly was not. I was so not clean at that point. I was right, though. This *was* the room where violations happened.

When that gloved pinkie went into my mouth? I'm sorry, but that was rape.

Once they were done with my mug shot, the lieutenant in charge came in and asked me if there was anybody I wanted to call. I wasn't sure if Lahna's cell phone was working down here, and I was pretty sure she wouldn't take a call from me even it was, so I told him there was nobody else for me to call.

"Okay, Mr. May. One thing. I don't really know what's happening, but a lot of people are coming here—all of my bosses—so be respectful when they come in."

Fifteen minutes later the head of Guam Customs, the federal prosecutor for the territory of Guam, the district attorney for that area, and another high-ranking federal official whose title I can't remember walk through the door of the holding area.

"Mr. May, we'd like to inform you that the transportation of a Schedule One narcotic such as marijuana through a federal facility is punishable by a five-thousand-dollar fine and five years in jail," the district attorney said.

"Since you've been to LAX, Honolulu International, and now Guam International, you're now facing fifteen thousand dollars in fines and fifteen years in jail," the federal prosecutor added.

They just let that sink in a little bit. I apologized and explained that I hadn't meant to do anything illegal, but that I was prepared to pay the consequences like a man. I could take that lick if I had to. That's the kind of shit you say when you watch *Shawshank Redemption* every time it comes on TNT.

"The only thing you have going for you, Mr. May," the federal prosecutor went on, "is that we have to prove intent in order to indict you with the full slate of charges. That you intended to bring marijuana to Guam."

"We just looked at the security footage," the head of Customs chimed in, "and it appears that you went approximately one hundred feet out of your way to pet a drug-sniffing dog that was wearing a vest that said DRUG DOG, DON'T PET. Then you did it again."

"Nobody is this fucking stupid," the other official said finally.

Agreed, motherfucker. Agreed!

"So how about this," the head of Customs said. "How about instead of this jail stuff, we give you a ticket for possession for less than an ounce of marijuana."

"Yes, yes, okay."

"It's a misdemeanor and you can pay it where you pay for airport parking tickets."

"Great, absolutely."

"On one condition: that you let us use the video at our Christmas party."

He was dead serious. It was so dumb and funny that they wanted to show everyone at the CBP and TSA in Guam. What was I going to say: No? I agreed and left as soon as they opened the door.

Walking out of Customs into the terminal with my backpack over my shoulder, I realized I was the last passenger in the airport for the day.* When I got outside to the cab stand, a cabbie was standing next to his car, waiting for me.

"Are you the guy who pet the drug dog?" I hadn't even left the airport and already the entire island of Guam was laughing their asses off at me.

The cabbie had taken Lahna and the kids to the hotel hours earlier. She told him what I looked like and paid him to come back and wait for me.

"She is *not* happy with you, bro."

"Oh, yeah, how bad is it?"

"It's bad, bro. You might not want to stay with her."

He was right. I didn't stay with her. I had to get a new room.

---

* I still have that backpack. I call it the Original Whitney because it's black and it was full of drugs.

———

A year and a half later I went back to Guam to do another set of shows. When I landed, the lieutenant in charge and another customs officers met me at the bottom of the escalator and presented me with two stuffed dogs.

"Here, you can pet these dogs," the lieutenant said. "They can't smell a thing."

17.

ELEVEN DAYS AND NIGHTS

In 2011, things in my professional life were starting to collide with things in my personal life in a way that affected both negatively. My run-in with the Guamanian K9 unit a year earlier was the first indication that all the benefits of being a rich stoner had begun to turn into liabilities. As the father of two young children, I couldn't be so casually and chronically ensconced in the pot-smoking world that I might end up in jail for years and risk not being there for my babies. I was already feeling like an absentee dad with all my touring. Even when we'd all be on the road together as a family, I still wasn't totally there. I'd headline until 2:00 a.m., not get to sleep until 3:00 a.m., then be expected to play Daddy by 7:00 a.m. when they woke up.

Life was crazy like that, and it was a lot to handle, especially now that Lahna was doing fewer gigs and less touring in order to care for our children. The impact that had on me, besides guilt, was a sense of tremendous pressure to work. I had to work constantly to pay for everything, to provide, and to make up for not being there as much as I wanted to be.

One of the events at which I agreed to perform was the Cowhead Cruise, put on by my buddy Cowhead, who was the morning DJ at 102.5 The Bone in Tampa, Florida. This seven-day Caribbean cruise left the last week of October out of Tampa on the *Norwegian Star,* destined for the Mayan Riviera, Cozumel, Belize, and Roatán Island. which is off the coast of Honduras. This was the fifth annual Cowhead Cruise, so it wasn't just some far-fetched radio stunt (like taking a Nolan Ryan fastball to the grill), this was a thing. A *real* gig. One I booked pretty early in the year, in fact.

By the time the cruise came around that fall, I had worked sixty-seven days straight, and I mean *straight.* I had gigs on sixty-seven consecutive nights, amounting to well over one hundred individual shows. I don't care how healthy you are, that kind of pace will catch up with you eventually. Three weeks before I had to be in Tampa, I was in New York for a stretch of shows, and I got super-dehydrated while trying to pass a kidney stone. The pain got so bad that they took me to Bellevue Hospital, where they take the dregs of society and, famously, all the fucking crazy people that Manhattan somehow accumulates. We went to the emergency room at first, but they decided to admit me and then put me in a shared room with a homeless man who had some kind of nasty chest cough that sounded like a chain saw getting fired up. I don't know what he had, but I walked out of that hospital with some version of it.

Initially I thought it was just the sniffles, but it only got worse as I continued my nonstop string of gigs. By the time I got to Jacksonville, which was my last set of shows before the Cowhead Cruise, I was legitimately sick. I had been diagnosed at some walk-in clinic along the way with mild walking pneumonia and given antibiotics and an inhaler. I didn't think too much of it at the time because over the years I'd gotten used to working sick. Usually I'd just lay off the weed for a while and try to let my lungs do their thing. So when my last show in Jacksonville was over and I'd taken the last photo with fans at around 2:30 a.m., I hopped in the car and drove straight through to Tampa to catch the boat.

Cowhead could immediately see that I was sick. He told me not to come on the cruise and just to go get myself better. I told him not to worry about it and that I'd just bought a bunch of medicine so I'd be okay. I thought I was going to be fine. My body is weird that way. I don't have high blood pressure, I'm not prediabetic, I don't have any of the markers for heart disease, but when anything viral comes around, it kicks me right in the dick for a little bit, lingers, and then goes away on its own.

I was not fine, by any stretch of the imagination.

We weren't out to sea more than a day before that walking pneumonia decided it was going to lie down right in my chest. Quickly I couldn't walk without wheezing. I couldn't catch my breath. People who didn't already know I was sick were concerned with just one look at me. After the first day, I quarantined myself in my cabin so I didn't become patient zero for whatever I was dealing with. It was scary. I spent those first three or four days wide-awake, afraid to fall asleep because I was worried I might stop breathing.

Every day when we pulled into a new port, I thought about getting off and going to a hospital. I was desperate. But Belize? Roatán? Cozumel? I love my Latino *hermanos* in LA, but I'm not trying to play doctor with any of them. *Fuck that.* It was only a couple more days, I could ride it out until we got back to Tampa.

I didn't quite make it.

On the last leg back to Tampa, I called the ship's 911 and had them come take me to the ship's infirmary. My lips were blue, my extremities were gray, my blood/oxygen content was at 48 percent, my heart rate was 250 beats per minute. The nurse immediately put me on oxygen and gave me as many antibiotics as they had on the ship. They took a chest X-ray once I was stabilized, and that's when they were, like, "Oh, shit, wake up the ship's doctor right now."

The doctor aboard the ship was a woman who had been an ER doctor at Walter Reed National Military Medical Center outside Washington, DC. She was ostensibly on vacation. Two minutes with me and she wanted to airlift me off the ship immediately and get me to Tampa General. But just my luck, guess what took off from southern Honduras the same day we took off from Tampa: a fucking hurricane. Hurricane Rina had been stalking us the entire cruise. As we went south and east, it went north and west. It was like a tango. The hurricane had dissipated into a tropical storm by the time we got north of the Yucatán Peninsula headed home, but as it weakened, it dropped a metric shit ton of torrential rain right between us and Tampa that a medevac helicopter couldn't, or wouldn't, fly through.

That poor doctor, she was not happy: "You know, I came on this ship to bandage small cuts, deal with the occasional broken bone, and distribute diabetes medicine. I didn't come on this ship to watch people die. Do not die on me. I seriously would not be able to take it."

She had a lot of fight in her, which encouraged the fight in me, but her sense of urgency let me know of the real chance I could die here. On a fucking cruise ship of all places. That's barely one step above dying on the toilet.

When we finally got back to port in Tampa around 6:00 a.m., we were met at the dock by Tampa Fire Rescue. They put me on a gurney and loaded me directly into the ambulance while they took my vitals. They had the same exact reaction as the nurse and the doctor on the boat: "Oh, fuck." That scared me *a lot*.

We got to the emergency room at Tampa General superfast. The EMTs off-loaded me and handed me over to the ER nurses. One of them scanned my chart, redid some of the vitals that the EMTs had done dockside a few minutes earlier, and said, "Oh, shit."

I started laughing.

"Why are you laughing, Ralphie?" she said.

"You're the first person that hasn't said 'Oh, fuck,' so I must be getting better."

I was in the ER from approximately 7:00 a.m. well into the night while the doctors ran tests and I waited for a room in intensive care to open up. Lahna had arrived by the time one finally came available just after midnight, which we were thankful for, though a little concerned about. When an ICU room opens up that late, I feel like the *C* part of that acronym probably didn't work out so well. I was not so interested in spending the night in an unlucky room.

To move me from the ER to the ICU, nurses called in the lift team to get me from the ER gurney to the ICU bed. The room was only like fifteen or twenty yards down the hall, so I told the team that I'd just walk. My oxygen levels had gotten back up to around 94 percent by this time, and they'd filled me up with about seven different drugs including a blood thinner called heparin, so I was feeling a lot better.

Five minutes later, Dr. Katz, the head of pulmonology at Tampa General, comes in to talk with me. I'd barely gotten more than a few words out when it started to feel like I was getting stabbed in my right shoulder, and the pain was radiating all the way into my lungs.

"PE, PE, PE," Dr. Katz started repeating to the respiratory techs. I was so doped up at the time, I was totally lost. *Physical education? Yeah, Doc, I get it, I'm fat. Fuck off!* Now I know that *PE* stands for "pulmonary embolism," which is the fancy way of saying "blood clot in the lungs," so the hospital can charge your insurance an arm and a leg . . . and a lung.

The respiratory techs came in, took the small oxygen mask off me, and put a *Top Gun*–style mask over my face that shot oxygen into my nose at fifty miles per hour to hyperinflate my lungs because they had already started collapsing.

It was fucking bad. People die in the hospital from that kind of embolism all the time. That I had mine right in front of the head of pulmonology, who had probably seen hundreds of these in his time, was nothing short of a miracle if you ask me.

As the oxygen did its thing and the pain subsided, Dr. Katz gave it to me and Lahna straight:

"Mr. May, you've experienced a severe pulmonary event. I believe a large blood clot has gotten into the blood vessels in your lungs. I have recommended that radiology come in here as soon as possible to place a filter in your vein so that no more clots make it to your lungs or heart. They have to go in through your neck to do this. Then they're going to go into another vein and chemically explode the remaining blood clots. If they get them all, and they get them fast enough, you'll be fine. You'll live. If they don't, you could die on the operating table. I want to be perfectly clear with you both: this is a last-ditch-type effort to save your life."

I was stunned.

Lahna was freaking out. "What are his chances? What are the chances this filter thing works?"

"Twenty to thirty percent."

"Oh my God, there's a twenty to thirty percent chance he'll die?"

"No, that he'll live," was Dr. Katz's reply.

This conversation took place at 1:00 a.m. The surgery was scheduled for 7:00 a.m., which seemed far away considering that in six hours I could well be dead. That wasn't the worst of it. Because I had no lung capacity, they couldn't put me under any kind of general anesthesia whatsoever during the operation. I would have to be awake for the surgery. They were going to have to strap me down because this was going to be hands down the most excruciating pain I'd ever experienced.

This is it, I thought. *I'm never going on a cruise again.*

Thanks to the oxygen, the blood thinners, and some other antiviral meds, I spent much of the rest of the night hacking up mucus out of my lungs. It was the nastiest thing Lahna and I had ever seen, and we had four years of diaper-changing experience under out belts. The mucus looked like peanut butter and had that consistency too. The techs were nerding out over it. They're used to seeing all manner of gross shit, but most of them had never seen anything like this before. They came in and out of the room frequently to check on me and keep track of the mucus volume. They said it was so they could calculate my lung capacity, but I was convinced they were running a pool out at the nurses' station.

By morning, I'd ejected something like 220 cubic grams, or ten ounces, of lung butter. To prep for the procedure at 7:00 a.m. they did another set of chest X-rays, and my lungs looked a lot better. The drugs were working and my lungs were now able to expand.

When Dr. Katz looked at the charts and the X-rays, he decided to call off the surgery. He came into my room to deliver the good news along with the full diagnosis of my issues: I had bilateral double pneumonia and pulmonary embolisms, which meant I had viral and bacterial pneumonia in my lungs and a blood clot blocking most of the remaining lung capacity.* I was basically drowning in an infection.

For the next seven days in the ICU I couldn't sleep. I didn't have insomnia; I mean, I wasn't *allowed* to sleep. My lungs were on a razor's edge, and the infection I was fighting was doing its best to try to drown me in myself. To beat it, I had to consciously force every breath in and out of my lungs until Dr. Katz said otherwise.

Breathing is an autonomic function that most of us take for granted (thank you, *Encyclopaedia Britannica,* volume *A*). We even have sayings about it when people are passionate about something: *Writing is like breathing.* What they're saying is they have to do it, they can't control it. Now I *had to* control it.

The idea that my body was so fucked that I was forced to make myself breathe so I wouldn't die was not only excruciatingly painful physically, it was also a total mindfuck. Lying there in the ICU, wide-awake in the middle of the night, often by myself, I started to make my peace. I wrote a letter to April about what it means to be a strong woman. I wrote a letter to August about what it means to be a strong man. Then I wrote a letter to Lahna and

---

* This was the same thing that killed Bernie Mac and Heavy D.

apologized for not taking care of myself. I wrote a long list of I Love You's and Thank You's to all my friends.

By the end, I was content. They say your life flashes before your eyes when you die, and it does, but it's not the career highlights or anything you place value on. At least not for me. It was all of the regrets I had: missing the first sonogram of my baby girl because I was making people laugh in Cleveland, or having to watch my son's first steps on video because I was making people laugh in Miami. Shit like that came to me constantly over what ended up being eleven straight sleepless nights (including the scary nights on the cruise ship).

I don't think anybody could have made it out of a situation like mine mentally unscathed—every waking moment thinking you're going to die if just this one time you forget to inhale or exhale and you let yourself go to sleep—but it did a number on me. It broke something in my brain.

I got out of the hospital after nine days, but it would be a couple months before I was strong enough to travel. My in-laws, who had retired to Sarasota since Lahna and I got married, were gracious enough to open up their home and let me stay with them while I recuperated. As much as we had our differences, they were fundamentally good people, and they showed it in those months after my scare.

Slowly my body got better, but something about my brain's not catching up as quickly fucked with me. Having my wife and kids float in and out because they had things to do and lives to live, while I lay there in a house owned by people who I knew would never think I was good enough, ripped open issues from my childhood that, thanks to the embolisms, I could no longer cover up. The embolisms had damaged my lungs so badly, Dr. Katz told me

I couldn't smoke weed anymore, which I had been using for twenty-five years to mask all the pain.

It was clear too as I worked to get out of there that my personal problems and my professional instincts were no longer just colliding. They were locked in a tug-of-war, and I was the rope.

18.
THE MAYS GO GAY

I've done some reckless, thoughtless, stupid shit in my time—as a young'un and as a grown-up—but as a poor kid from small-town Arkansas who grew up in a shotgun shack, one of the things I will always be proudest of as a father is being able to show the world to my kids and to expose them to new and different experiences. I don't say that to sound like some kind of humanitarian hero. It's not like it's been hard. I'm not Atticus Finch. Living in Los Angeles, it's been a breeze. All I have to do is take April and August to school or to a restaurant or just open the front door and let them play outside. In any of those situations, I'm basically dropping them into a kaleidoscope of humanity where each sparkly bit belongs just as much as any other. As a result, I've been able to teach my kids one of the most important lessons of all: that there is no excuse for hating people as a group when there are so many reasons to hate them individually. Even as young children they know not to judge people based on their skin color or gender or sexual orientation, but rather on more important things, like whether they know how to merge onto a fucking highway or if they hold the door open for the person behind them or if they text in a movie theater.

The thing is, you never know how well you're doing as a teacher or as a role model with that stuff until you see how your kids respond in a totally foreign environment, around people who are nothing like them. My first big test came when I took the entire family to the gay wedding of our next-door neighbor Gay Tony and his longtime partner, Aunt Tim.* When Tony and Tim got married, April was six years old and August was four. I wasn't concerned about how April would handle being at the wedding of two men because she was *in* the wedding. She was part of the whole production as one of the flower girls in the processional. She couldn't see what we saw. She didn't have the good fortune of being able to sit back and take in the entire scene. Even if she had, girls are light-years more advanced than boys at that age, and she'd already been exposed to two years of structured public school where the focus is on sitting still and being quiet. If she had questions, she also had enough social grace to lean over and whisper them in her mama's ear. August, on the other hand, was at that age where boys get *super*verbal but also haven't developed an inner monologue yet. If a thought entered his brain, it was comin' outta that little mouth. Like a baby eating pureed sweet potatoes—it's coming out in pretty much the same form it went in . . . *and quick.*

I had no idea what to expect from August, mostly because I had

---

* Gay Tony and Aunt Tim aren't their real names obviously, it's just how they're saved in my cell phone.

no idea what to expect period. None of us had been to a gay wedding before. Since moving to Los Angeles, Lahna and I had made a bunch of gay friends, but gay marriage had only been quasi-legal in California since 2008, and it had *just* become Supreme Court official when Tony and Tim got hitched, so these were our first legit, real-deal gay nuptials. It wasn't just a symbolic gesture of commitment anymore. One of these guys could lose half his shit now. This was serious business.

The ceremony was completely unremarkable in that it was impeccably decorated, the orchestral music was beautiful, and none of the flower arrangements were shaped like giant dicks. The grooms and the groomsmen were in perfectly tailored suits, and Tony and Tim exchanged vows that sounded more or less like every other set of wedding vows you've heard and only half-believed. It was just . . . a wedding. Which was the exact opposite of what I was prepared for after sitting through a pre-ceremony singing performance that has forever changed how my son looks at me as a man.

Prior to the live taping of every sitcom or late-night talk show, a person comes out to warm-up the studio audience. Usually it's a decent stand-up comic who is good at crowd work, though sometimes it's the star of the show themselves—Robin Williams used to warm up the crowd before tapings of *Mork & Mindy*. These warm-up guys are a lot like hosts at a comedy club or the opening act for a headliner at a theater gig. Their initial goal is to fill time while the audience settles in, and the performers and crew get locked in. But their larger purpose is to get the audience in the mood to laugh so they are more receptive to the jokes the performers are going to try to land.

Weddings have their own version of this. It's the perpetually single fat-girl cousin who gets up and sings that horrible song from *Frozen* or *Titanic,* but prefaces it with some rambling five-minute story about that time she went bowling with the bride and groom, and they had pizza, and they each grabbed for the last slice of pizza, then they decided to share it, and that's what true love really is. Or sometimes it's a possibly retarded brother, like my buddy Rusty Dugan, whose parents thought it was sweet that he wanted to learn how to play "Moonlight Sonata" on the recorder in his occupational-therapy class so he could surprise the bride and groom on their special day; only he ends up with a raging boner in the middle of the song and all you can think is *Rusty must really love that recorder. Will you look at that, sweet Lord Jesus, is that boy musically* inclined*!*

Tony and Tim went a different direction with their pre-ceremony warm-up guy. Specifically they went deep, dark, and vertical: a six-foot-four-inch black male transvestite Cher impersonator named Sugar, with a *Ch,* who wore eight-inch platform boots, fishnet stockings with garter belts, a bustier, *and a cape.* Because looking like the love child of Grace Jones and Dikembe Mutombo was too subtle for Mr. Chugar, apparently.

April didn't get to see Chugar. She was back in the wings with Lahna preparing for the ceremony. August was in the audience with me, and he had so many questions.

"Daddy, what is *that?*"

"That, Son, is a transvestite."

"Wooo, that's a big transmesmite, Daddy."

"Yes, Son, I reckon that's about as big as they come."

"Yep, that's a big'un." Like every four-year-old who thinks he's a big boy, August was now an expert on transvestite culture. "Biggest one I ever seen, Dad. Biggest one for sure. Transmesmites is big, Dad."

That satisfied August's curiosity through the beginning of Chugar's routine. And he was killing it. Or at least I assume he was. Cher always sounded like a bluetick hound to me, and that's exactly what Mr. Chugar sounded like, so I just took for granted that he was great. His dance moves were on point too. During a catwalklike pivot-and-spin move, August finally noticed Chugar's cape, which led to more questions.

"Look, Daddy! Mr. Chugar has a cape. Do you think Mr. Chugar likes sword fighting?"

"Oh-ho! I bet he does, Son!"

"Do you think he brought his sword with him, Daddy?"

"I'm pretty sure he packed it."

"Do you think he'd want to sword fight with me, Daddy?"

"Maybe when you're a little older, Son. Mr. Chugar's only allowed to sword fight with boys near his age. That's the rules."

I'm not much for reenactments and cover bands and impersonators, but I know enough about live performance to know that Chugar was as good as they come. Tony and Tim did not find this dude hanging out in front of Donut Time on Santa Monica and Highland.* He looked nothing like the kind of transvestite that Doug Stanhope and I saw ten or fifteen years earlier pick up a midget, set him on top of a newspaper box, and suck his dick. No, this was a trained professional. Thankfully too, because about halfway into his performance, his big ol' dick and one of his balls fell out. Like any normal person, Chugar's instinct was to panic, but that's where the similarities ended between him and, say, a female Cher impersonator. If some woman's 'giner lip falls out in

---

* The stretch of Santa Monica Boulevard in Los Angeles between La Brea Avenue and Highland Avenue has long been notorious as the hangout for LA's black transvestite sex-worker population. Donut Time used to be nicknamed Tranny Time or the Tranny Donut Shop.

the middle of a performance, do you really think she'd be so composed? Do you really believe she'd just fold that little meat curtain back in and demur to the crowd, like, "Hee hee, don't judge. I made some bad choices in college. We're good now." Hell no! That show is *over*. Not Mr. Chugar. As a seasoned performer, muscle memory kicked in. He grabbed some double-sided tape from his pocketbook, turned around, stuffed all that junk back in, taped it in place, and finished the song.

He also finished any shot I ever had of impressing my little boy.

There's an old joke about how dads sometimes engineer it so their young sons walk in on them peeing, because with their tiny little bodies and itty-bitty little wieners, young sons will think their dads have the biggest dicks the world has ever known. It's like a cheat code for admiration, for feeling like a man, and Chugar had just taken it from me by accidentally exposing my son to a dick so big it had an elbow in it.

It didn't *have* to be this way. Chugar could have gone with a Young Cher look with long flowy pants, or even a 1986 Cher look with that big black Vegas-showgirl dress she wore to the Oscars. With outfits like those, this kind of wardrobe malfunction would be near impossible. But, no, Tony and Tim had to hire Chugar to do a modified 1989 "If I Could Turn Back Time" music-video Cher look—the one on the battleship with the fishnet bodysuit and the fabric *V* that covered her boobies and her 'giner meat—that made this slippage almost inevitable. I mean, what do you think is going to happen with a guy like Mr. Chugar, packing a python and a couple of gator eggs in those skimpy little britches?

"Daddy," August said finally, "Mr. Chugar sure has got a big ol' pee-pee."

I couldn't lie to my boy. "No, Son, you and I have pee-pees. That's a *dick*."

"Yep," he said reassuringly, "transmesmites gots dicks, Dad."

After the ceremony, Lahna and I sent the kids home with a babysitter and went to the reception by ourselves. Kids have no business being at wedding receptions of any kind, in my opinion. They're loud and run late, and the last thing you want is to be cradling a couple of tired, whiny babies at 11:00 p.m. while three hundred people are getting stupid and dancing their faces off. I had absolutely nothing to base this on, but I was also sure this unsuitability would be even truer at a gay wedding reception.

And I was right. This thing was gayer than a George Michael concert, by which I mean it was the best wedding reception I've ever been to in my life.

The reception started at 7:00 p.m. Being straight white people, Lahna and I arrived unfashionably on time. The other guests trickled in over the next half hour or so, which gave us time to scope out the refreshments and find our table. The food and drink was fabulously awesome. These gay boys went all out. They brought in at least one hundred cases of champagne. There was a prime-rib station. Not one of those cheap Palace Station Casino buffet types either. This meat was clearly from a cow—a *fresh* one. There was a seafood station too, where you could just walk up and grab a whole lobster like it was nothing. *A whole lobster?!* Red Lobster can officially suck my dick. *This* is for the seafood lover in *me*, motherfucker! There was even a real sushi bar, with real fresh fish, and real bona fide Japanese-y Japanese slicing and rolling it. Other weddings that try to do sushi end up relying on their caterer, who just plucks some Vietnamese guy named Hoa from the crew and the

Hispanic guy from the kitchen with the lightest skin. Ideally, one who has narrow eyes because his great-great-grandmama fucked an Aztec or whatever. But not this time, jack. These fellas straight-up Tokyo-drifted over here.

Our table was set toward the back behind the dance floor. Other people might take our distance from the head table as a personal slight, as a reflection of the thinness of our friendship bond to Tony and Tim. I took it as recognition of our closeness as neighbors—because they put us closer to the food. The tables were decorated with the same style and taste as the wedding ceremony itself. There were even party favors. At each seat, in front of the place cards (handwritten in calligraphy, of course), were three little pills.

Lahna says, "Is that candy?" She thought maybe they were palate cleansers or mints for between courses.

But I knew better. "Honey, I'm pretty sure I know every candy ever made." I was especially familiar with every type of hard candy for which pills might be mistaken—Nerds, Tic Tacs, Jolly Ranchers, Pop Rocks, Necco wafers, Smarties, Pez, Atomic FireBalls, Now and Laters, Skittles (original *and* tropical), Jelly Belly, Life Savers, Werther's Originals, Jordan almonds, Bit-O-Honey, those individually wrapped peppermints at restaurants that have little bits of poo on them according to *Dateline*. These pills were not those.

"I don't know what those first two are," I told Lahna, "but that last one looks like pharmaceutical-grade MDMA from the early nineties."

"What's MDMA?"

"That's ecstasy."

"Ohhhh-ho-ho-ho-ho-ohhh." Lahna's eyes dilated in recognition like she'd already started rolling on the shit. *Yeah, you remember that now, don'tcha.* It was a welcome moment of free-spiritedness from her, since we had not been getting along all that great after the little Guam incident.

We didn't have to wait long to find out what the other pills were. As everyone found their seats, one of Tony and Tim's friends grabbed the microphone and got the festivities started. A little gay Ricky Ricardo–type fella named Diego, he was, I guessed, going to be the emcee for the evening. I don't know if he was the best man, but when he turned on the mic, he gave the best wedding speech I'd ever heard:

"Hello, party people, hello! Tonight, baby, we are going to party until three a.m., baby!"

It was 9:20 p.m., jack. The nightly news hadn't even started yet, and my man is calling *3:00 a.m.*? I don't think so.

"Tonight, baby, we are going to wonderland, baby, just like Alice!"

According to the 1951 animated film, Alice spent hours in a fever dream running from a crazy lady, being pushed along by some bipolar schizophrenic in a top hat, Flavor Flav dressed as a rabbit, and two fat guys on mopeds. All I wanted was some surf 'n' turf.

"On your table you have three pills in front of you: one will make you smart, one will make you talk, and one—the little Goldilocks pill—is just like Diego, it makes everything feel *allllll riiiiiiighttt.*"

Well, when you put it that way . . .

"So let's take this pills, okay, baby? On three, everybody. One . . . two . . . three!"

Diego popped all three at once like they were . . . well . . . *candy.* Most of the guests followed suit. Lahna and I paused. Lahna paused because she wasn't sure. I paused because Lahna paused.

"Should we take these pills?" Hesitation was in her voice, but also that little bit of mischief that was asking for permission to get e-tarded.

"Fuck yes! These are *gay* drugs. You're damn right we're taking these."

I'd slang enough weed to enough people in my day to know where all the good, designer shit comes from. And gay drugs are the best kind they make. So we popped the pills together. No one was seated to my left, so I grabbed those pills and popped them too. Fuck it. Where I come from, if you're gonna dance with the devil, you might as well lead.

To this day I have no idea what those other two pills were, but let me tell you something: they worked. Have you ever eaten fresh lobster on ecstasy? It's like burying your face in sweet, briny 'giner meat that's made out of soft, milky titty flesh. The prime rib felt so good on my tongue and my lips and my teeth and all over my face that now I know where Lady Gaga got the idea for the meat dress she wore to the MTV Video Music Awards. She went to Lawry's on La Cienega for dinner one night rolling her ass off.

Together, the pills created a kind of sensory awareness that was otherworldly. Headed back to our table from the dessert station, Lahna and I were talking, entirely unaware of our surroundings except for each other, when a beam of light reflected off something shiny in my peripheral vision. It was a sequin, attached to a G-string, covering a nutsack, attached to a half-naked Puerto Rican man (according to the flag on the butt floss) gyrating on one of the four risers that sat on the corners of the dance floor. As I turned, I found myself momentarily eye to eye with the man's junk. The five-pointed star in the middle of the flag G-string was pasted over his wiener and sticking straight out toward me like the tip of a Phillips screwdriver. With all the gyrating, the man's dick was a split second ahead of the rest of his junk, which gave me just enough time to dodge a bulging ballsack headed straight for my nose and upper lip. Keeping my dessert plate perfectly level like a buffet veteran, I dipped my inside shoulder and arched my back, bringing my head down with it and sending a set of Puerto Rican meatballs sailing just over my face.

I had *Matrix*'d nuts. It was quite possibly the most instinctive, athletic move I'd made in the last thirty years. What was more incredible was that I never have that kind of luck—not as an adult, not in social situations like this. My usual luck would involve a de-layed surprise reaction, which would produce a gaping jaw, which would in turn give the guy's nuts a perfect place to come to rest and a direct path for his dick to drop flush onto my face. A true, full-on teabagging. Then, with a deviated septum that makes breathing through my nose difficult at times, I would have to struggle to say, with my mouth full, "Sir, would you get this off my face, please?"

Twenty minutes later, my consciousness expanded even further, and I found myself thinking about the multidimensionality of the universe in which we live and the seemingly diametrically opposed nature of infinity. One kind of infinity goes on forever and is so large as to be incalculable—like the universe, or pi. But then there is the infinitely small. The kind where, because you can't divide by zero or divide to *get* to zero, you can split something in half into infinity, but not into nothingness.

I started thinking about that in the context of an atom. If my car, sitting in the parking lot of the reception hall here in Los Angeles, were the nucleus of an atom, the electrons orbiting us would circle over New York City, the Panama Canal, Hawaii, Alaska, the bot-tom of the arctic circle maybe. And in theory, because there are an equal number of negatively charged electrons and positively charged protons in a stable element, we should be able to count on the path of those electrons orbiting us in the car out in the park-ing lot. But we also know that an electron can dip up and down from an excited state to its ground state, emitting light. Because of the physics of light, the electron and the light it emits don't, in theory, have to stay on their orbital path around the nucleus. They can take an infinite number of circuitous routes through time and space to get from point A to wherever point B is. Then I started to contemplate that maybe it's those electrons that make up the thread that holds us to this dimension, that keeps all of us at this wedding reception right here, right now. That's what was going on in my head.

My body had other ideas. Turns out, while my mind was expanding in an attempt to unify myself with all earthly forces, I was actually standing by myself on the edge of the dance floor tweaking my nipple, holding my crotch, matching the gyrations of my junk-swinging Puerto Rican friend as we swayed to the rhythm of a Kesha song.

I told you, these pills fucking *worked*.

Diego ended up being spot-on. We went until 3:40 a.m. It was a hell of a party. If you ever get invited to a gay wedding or a gay party of any kind, let me give you some advice: *go*. Do not second-guess it. Do not worry about what your coworkers might think. Just go. I'm so glad I went, and not even for the drugs. Okay, maybe a little for the drugs. I was mostly happy that I went and could be an ambassador for my accent. Most gay men, especially in places like New York and San Francisco and Los Angeles, think that people who sound like me hate guys who sound and look like them. Nothing could be further from the truth, and I got to be proof of that for at least one night.

If there is anything I regret from that night, though, it's not having August and April there with us. Sure, they would probably have been asleep under the table by eleven thirty. And sure, after seeing all those giant swinging dicks everywhere, they might not ever look at me the same way again as a father figure or a male role model. But I wasn't much older than April when I noticed how little girls could already be little bitches to each other at that age based on who they were friends with, what they wore, and what things they liked. I wanted April to be friends with everyone—with *anyone*. And I wasn't much older than August when I started being taught that one of the worst things that could happen to you as a man is getting hit on by a gay guy. It meant that they'd identified something soft and fairy in you. It was ridiculous shit, and I didn't want August to ever think that way. I knew his school and some of his friends' parents would do a lot of the heavy lifting on that front in the years to come, but still, it would have been nice to have laid some of that groundwork myself in an experience that was new to each of us.

What I regret most of all, though, was that this was one of the last fun things we did as a family before the wheels fell off.

19.
THIS IS THE END

Lahna and I both changed after my pulmonary embolisms. Once I was physically recovered enough to travel and work, we started fighting day and night. It was neither of our faults. Lahna was feeling my mortality more closely than she ever had before, which kicked in her maternal, caregiving drive to make me get healthy. And since I was no longer able to self-medicate the demons away with weed, my behavior got erratic.

For a good year, I was hostile and easily agitated. In some periods I was totally out of control. Like the time I attacked a barista at the Starbucks on Sunset down the street from the Comedy Store because one of his dirty hippie dreadlocks kept dropping into the large frothing pitcher he was using to steam the milk for my Venti caramel macchiato. Do you have any idea what it's like to watch an out-of-work actor dip his furry granola tentacle into your lunch without a care in the world? Every red-blooded American would be horrified and livid if that happened to them, and I believe they would be within their rights to throw the tainted coffee right in that barista's fucking face. That said, I also believe they would not have gone on a tirade that involved threatening to wash/drown him in the prep sink. Instead, most reasonable people would have just left and walked the three blocks down Sunset to the next Starbucks.

In my defense, I *was* on drugs. All kinds of prescription medications for my other ailments and aches and pains. They made me crazy. I would regularly lose track of time. I was constantly awake, usually for days on end. The only times I did sleep were when I was home from the road, but then I'd sleep for two straight days and end up spending even less time with my babies than I did back when we were all on the road together.

Eventually I started having panic attacks and bouts of severe anxiety, so doctors added Xanax to my list of prescribed meds. I used them primarily when I had to fly, like I used the THC strips. I'd pop one and knock myself out.

Unfortunately, Xanax ended up being too much for me. The final nail in the coffin came after flying back to LA from a gig in Tampa, of all places. Lahna was set to pick me up at the airport, but I was so out of it that I forgot and went over to Hertz to rent a car. That doesn't sound like such a big deal on the surface, but if you've ever rented a car at Los Angeles International Airport, you know it's a long, exhausting process that even sober, well-rested people screw up: you have to walk all the way out of the terminal, wait on the center island for a bus to pick you up, ride two miles in shitty airport traffic, stand in line for heaven knows how long, pray they have cars available, refuse all the extra bullshit they want to offer you that turns a car rental into indentured servitude, then once you've found your car and exited the lot, you have to figure out where you are because an LAX rental-car lot is the most disorienting place on planet Earth. I've walked out of the Arkansas forest in the middle of the night baked like a Virginia ham and had a better sense of my bearings.

If the myth of Sisyphus were written today, it would not feature a man pushing a giant boulder up a hill only to have it roll back down just as he reaches the top. Instead, he would be endlessly circling the arrivals level at LAX during that two-hour period in the afternoon when all the flights from Asia and the Middle East come in. By the time Lahna figured out where I was, she had lost count of how many times she'd circled the airport waiting for me to show up at the curb. When she finally got to me, I was standing outside the bus entrance to the Hertz lot waiting for the tongue-lashing of a lifetime. Instead, right there in the car, on the side of the road, Lahna did an intervention. She wanted me to go to rehab. Today.

I don't know if she was planning to take me somewhere like on the TV show *Intervention* and I messed up the logistics, or if she got so fed up that she couldn't wait any longer, because my door wasn't even closed yet when she just started talking and talking. At first, I had no idea what she was saying. All I heard was noise coming from the hole in her face. That sweet, melodic voice I fell in love with now sounded like Freddy Krueger trying to get his change out of a vending machine. Worse, I was in no mood to talk. My head felt like a sack of mashed potatoes, and I just wanted to be left alone. None of that stopped Lahna. She had to say her piece while she had me as a captive, barely functioning audience or God only knew when she'd have the next chance.

Finally, she got Jay Mohr on the phone. I tried to turn my ears off as he added his perspective to this mess, but it's hard to shut out a Jersey accent, and it's even harder to ignore the guy who literally changed my life. I was still pissed and irritable and tired—not even Jay could change that—but eventually they wore me down. I agreed to go to rehab in the shittiest, least confidence-inspiring way possible.

"Fine. Fuck it!"

We drove right from LAX out to the Canyon rehab center in Malibu. You want a real mindfuck? Take a drive from the dirtiest, busiest, most run-down airport in the country, up one of the most picturesque stretches of road on the West Coast, to a secluded hillside paradise in one of the wealthiest zip codes in the country, all because your wife thinks you're a drug addict and your life is falling apart. There isn't enough Xanax in the world to make that not sting.

Checking me into the Canyon, Lahna told them unequivocally that I was a drug addict. I told them that wasn't the case at all. I was only taking the drugs that had been prescribed to me, and never more than the recommended dosages. I told them that I did have a ton of weed in my system, though. Dr. Katz, if you're reading this, sorry, brother, old habits die hard.

The intake workers took all of my belongings, drew my blood, and gave me a tranquilizing dose of Ativan so I wouldn't experience any kind of withdrawal. By the time I woke up two days later, in a puddle of my own piss, the drug counselors had the test results back: no opiates in my system, just like I'd told them.

They were confused because Lahna told them I was hooked on pain pills. I can see how she thought that, what with all my prescriptions, but she was just focused on the wrong kind of pain. I was managing my *physical* pain just fine. But the *mental* pain was fucking with me and pulling me back to self-medicating by smoking weed with two hands.

Everyone acknowledged that I did not have any kind of narcotic or alcohol dependency that one could responsibly classify as an addiction. That didn't mean I didn't have any problems, Lord Jesus, even I knew that, so they put me with a psychiatrist. By the end of the session, I was diagnosed with severe PTSD. When she explained what PTSD was, how it worked, and what the symptoms looked like, it felt like she was reading from my emotional *Wikipedia* page. My parents' divorce, my car accident, the torment from the old Houston comics—it had all cascaded over the years, and instead of dealing with it, I'd obscured it in a giant cloud of pot smoke.

I could have left the Canyon at any time, whether they labeled me an addict or not, but I decided to stay and start working through some of these things. That was the greatest thing about the Canyon, even better than the view. I got to work through all of the trauma that I'd had in my life. We tinkered with different meds and found an antidepressant that worked for me. I learned to meditate. After two weeks, I was exercising during the day and sleeping well at night.

Still, I was in a precarious position with Lahna. She put me in the Canyon and told me I had to stay there to get better, otherwise she and the kids wouldn't be at home when I got back. Yet she was upset at how expensive it was for me to stay there. I understood her anxiety and frustration—we had a big nut and I was the primary breadwinner. But, you can't have it both ways, sweetheart. There's no such thing as getting better on *your* terms. It's either get better or don't.

When I finally left the Canyon and went home, I was still angry at what I felt was a cruel and selfish double standard. I got over it because I knew Lahna meant well, but you can't tell somebody what to do and give them no choice in the matter without their resenting you for it. That's where my real anger was coming from. She'd given me no choice about going to the Canyon, and I did the work. Now, probably because she was afraid I'd backslide like I'd done before with the weight loss after gastric bypass and the pot smoking after my embolisms, she wanted to be in control of *everything*—my diet, my exercise routine, my schedule. *Everything*. And that just wasn't going to work.

By 2014, our relationship was in a rough place.

Not long after my stint at the Canyon, our dog Pimp died. Lahna and I had gotten Pimp together way back when she first moved to LA to be with me. For a boxer, Pimp lived a long time, and in some ways he was like a metaphor for our relationship—against all odds and conventional wisdom, he just kept on chugging. His death fucked me up.

I don't know if it was related, but at the same time I started spending more time at our place in Nashville and treating Zanies as my home club like I had with the Comedy Showcase in Houston and the Laugh Factory in Los Angeles. I used touring logistics as my reason for camping out in Nashville as much as I did, but I knew that was just an excuse—one Lahna was not going to let me skate on. She'd fly out from LA with the kids and our other dog, Hoochie Mama, for a visit and spend the majority of our waking moments together yelling at me for not being a good enough father. I was barely keeping it together enough as it was. Trying to manage this shit on top of it? It was too much to bear. Eventually I snapped.

One day I had what doctors call an insomnia-induced dementia event. I didn't know any of this at the time, but I made more than one hundred calls to Lahna, my assistant, and a number of other people who I can't (or won't) remember. When the phone wasn't good enough, I fought with Lahna on FaceTime and showed her a gun. I threatened to use it to kill myself. As all this was happening, I casually drew myself a relaxing bath before bed. Just as I was about to hop in, I heard a loud banging that didn't seem to stop. At first I thought it might be the wind slamming into something across the street, but soon I realized the sound was much closer. It was at my front door. I threw some clothes on and went downstairs. When I opened the door, I was greeted by a handful of cops. I had no idea why they were at my house. I was genuinely perplexed. They explained that they had received a call that someone at this address had threatened to kill himself. I thought they had the wrong house. I told them that was impossible because I hadn't talked to anyone all day.

The police were cool about everything. They found my wallet and keys, gathered up my medications, and escorted me to the Vanderbilt University hospital emergency room, where I had a great conversation with the doctors. I told them exactly what the police told me, and for a minute they were as confused as I was, primarily because I seemed totally lucid. Still, they didn't want to take any chances since I'd come in under threat of suicide, so they placed me in their psychiatric ward on a seventy-two-hour hold.

I spent Friday night, all of Saturday, and Sunday morning in their care without incident and without much sleep. Then, on Sunday night, the crazy came back. I was out of my mind. The hospital staff thought for sure that I'd gotten my hands on some drugs, but they did a toxicology screen and found nothing. By process of elimination, the doctors were finally able to diagnose me with insomnia-induced dementia. They explained that the loud banging at my front door probably triggered an adrenaline dump that brought me out of my dementia that was responsible for my having no recollection of the phone calls or the FaceTime conversation or the gun. I was lucky, they said.

I stayed in the ward for a few more days while they tinkered with my antidepressants and I went through some intensive counseling. Eventually I was referred to a doctor who gave me medication to sleep, anti-inflammatory drugs for my pain, a bipolar medication, and supplements to correct a pretty substantial vitamin and mineral deficiency. Within a few weeks I started to feel better than I had in a long time. Of course the meds helped, but regular sleep, a better diet, and a newly balanced mood were a godsend. Without them, I'm not sure I would have been able to get over the whole humiliating experience as quickly as I did. Who wants to be known as the big fat funnyman that had to spend a long weekend with a bunch of schizophrenics and meth heads down at the ol' psych ward? Half these fucking people had to be tied down. It was bananas. This was not me.

Lahna is a storyteller. I have admired and supported this talent of hers since the day I met her in Houston. We share this talent, which meant that there would always be something that bonded us besides our babies. It was a comforting feeling in the more turbulent times. In early 2015, she had the idea to do a documentary. She wanted to scratch that storyteller's itch by telling a story about our lives. My immediate reaction was entirely negative, though I tried to keep as much of that to myself as possible. You want to tell the story of *this life*? Right now? That's a sad fucking movie, jack.

All I was doing was working. All Lahna was doing was taking care of the kids. The littlest things set us off. If I was five minutes late to something, she'd lay into me like it was a personal affront to her, even when I was late because I had been working out trying to keep myself alive. Inevitably we'd land in an argument where I'd get mad and exasperated, then she'd bring up my bouts of craziness or how much money I spent while I was in rehab. I would breathlessly explain how hard it was to bear the burden of providing for the lifestyle our family had become accustomed to, and she would then turn that against me by reminding me what a fuckup I was, and how if anything happened to me, I'd be shifting that burden solely onto her. I knew she was scared for me and worried about our future, but just once I hoped she might dial it down to a 7 instead of going nuclear all the time. She had no incentive to do that, however, because little was still holding us together. Our connection had so weakened that our sex life was effectively nonexistent. That's an important part of a relationship that reconfirms connection and galvanizes a partnership. To have that gone was brutal. And she wanted to make a documentary about it?

Still, she was my wife. I loved her and I wanted her to be happy, so I agreed to participate in the documentary. One of our first shooting days was in Madison, Wisconsin. I was on the road for a fairly long stretch, living out of the tour bus we bought off Dave Matthews back in 2012, and she wanted to capture what that was like. It sounds romantic in the literary sense, but it's a constant highwire act. The logistics of travel, ticket requests, morning radio spots, and merch sales are enough to drive anyone nuts; but I had the additional psychic load of dealing with my health. Eating right, sleeping enough, getting some exercise, were all important for my health, and difficult to accomplish day to day.

Wouldn't you know it, the day before Lahna and the kids came out, I got sick again with an upper-respiratory infection. That did not sit well with Lahna, who had hired a personal trainer to come out to Madison to help with the exercise part of my health regimen. The personal-trainer bit didn't sit well with me. What the fuck is that about? I'll tell you what it's about: she was trying to manipulate me to lose weight. She thought she could play to my vanity by sticking a camera in my face. How could I possibly respect that?

I'm sick as a dog in the middle of Wisconsin. I'm with my wife, two kids, a trainer, a documentarian, my tour manager, and my driver on my tour bus. I'm wearing six hats at once, and all I should have been doing was resting, not spinning all of these plates. It was too much. I couldn't process everything that was happening, and I was getting increasingly agitated with everyone around me. Before I knew it, it had descended into a huge knock-down, drag-out fight, which was the last thing I needed, because I had to get some rest before my shows started at 8:00 p.m. Finally I retreated to the bedroom in the back of the bus and closed the door, but she wouldn't let it go. She woke me up at 5:00 p.m. and then a couple times after that. Eventually I snapped on her and told her to leave me the fuck alone, but by then there was no chance I'd get back to sleep. I was too heated. I had to hop in the shower for a little bit to cool myself off mentally.

When I was done with my shower, it was close enough to show-time that it made sense to get ready. I was starting to brush my teeth when I realized we were out of potable water for the sinks, so I asked Lahna to hand me a bottle of water, and I'll got from her was this shitty look, which set me off again. That was all it took for us to be at each other's throat again.

In the car on our way to the gig from the parking lot where we parked the bus, Lahna pulled out her phone and called my assistant Aaron. Right in front of me, she asked him to change her flight to the next morning. She was leaving town early. I was absolutely livid. Not just because she was my wife, not just because she was the one who hauled this fucking documentarian out here, but also because she was my opener!

I made my tour manager stop the car. I couldn't be in the same car with Lahna in that moment. I got out and walked back to my tour bus. I would rather take a cab to the venue, that's how much

I could not be around her anymore. It wasn't over, though. When I got to the club, the hits just kept on coming. Lahna decided she wasn't going to perform that night. She was going to leave the club and go back to the bus. Instead of leaving right away, though, she thought it would be better to stay in the greenroom for a while to continue chewing me out.

While she read me the riot act for the litany of crimes I had committed and we had litigated over and over the last three or four years, I watched the fill-in feature act, a local female comedian, on the CCTV mounted to the wall in the greenroom.

"Lahna, while you're bitching at me, that girl is working in *your spot*! Why don't you worry a little less about me and a little more about your own work? You're fucking around missing your set? I don't believe this." I was at my wit's end, at a complete loss. "I've never done this in twenty-five years of stand-up, but I have to fire you. You cannot cause a bunch of drama, miss your gig, and cost us repeat work. I can't believe you did this. You're fucking fired."

I'd reached my breaking point. Then I pushed beyond it. I grabbed her guitar and threw it on the floor.

"You see this five-thousand-dollar guitar? I should stomp this thing to pieces. Why not? I paid for it. You don't want to use it and I damn sure don't play. You probably don't even give a shit."

I couldn't stay in the bus that night. It would have crushed me. I didn't have another place to stay, so I just sat up in the car all night looking at the bus. Wrapped in black, with my name and my big stupid face plastered all over it, the bus represented pretty much everything that I had worked for—that *we* had worked for.

I stayed up until 7:00 a.m., when my tour manager was scheduled to drive Lahna and the kids over to Milwaukee to catch their rescheduled flight home. Right at seven, the door to the bus flew open and my kids came over and hugged me and started crying. They didn't want to leave. Lahna didn't want to hear it. She had snapped in her way, like I had snapped in mine.

"You can't be around me or your kids right now. I'm sick of this shit. I'm going home."

Madison, Wisconsin, is a beautiful pastoral town in the late spring, but in that moment it was the ugliest place I had ever been. I have never felt so much despair in one place, at one time. I finished the week in Madison, but it fucked me up so much that I canceled the rest of the gigs on that leg of the tour, sent the trainer and the documentarian home, and went back to Nashville.

A few days later I spoke with Lahna and delivered an ultimatum: if she wanted to stay together and make this thing work, she had to leave Los Angeles and move out to Nashville with me. This was not new ground for us. We'd taken a ride on this merry-go-round more than a few times. No matter how fast I got it spinning, it always stopped on one thing: Lahna thought moving to Nashville would be bad for her career. I couldn't have disagreed more. LA is one of the most undesirable places to live for a comedian in my shoes and a comedian in Lahna's shoes. I'm a salt-of-the-earth Texas comic and a headlining road warrior who fills big clubs and theaters. LA couldn't be more inconveniently located in relation to the places I do best in. As a musical comedian trying to get as many reps as possible when she was not busy being an awesome mom, LA clubs were not the venues where she was going to get to flex her comedy muscles the way she needed to.

But all of that work stuff was beside the point to me. We never wanted to raise our kids in Los Angeles. For all the good things that big cities have going for them, raising kids isn't one of them. I wanted us to move to Nashville so we could have as close to a normal life as possible. I wanted the kids to grow up in a place with seasons. I wanted them to go to good public schools. I wanted them to have a big vegetable garden where they could experience the pleasure of eating something you've planted and harvested. I wanted them to learn how to respect religiosity instead of ridicule it. I wanted August to develop a Southern accent like me, and I wanted April to learn how to say "Bless your heart" when she really meant to say "Go fuck yourself." I wanted to be a real family again.

Lahna said no. Two weeks later I filed for divorce.

20.
BACK TO THE FUTURE

The conference room at a divorce lawyer's office is a lot like the room at the animal hospital where the veterinarian brings you when it's time to put the family pet to sleep. It's claustrophobically small. It feels like sadness, and it stinks like death. For all the good times you've had, this is where you'll have your last moment together. For some reason, it is always right off the reception area in full view of people anxiously waiting their turn, hoping for good news but preparing for the worst. It's like they do it on purpose, the way kings and tyrants used to string up traitors and liars right outside the gates of the castle, as a warning: do what we say or you might end up here too.

For a year I dreaded walking into that room and sitting across from Lahna as we negotiated our way apart from each other. Don't worry: I won't go into too many details. Not only is it plain impolite, but no one wants to hear the play-by-play of someone else's divorce. It's like narrating the demolition of an abandoned building that has finally been officially condemned. Just let me know when the dust has settled, the rubble has been cleared, and it's time to rebuild.

I read once that the opposite of love isn't hate, it's indifference. I saw it on Twitter, so it's probably scammy clickbait, but the more I thought about it as the divorce inched along, the more that statement felt true. If you don't give a shit about someone, it's virtually impossible to muster the energy required for hatred. So if you *do* hate them, it must mean you still care. In a divorce—one you never wanted—that realization can be intoxicating because it feels like a glimmer of hope. Lahna was full of vitriol for me. She said and did a litany of spiteful, hurtful, unnecessary things. For a while, thanks to Twitter logic, my brain told me, *Boy, that must mean she still cares a whole hell of a lot.*

There was only one problem: by the fall of 2016, I was the one who didn't care. Let me rephrase that: I cared deeply about our kids, about my life, about my work and my happiness—all the important things. I just didn't care anymore about how Lahna felt about me. I was indifferent, and it was completely liberating. The only times in my life I'd ever felt this free were in the moments right after Thanksgiving dinner each year when I changed into sweatpants.

They say that when God closes a door, He opens a window for you. (I saw that one on a pillow.) If it's true, when God closed the door on my marriage, the window He opened seemed to look right out onto the bright lights of the Las Vegas Strip.

The older I get, the more Las Vegas reminds me of my own stand-up career. By many accounts, it has no business existing, let alone thriving—especially when you consider how it began—yet there it stands year after year, getting bigger, continuing to draw people from all over the country looking to have a good time.

I've always had an interesting relationship with Las Vegas. From the outside, with its glitz and ostentatious displays of wealth and excess, a guy like me doesn't seem to fit in a city like Las Vegas. Mine is not a face you expect to see on a fifty-foot-high marquee as you ride from the airport to your hotel. Yet all you have to do is take one look beneath the surface to realize that the heart of Las Vegas is made up of my people. Whether it's the cocktail waitresses and pai gow dealers who live and work there, or the college buddies and married couples who come in for their annual trips, the people who keep Vegas ticking are the same people I see at my shows all across the country. You can only come to that understanding after you've both toured the country multiple times and played Vegas enough to see the overlap with your own eyes.

The first person to bring that to my attention was Damian Costa, who booked me at the South Point Hotel Casino and Spa for a number of years when he was their director of entertainment. Damian is a great guy, and after shows we'd grab a late dinner and shoot the shit about comedy and the golden era of the Vegas lounges. We'd lament that no comics were doing what the all-time greats did back in the 1940s, '50s, and '60s, when Las Vegas was still just a small collection of hotels with names like Last Frontier and Desert Inn. Guys like Milton Berle, Dean Martin and Jerry Lewis, George Burns, Edgar Bergen and Charlie McCarthy, and the great Don Rickles would come into town and do five or six shows a night, six days a week, for weeks at a time. Rickles, especially, was famous for starting his first show just after midnight and going until five or six in the morning, each show just getting meaner and dirtier (relative to the time, obviously). Those Vegas shows made Rickles's career. Most people think it's because that's where he met

Frank Sinatra and Dean Martin and the rest of the Hollywood set who made sure Mr. Warmth was always taken care of. But that wasn't it at all. Buddy Hackett explained it to me one day:

"The great thing about Las Vegas is that America comes to you, you don't have to go to America."

What he meant was, the coolest of the cool would come out there, they'd see Rickles's act, then they'd go home and tell all their friends about him. The beauty is, Las Vegas is like Disneyland: no one has ever come back home having lost money or had a miserable time, at least not according to the stories they tell their friends. In reality, the trip may have been a hot, sticky hell on earth full of vomit and rejection and poor decisions—and that's just Disneyland—but who wants to hear a story about that? I'd rather hear you talk about your divorce! As a result, by the time the lounge era ended in Vegas, Rickles was a legend.

One night in late 2012, fresh out of rehab, I was having dinner with Damian after a show, and he made the point that no one does anything like those Rickles shows anymore, and they haven't for a long time. A bunch of lounge acts impersonate the guys from the golden era, but nobody is doing their own version of it, which meant a huge opportunity was just sitting out there, unrealized. Over the next couple hours, Damian and I came up with a show called *Dirty at 12:30*. It would be toplined by me and my buddy Gabe Lopez, it would be every Friday night in the main lounge of the South Point, it would be free, and it would be fucking filthy.

Dirty at 12:30 opened in May 2013 and was an immediate success. Just my luck, as its popularity grew, my marriage started to fall apart. Before long, I had to step away from the show and hand it off completely to Gabe. Earlier in my life, having to do that might have pissed me off and I would have looked for people to blame, but I was good with it when it came time to pull the trigger. Gabe was too funny to be living in some shitty little apartment and working a real job to make ends meet. This was a chance for him to stand his career up on its own two feet and give it a real go. Joey Medina had done something similar for me when I had to get the hell out of Houston and he vouched for me at the Latino Laugh Festival and then gave me a place to stay when I got to Los Angeles. Besides being the right thing to do, handing off the show in its entirety to Gabe was a chance, finally, to karmically return the favor and pay it forward.

My relationship with Las Vegas did not end with the *Dirty at 12:30* move. At the end of 2016, I threw away the condoms and we moved in together. That September, just as I was mentally coming through the other side of all the divorce stuff, I was in town and had dinner with Damian Costa again. In the years since he'd inked the *Dirty at 12:30* deal with us, he'd moved up the strip to Caesars as their vice president of entertainment operations. Our conversation meandered like it always does, landing on the familiar topics that we could talk about until the whiskey bottle was dry, and this time I was the one who brought up a point that had been gnawing at me.

On the ride in from the airport, I'd noticed something about all the billboards and marquees: almost no stand-up comics. The ones whose names I did see were only there for the weekend. Otherwise, all the way from McCarran to South Las Vegas Boulevard and Flamingo Road, it was magician, magician, naked dancing men, nightclub, nightclub, *day* club, "illusionist," Britney Spears, magician, Muppet (Celine Dion), Blue Man Group, Cirque du Soleil, Cher. The only comedians with a permanent presence in town were Carrot Top and Jeff Dunham—both funny guys, but with their cases of props and ventriloquist dummies, respectively, not traditional stand-up comics. It was time, I argued to Damian, for a real stand-up comic to have a real Vegas residency.

"Put me to work!" I said.

"I don't think lack of work is your problem, buddy."

Damian was missing my point, and so was I frankly, until I took a beat to think about it. I didn't *need* this residency, I *wanted* it. I'd forgotten what that felt like. Recently, for the first time in my life, stand-up comedy had felt like a *job*-job. Like something I had to do, rather than something I loved to do. The idea of a residency was as invigorating to me as a forty-four-year-old as the prospect of moving to Houston was when I was an eighteen-year-old.

Damian was into the idea. A month later we had contracts for a full residency at Harrah's, a Caesars property just across the street from the Palace. My first show was January 26, 2017, and it was fantastic. The cliché thing to say here is that I had massive butterflies; that I was just as nervous for this show as I was for my first set at the Comedy Showcase in Houston or opening up for Sam Kinison in Fayetteville; that this was the first night of the rest of my life. None of that is true.

What *is* true is that my first show at Harrah's felt much more like starting over than it did finishing up—which is how a lot of people think about residencies of any type, whether it's in Las Vegas, the Poconos, Branson, or Atlantic City. That's where careers go to die, conventional wisdom says. Well, what about my life or my career has been conventional? Sure, a Vegas residency is not the most likely place to pick for a fresh start. But then, Clarksville, Arkansas, is not the most likely place to find a comic. A Shakey's Pizza is not the most likely place to find your first mentor and your first big break. The first season of a reality competition show is not the most likely place to get your biggest break. I could go on.

The point is, for me, the Harrah's residency was the rebirth of my spirit. The darkness lifted, the weight of it all fell away, and the buoyant, energetic good ol' boy with the foul mouth and the baby face was back. Who knew taking a ride in the wayback machine for a little old-school Vegas comedy inspiration would be just the thing I needed? I sure didn't, but I am definitely grateful.

I'll tell you, for somebody who came of age in the world of comedy, there sure has been a ton of drama in my life. That used to grind my gears. It felt like the world was aligned against me. Eventually, though, I realized that drama is the lot in life of the comedian. Just as there is no hot without cold and no light without dark, there is no comedy without drama.

Drama is life. Drama is reality. Drama is the red pill.

You can refuse to swallow it if you want—you can take the blue pill instead—but if you do, you'll never live. You'll never know the highest highs because you've never exposed yourself to the risk of the lowest lows. That's why love is so exhilarating, because the opposite is indifference, which is just another word for complete rejection. It's a gamble, to be sure, but if you turned back time tomorrow and fate handed me the dice again, I'd have no problem rolling them and hoping for the same numbers I rolled the first time, with Sam Kinison words burning in my ear:

"They're not gonna be nice to you, kid, but you'll learn a hell of a lot."